David Hepworth has been writing, broadcasting and speaking about music and media since the seventies. He was involved in the launch and editing of magazines such as *Smash Hits*, *Q*, *Mojo* and *The Word*.

He was one of the presenters of the BBC rock music programme *The Old Grey Whistle Test* and one of the anchors of the corporation's coverage of Live Aid in 1985. He has won the Editor of the Year and Writer of the Year awards from the Professional Publishers Association and the Mark Boxer award from the British Society of Magazine Editors.

He lives in London, dividing his time between writing for a variety of newspapers and magazines, speaking at events, broadcasting work, podcasting at www.wordpodcast.co.uk and blogging at www.whatsheonaboutnow.blogspot.co.uk.

He says Chuck Berry's 'You Never Can Tell' is the best record ever made. 'This is not an opinion,' he says. 'It's a matter of fact.'

For more information on David Hepworth and his books, see his website at www.davidhepworth.com

Praise for *Nothing is Real: The Beatles Were Underrated and Other Sweeping Statements About Pop*

'This collection of Hepworth's journalism offers counterintuitive takes on everything from Sixties B-sides to wedding music' *GQ*

'A collection of essays that stretch and soar across a career spanning five decades' *Guardian*

'Hepworth's books are always a treat . . . a collection of music journalism [that] considers the real legacy of the Beatles, the importance of the drummer, the demise of the record shop – and much else besides' *Choice Magazine*

Praise for *Uncommon People: The Rise and Fall of the Rock Stars*

'[A] colourful, richly marinated survey of the phenomenon of the rock star . . . After almost an adult lifetime of witnessing the music industry at close quarters, Hepworth is, in many ways, a dream author' *Guardian*

'A celebratory but multifaceted look at this strangest of occupations' **** *Mojo*

'*Uncommon People* attempts to preserve this vanishing breed in a kind of rock star bestiary . . . A composite biography of an almost folkloric figure, one made of bits of Bob Marley and Madonna, Prince and Ian Dury' *Sunday Times*

'Knowledgeable and entertaining' *Daily Mail*

'Shrewdly charts the rise and fall of the rock star' *Guardian* Music Books of the Year

'The effect is that of faded, evocative, partisan Polaroids scattered from the memory of one obsessive music fan . . . *Uncommon People* emerges as part of the drive to capture, analyse and archive key moments in musical history that might otherwise vanish from popular memory before we know it' *Observer*

'Perceptive, charming and often humorous' *Sunday Post*

'Something of an exercise in nostalgia, but Hepworth is such an engaging writer that you're happy to go along for the ride' *Irish Independent*

'David Hepworth is such a clever writer . . . *Uncommon People* is a gorgeous read, celebratory and bittersweet, both pep rally and memorial, throbbing with insight and incident' Julie Burchill, *Spectator*

'Hepworth's wry, lively prose pulls the reader along' *The Times*

'In a lifetime's devotion to the music and several decades as a journalist and TV presenter, he has acquired deep reservoirs of knowledge and a towering stack of anecdotes. He deploys his weaponry wisely and writes in an easy, fluid style . . . Hepworth is an inspired phrase-maker' *New Statesman*

'An obituary of rock 'n' roll' *Radio Times*

'Packed with pub-friendly facts and peppered with Hepworth's own memories from 30 years on the frontline, it celebrates rock while also mourning its demise' *Classic Rock*

'This book is a kind of elegy for a glorious but passing phase in entertainment history . . . brim[s] with insight, humour and a certain genial astringency . . . terrific' Stuart Maconie, *Mail on Sunday*

Praise for *1971: Never A Dull Moment*

'This is no "my generation is cooler than yours" nostalgia trip. Just as movements in art, jazz or TV undeniably had Golden Ages then so too with the long-playing record and its seismic effect on subsequent generations. David Hepworth's forensic sweep of this astonishing twelve months is thoroughly absorbing and appropriately rollicking, expertly guiding us through one miraculous year in all its breathless tumble of creation' Danny Baker

'Full of fascinating detail and obviously a labour of love, a must for anyone who can remember the Seventies or who was there' Rosalind Miles, author of *The Women's History of the World*

'A trawl through the year in which albums took over from the pop single as the primary unit of consumption' *Guardian*

'Full of analysis and anecdote' *Sunday Times*

'A richly entertaining reminder of when LPs ruled the world' *Spectator*

'Reliving those heady days of rock' *Mail on Sunday*

'A witty, self-deprecating history of Hepworth's own *annus mirabilis*' *The Times*

'This lively month-by-month study argues that it was the greatest year in pop' *Telegraph*

Also by David Hepworth

1971: Never a Dull Moment
Uncommon People: The Rise and Fall of the Rock Stars
Nothing is Real: The Beatles Were Underrated and Other Sweeping Statements About Pop
The Rock & Roll A Level

A FABULOUS CREATION

HOW THE LP SAVED OUR LIVES

David Hepworth

BLACK SWAN

TRANSWORLD PUBLISHERS
61–63 Uxbridge Road, London W5 5SA
www.penguin.co.uk

Transworld is part of the Penguin Random House group of companies
whose addresses can be found at global.penguinrandomhouse.com

Penguin
Random House
UK

First published in Great Britain in 2019 by Bantam Press
an imprint of Transworld Publishers
Black Swan edition published 2020

Copyright © David Hepworth 2019

A CIP catalogue record for this book
is available from the British Library.

ISBN
9781784162085

Typeset in 10.58/14.51pt Minion by Jouve (UK), Milton Keynes.
Printed and bound in Great Britain by Clays Ltd, Elcograf S.p.A.

Penguin Random House is committed to a sustainable
future for our business, our readers and our planet. This book
is made from Forest Stewardship Council® certified paper.

MIX
Paper from
responsible sources
FSC® C018179

1 3 5 7 9 10 8 6 4 2

This book is dedicated to those who knew how it felt to carry an album down the street.

CONTENTS

Foreword   xi

A Fabulous Creation   xv

1967: 'People were smiling and giving us the thumbs-up'   1

1968: 'The Rock Machine is a machine with a soul'   17

1969: 'Fucking incredible'   32

1970: 'The Man can't bust our music'   47

1971: 'The annus mirabilis of the rock album'   62

1972: 'There's a new sensation, a fabulous creation'   76

1973: 'There is no dark side of the moon – it's all dark'   92

1974: 'Rock is dead. Long live popular music'   108

1975: 'Take Donna home and make love to her'   124

1976: 'What's the worst job you ever had?'   139

1977: 'With their fretboards pointed directly at the
        music of the spheres'   154

1978: 'The kids need new shoes'   167

1979: 'Oh I just don't know where to begin'   182

1980: 'Suddenly we were floating'   196

1981: 'Home Taping Is Killing Music'   209

1982: 'We're here to save the recording industry'   222

After 1982: 'Who cares about the box?'   235

Beyond 1990: *Played Just Once*   251

A Hidden Track   269

Shelf Life – An Appendix   271

Select Bibliography   323

Acknowledgements   327

Picture Acknowledgements   328

Index   330

FOREWORD

'I let my LPs go.'

Those are words I hear a lot nowadays. They usually come from somebody around my age, somebody who grew up in the fifties or sixties, in an era when it seemed the only material possessions anybody truly coveted, or could reasonably expect to acquire, were long-playing records.

When I ask what happened to their precious LPs these people mutter something about storage space, about kids and spouses, about having replaced them with CDs, then downloads, and finally with a subscription to a streaming service. Some offer this explanation apologetically. Others are quite proud that nowadays, thanks to digital technology, they can access the music – and, after all, isn't that what it's all about? – without having to deal with its attendant clutter.

I know what they mean. Over the last twenty years I've taken as much boyish delight as anyone in the way all the recorded music in the world is now suddenly at my fingertips. I'm not a vinyl fundamentalist. I will not engage in conversations about matrix numbers or the superior quality of a first pressing. On Record Store Day I avoid record stores altogether. I find it irritating beyond belief that people are prepared to make a fuss about a kind of scarcity which has been contrived purely in order to encourage them to make just such a fuss. The hype the record industry is perennially accused of visiting on fans is nothing to the hype that fans visit on themselves.

Music is just as popular now as it was in the days of Michael Jackson or Enrico Caruso. What changes is the way we consume it. And every time we change the way we consume it we also change our relationship with the music and the people who make it. This book is about a time when we consumed recorded music in a very particular way. This book is about the era of the LP. The era of the LP is not the same as the era of the album. Although all LPs were albums, not all albums were LPs. CDs were not LPs. Cassettes were not LPs. Downloads are certainly not LPs. The story begins, for obvious reasons, in 1967 and ends, for reasons only becoming clear to us now, in 1982. A lot happened before and after those dates, which we'll get to, but it's the time period between those two dates that marks the era of the LP.

But surely, you say, the LP is making a comeback, isn't it? We keep hearing about it. If it is, which is a big question, that simply means that there must be something about the LP, and the attendant LP experience, that means a great deal to us, whether we lived through it, as I did, or simply yearn for it, as the hipster I recently passed in east London, dangling a copy of the first Led Zeppelin album by one shrink-wrapped corner, presumably does.

Why do bands still feel the need to parcel out their music in denominations of forty minutes? Why is the long-playing record the only music carrier we feel emotionally attached to? Is the current vogue just a retro fad which will pass or the harbinger of something more profound? Why do today's young performers, who by rights should be enjoying the immeasurable advantage of being able to send their music through the air without the attendant inconvenience of manufacture and distribution, still yearn for the benediction of this anachronistic product first invented in 1948? What makes the LP a fabulous creation, to borrow the line from Roxy Music's 'Do The Strand' – a great opening track on *For Your Pleasure*, a record that was in many ways the apotheosis of the LP? That's what this book attempts to discover.

I don't really have a record collection. The word 'collection' implies something which obeys an organizing principle. What I have is more like an accumulation of records. I have these particular ones because they attached themselves to me in the course of my life and work. In a lot of cases I can tell you exactly how I came to have those records. That doesn't apply to most of the things in my house. LPs look their age, with all that implies, which is one of their unique features. As in any accumulation of items that have been acquired over a lifetime there are a few I'm not even sure are mine. I've just noticed that I've got a copy of the first Jimi Hendrix album from 1967 where I've crossed through the name of the original owner on the cover. Sorry about that, 'N. P. Rich'. I'm intrigued by the fact that he used his initials. Interesting how formal we grammar-school boys were back in the Summer of Love. But back then we weren't aware it was the Summer of Love. Back then pop music seemed to be experienced purely in a forwards direction.

I got that record over fifty years ago. I don't believe music was better back then any more than I believe it's better now. I've been fortunate enough to be able to witness both eras. I don't believe in new music any more now than I did at the time of the Beatles. There is no new music. Mostly that's just old music played in a new way by new people. I do believe music is very different now, though. It's different because the world is different, the technology is different and we are different. What has always interested me about music, and made me want to write about it, is the way it reflects and shapes our behaviour. I don't believe in records changing lives. What I do believe is that the records we liked can lead us back to the lives we once led and the people we once were. That's what I hope this book is about.

Let's say it's dedicated to anyone who let their LPs go.

David Hepworth
London 2018

A FABULOUS CREATION

In the days of 78s, a record had just one tune on it. That tune was on the A-side. You could flip it over and there would be a slightly less appealing tune on the other, but that would be entirely at your own risk. You could sit down to listen to the tune but you'd have to stand up again pretty soon and take the needle off the record. From the age of Sousa to the end of the Second World War single records were the rule. It wasn't until the late 1940s that two big American record companies, RCA and Columbia, agreed on a way of bringing to market a new product which could finally break through the time restriction of a few minutes a side. They called this the long-playing record or LP.

This new product would be able to fulfil their dream of carrying an entire symphony – normally running around thirty-five minutes – without the listener having to do more than get up and turn the record over at the end of side one. Before the long-playing record, lovers of classical music had to tolerate symphonies being divided over up to a dozen discs. To make it easier to keep track of those collections the retailers would sell wallets to keep the individual records in. Because these looked like the kind of book into which you might post family snapshots, the wallets became known as 'albums'.

The new microgroove LP went round at 33⅓ revolutions per minute, which meant people had to have a new turntable. The new LPs were made of a plastic compound which was a fraction of the weight of the old shellac 78s. The grooves were smaller, which called for a more delicate stylus and a less weighty arm. The new LPs were not always twelve inches in diameter. It was initially thought that in order not to put too much pressure on the purses of the fans or the limitations of the performers, LPs by pop stars should be restricted to ten inches, which was enough playing time to have four songs on each side. As late as 1954 Frank Sinatra albums were still being produced in the ten-inch format.

At the same time the music business was casting around for entertainment that was suited to this new long-playing format. It proved perfect for cast and soundtrack recordings of hit musicals – Act One on the first side, Act Two on the other. You could even replicate the theatre-going experience by transforming your lounge into a playhouse and serving drinks to your guests at the interval. When *Billboard* introduced its first chart of Best Selling Pop Albums on 24 March 1956, the same week that the first Elvis Presley LP was released, five out of the top ten albums were soundtracks.

Comedy was another strong seller in the early days. In a world where you couldn't rewind or repeat radio or TV, people loved the idea of being able to hear their favourite stories, punchlines and funny voices whenever it suited them. A new comedy LP was a good enough reason to invite friends round for an evening of listening together. An evening with the record player, with friends bringing along their copies of *South Pacific* or *An Evening Wasted With Tom Lehrer*, was the preferred entertainment of many sophisticated young marrieds of the fifties.

The long-playing record did more than deliver the experience of going out without the need to leave the home: it also delivered further experiences that were entirely new. Just as in the era of 78s you'd been able to turn your living room into a dancehall, with the LP you could turn it into a theatre. With the aid of one of the many LPs whose titles boasted they provided *Music For . . .* it was suddenly possible to temporarily transform that room into a boudoir, a Polynesian beach at sunset or an exercise class.

In the 1960s the record business began to boom as more and more households equipped themselves with machines to play records on. Between 1951 and 1962 the price of the popular Dansette range of home record players came down from a substantial thirty-three guineas to a pocket-friendly eleven guineas. Even then the majority of those were paid for through hire purchase schemes. The LP was still not for everyone. It was predominantly the domain of lovers of so-called 'serious music', jazz fans or pipe-smoking uncles who were naturally worried about anyone playing trashy pop music on their jealously guarded radiogram. Even in the late sixties a friend remembers his father refusing to let him play Donovan records for fear 'it might damage the needle'. A radiogram was primarily a piece of furniture. The sound it produced was secondary. What mattered most was the visual impact it made on a visiting neighbour. Some designs even provided a space for one's own cocktail cabinet, enabling the host to display his bottles of Warninks Advocaat or Harvey's Bristol Cream alongside his collection of records by the Swingle Singers.

The LP was not regarded as being for young people or for the artists whose music they favoured. The beat boom which swept the world in the 1960s was powered overwhelmingly by seven-inch 45s. The idea of forty minutes of music from just the one artist as being in any way pleasurable was something the public rarely thought about. For pop groups an LP was a prize, a recognition of their efforts, something they might get the opportunity to make once they'd had enough success with singles. An album was never a priority for Elvis or Buddy Holly or, in the early days, even the Beatles. When the Beatles did their climactic show at Shea Stadium in August 1965 in front of what was then the largest audience that had ever attended a pop show, they played for about thirty minutes. This was less than the running time of their recently released LP, the soundtrack for *Help!*

Though Bob Dylan changed the formula in 1966 with his two-LP set *Blonde On Blonde*, the record that changed everybody's expectations was by the Beatles. *Sgt Pepper's Lonely Hearts Club Band* came out in the summer of 1967 and pointed the way things would go. The Beatles had already established the idea that a pop LP could be more than Phil Spector had traditionally thought it should be – two hits and a lot of filler – but this was something different. It was the first album the Beatles made without any thought of performing any of the individual songs live. There was no single taken from *Sgt Pepper* any more than there had been a single taken from Beethoven's Fifth. For the first time the LP was presented as a complete piece of work. They hadn't collected a number of songs and put them on an album. They had done something new: they had 'made an album'. In doing so, they changed the game.

Artists – and many began to call themselves 'artists' – would henceforth make albums. That's what they did. Everything else was a distraction. As far as the artists were concerned these albums would ideally be treated as statements, much as new novels had always been. Moreover, from the beginning of this era musicians expected a degree of control that novelists weren't allowed. The artists often decided the outside of the package as well as what was inside. The records were offered for sale in jackets that were as much part of the experience as the music on the record, covers that would often have the happy effect of making the music seem slightly grander than it was. The cover was as much the thing as the record itself. While George Orwell's *1984* is regularly republished in a different livery, *Sgt Pepper's Lonely Hearts Club Band* looks the same today as it did in 1967. The world would not have it any other way.

The artists weren't the only ones whose worldview was transformed by the new album experience. Similar changes came over us, the people who bought the albums. When we went home from the record shop on those blessed days when we had been able to afford to buy an album, we felt we had done something more than exchange cash for an item of fast-moving consumer goods. We had 'bought the album'. This was in itself a token of a new degree of seriousness. We had graduated from short form to long form. We had put away childish things. We had demonstrated a commitment nobody had previously thought us capable of. We had moved from the world of liking to the world of loving; from the fickle world of fandom to the adult sphere where what was valued was commitment, where we listened again if we didn't get it all the first time, where we were clearly in it for the long haul. We had become, in a teenage way, patrons of the arts. We had become the kind of people who bought albums.

There have been many music carriers before and since the LP. There have been cylinders, 78s, cassettes, eight-tracks, CDs, downloads, and finally no carrier at all, simply a sequence of instructions dispatching a series of noughts and ones through thin air. Yet there has only ever been one carrier to which we have an emotional attachment and that is the twelve-inch long-playing record. The CD has now been and gone and yet the LP lives on for a minority of enthusiasts, many of whom were not born when the LP truly roamed the earth.

That era began in 1967 with *Sgt Pepper*. It ended in 1982 with Michael Jackson's *Thriller*. It's at that point that making records changed from an art to a science. By the era of *Thriller* the total sales were greater, far greater than ever, but an increasing number of them were on cassette, which people found more suited to the way they preferred to listen. Soon the majority would be on CD and then the majority would be downloaded. Then they would be streamed. Ultimately nobody would actually buy anything at all. They would simply access music much as they would water from a tap – with roughly the same level of emotional engagement. It's at this point that people started to talk about wanting to listen to a tune rather than an album.

Between 1967 and 1982, between the establishment of the youth market and the arrival of the home entertainment industry, between Bob Dylan's *John Wesley Harding* and the heyday of Donkey Kong, between *The Forsyte Saga* and the Kids from 'Fame', between the Dansette portable and the Sony Walkman, lies the era of the LP.

During that time this fabulous creation played so many different roles in our lives that we are in danger of forgetting many of them. It was a semi-precious object, a mark of sophistication, a measure of wealth, an instrument of education, a unit of currency, a banner to be carried before one through the streets, a poster saying things one dare not say oneself, a means of attracting the opposite sex, and, for hundreds of thousands of young people, the single most cherished inanimate object in their lives.

This is the story of that time. It's the story of how the artists made these LPs and also how we the people played them. It's a story that takes us from recording studios where musicians were doing things that had never previously been done (and nobody thought to stop them) to the sparsely furnished living quarters where the products of their efforts would be spun in wonder. It's a journey back to a time when music was central to our lives. It's a story that recalls a time when there were few computer games or mobile phones and seventeen-year-olds were deemed capable of sitting down alone with no distractions and devoting thirty-five minutes of their attention to whatever issued from the speakers.

The era of the LP was such a moment as had never happened before. By the time the iPod came along in 2001 it had already passed; as far as most people were concerned the whole idea of the LP was already one with Nineveh and Tyre. In the present century cultural commentators point to a burgeoning cult around antique long-playing records and wonder aloud if this indicates a more general desire to get back to feeling about music the way we used to feel. Are our lives now so altered that they can no longer accommodate the experience that was the LP? To answer that question we must return to the day that era began and see what our lives were like then.

1967

'People were smiling and giving us the thumbs-up'

The first day of June 1967 was a Thursday. I was on my way home at the end of a school day, a boy just three weeks away from his seventeenth birthday, in the uniform of a grammar school in the north of England. My route to the bus took me past my favourite record shop. I always went this way to replenish my spirits. This was the first of many favourite record shops I was to have in the years to come. At the time proper record shops were only just starting to exist. Prior to this time most people bought their records at electrical dealers, at traditional musical instrument shops or, most likely, at a local branch of a chain of high-street chemists. Here the latest records would be dispensed dispassionately by tightly permed middle-aged women who would clearly rather have been advising on hair spray. There wasn't much romance about these places.

I had only recently discovered that there was another way to buy

1

music. This was in a shop where the people behind the counter seemed to feel the same way about records as the predominantly young people in front of it. This particular shop was called the Record Bar. It was situated in a kiosk attached to an old cinema, in a tiny space that had presumably been used to sell sweets to film-goers back in the golden age of the movies. The Record Bar had only been open a few months but I had already spent a lot of time in there flipping through the new releases, combing their sleeves for names that suggested connections with earlier records, and in some cases actually committing their entire track lists to memory. In the course of these hours I had learned it was run by Ken and Betty.

Ken and Betty seemed, at least to my teenage eyes, middle-aged. Ken wore a suit and Betty was always smartly turned out. I suppose if I had thought about it I would have regarded them as Sinatra people, which would have placed them on the far shore of adult-hood. They were probably only in their late twenties. I remember the small shop was always wreathed in their cigarette smoke. They would place their cigarettes in the ashtray while they took the sleeve of *Motown Chartbusters* or *Five Live Yardbirds* or *A-tom-ic Jones* which the customer had selected from the racks. They would then reach behind them for the actual record which was always kept at the counter. They would carefully reunite the record with its sleeve, slip it into one of their candy-striped paper bags and then resume their gasper before taking the customer's money and putting it into the cash register, finally snapping the clip that kept the ten-shilling and pound notes safe.

Although in 1967 there was nothing remotely resembling the level of hype that nowadays attends the release of a new blockbuster film or smartphone, I knew there was a new Beatles LP coming. I had even seen some pictures of them at work in the studio in one of the music weeklies. In these pictures they all had moustaches and were wearing scarves and ponchos of vivid design. Don't worry, said the caption, EMI haven't rented their studios to the gypsies – it's just the Beatles and their new look! The hippies of Haight Ashbury may have declared this the Summer of Love but the war in Vietnam was continuing unabated and the Six-Day War was about to begin in the Middle East. This may have been the Swinging Sixties but in most respects they were indistinguishable from the fifties. Television was still black and white; indeed BBC1's big-rating Saturday night show was *The Black and White Minstrel Show*. On the evening of 1 June Simon Dee's guests on *Dee Time* were Thora Hird and Stubby Kaye. The story dominating the news that day was about Francis Chichester, the sixty-six-year-old Briton who had become the first man to sail singlehandedly around the world, returning to Greenwich where he was welcomed by the forty-one-year-old Queen. News about pop music still travelled exclusively along the frail filaments of the music press. The grown-up media organizations weren't very interested.

Living in the north of England I hadn't been able to hear the first broadcast of the new record, which had been on the pirate station Radio London on 12 May. I had heard Kenny Everett on the BBC's Light Programme the Saturday before release. He had featured an interview with Paul and John, playing every track from the new album but one. The BBC had banned this final track because they thought it was about drugs. The song that actually stuck in my head after just one listen was 'Lucy In The Sky With Diamonds'. It had that phasing effect which Lennon had described as 'double flanging'. However, this being the Beatles, it also had a driving chorus that was as much R&B as what Everett had parenthetically called 'psycho-delia'.

Hence I knew I was looking for something but I wasn't entirely sure what. The Record Bar had a small window, which was always full of the latest releases. That week there was the first LP by a new artist on Deram called David Bowie, *The Supremes Sing Rodgers &*

Hart and the Monkees' newly released *Headquarters*. This was the Monkees' third album in less than a year. They had swarmed into the space left vacant by the Beatles' withdrawal from touring. The newspapers seemed to have accepted the idea that since they had stopped personal appearances in late 1966 at least some of the Beatles' thunder had been stolen. Indeed their manager Brian Epstein was sufficiently concerned about the ground they were losing that he insisted the Beatles needed a single before the album was finished. Thus 'Penny Lane' and 'Strawberry Fields Forever' were taken from the sessions and paired for a double A-sided single which came out in February. When it failed to go to number one, thanks to the sales being shared between the two songs and the less than scientific methodology of the charts at the time, the murmurings grew louder.

I must not have seen an advert or newspaper story alerting me to what I should be looking for because when I first clapped eyes on the cover of *Sgt Pepper's Lonely Hearts Club Band* in the tiny window of the Record Bar I wasn't entirely sure this was what I was seeking. It took me a couple of seconds to process the signals that confirmed that I was looking at it. It was an unusually densely populated cover. Cut out like a horizon on a background of cyclorama blue was a montage of a sea of faces, either in antique black and white or childishly hand-tinted. Standing front and centre, in the yellow, pink, blue and red uniforms of fantasy bandsmen, were John, Ringo, Paul and George. They stood behind a bass drum announcing them as Sgt Pepper's Lonely Hearts Club Band. In front of them, spelled out not in the crisp graphics of consumer advertising but in the heartfelt medium of flowers, was the word 'Beatles'.

In the fullness of time most of the Beatles covers would be pastiched. The faces half in shadow on *With The Beatles*. The semaphore signals of *Help!* The photo-booth effect of *A Hard Day's Night*. However, this new one would be pastiched more widely and more quickly than most. Indeed within one short year it would be sufficiently seared into the mass consciousness of the world for Frank Zappa to line up his own basket of deplorables for a rejoinder he called *We're Only In It For The Money*. Within a few years the merest glimpse of a motley multitude lined up behind an antique bass drum in the same fashion would subliminally transport people back to the day they first laid eyes on *Sgt Pepper*.

For me, the tingle of excitement triggered by my epiphany at the shop window arrived a microsecond ahead of the by-now-familiar stab of thwarted desire. I looked at my watch. If I was to buy a copy today – and I clearly would not sleep if I did not buy a copy that day – I had two hours to do it. Although Britain's first cash machine was unveiled in the same month as the record's release, credit as we understand it now was not invented in 1967 and it certainly wasn't extended to teenagers. In 1967, like all sixteen-year-olds, I could conduct a detailed audit of my entire worldly wealth by thrusting a hand into my right trouser pocket. In there was about ten shillings, which was less than a third of the purchase price of *Sgt Pepper's Lonely Hearts Club Band*.

If you were a teenager in the sixties, records of any kind were purchases that had to be postponed until there were available funds. There was no buy-now-pay-later plan. This even applied to singles. It also applied to EPs. It applied on an entirely different level to LPs. LPs, which were the primary currency through which teenagers calculated worldly wealth, had to wait for Christmas or birthdays. The purchase of LPs was usually dependent on the intercession of kindly relatives. There was no credit to be had other than that which could be secured by promising to pay the sum back in sweated labour for the family member capable of advancing the sum. To this end I hurled myself on to a passing bus and like a wild-eyed jockey urged it to carry me the four miles to my father's place of business.

My father, like most of his generation, had grown up regarding recorded music as something far down the list of personal priorities. Since these included surviving a Depression and then a war this was not in itself surprising. He sometimes described the record player, the only item of household furniture I had any attachment to, as a 'tingle-airy'. This I found out was a Victorian music maker that he couldn't possibly have remembered. However, even my father recognized that a new Beatles album was something out of the ordinary and without fuss he advanced me the twenty-five shillings I would need to cover the thirty-two-and-six purchase price. I promised to work for him the following Saturday to repay the debt, then took the bus the four miles back to the Record Bar, again urging it to complete each agonizing furlong more quickly. I got there minutes before the shop closed, conducted the transaction with shaking hands, and then took the bus back home. It is not a figure of speech to say I was trembling with excitement.

Once home I lugged the family's pink and grey Bush portable mono record player into the front room and introduced it to its new companion. Bringing a new record home in those days had the effect of introducing something flashy and new that inevitably eclipsed the small number of records one already owned. *Sgt Pepper* was something else. This was a step change. It was the first album I'd owned that had a gatefold sleeve. It was the first one that anyone had owned with the lyrics of the songs on the back. If you didn't count the Andy Warhol banana cover of *The Velvet Underground And Nico*, which had come out two months earlier – and most people didn't – it was the first pop record that came in a package that didn't appear, like the Beach Boys' *Pet Sounds*, to be an afterthought.

Clinchingly, in contrast to the Warhol banana, the teeming cavalcade on the cover suited and prefigured a record which seemed similarly bustling with characters, as I was soon to discover: the good

Sergeant himself, the boy Billy Shears, the lady Rita who handed out parking tickets, the Hendersons late of Pablo Fanque's fair, the aristocrat who blew his mind out in a car, even the seaside postcard family Vera, Chuck and Dave. At the same time *Sgt Pepper* described an English dreamscape of marshmallow pies, plasticine porters, angry young men, chaps from the motor trade, hogsheads of real fire, cottages on the Isle of Wight, girls known as 'skirts', Blackburn, Lancashire, the House of Lords and even the Albert Hall. The passionate parochialism of *Sgt Pepper* was to make a nonsense of every argument mounted before or since for making yourself understood in America by playing down the Englishness. *Sgt Pepper* could not possibly have been more English. It was as English as a biscuit.

As soon as I took it out of its pink inner bag, ignoring the toy moustache and Pepper decals you were supposed to cut out and wear, I could see straight away that it was not like other pop records in that it barely had any gaps between the tracks. I eased the disc over the spindle in the middle of the deck, slipped it past the auto changer that usually held singles, and lowered the stylus on to its surface. *Sgt Pepper* was not to leave that platter for at least a week. In this my copy was not alone. The release earlier in the year of 'Strawberry Fields Forever' and 'Penny Lane' had alerted everyone to the prospect of the Beatles coming up with something unprecedented. Now it was here it was not just unprecedented, it was also, even by their standards, shockingly appealing. Ever since the release in 1964 of their first entirely self-penned LP *A Hard Day's Night* the Beatles, alone among their peers, had appeared to have no difficulty coming up with a dozen songs at a time that were not merely catchy but inexhaustibly so. They also came up with songs that were more sophisticated than they seemed. The more you heard them the more you wanted to hear them. For all its 'psychedelic' habiliments and cannabis-fired flights of imagination, *Sgt Pepper* was clearly the best pop LP anyone had ever heard.

And it clearly demanded to be listened to as an LP. Even if you didn't buy the idea that it told a story, the simple ruse of starting and almost finishing with the same song gave it a circularity that meant that when you took the stylus off the repeating run-out groove at the close of side two the only sensible thing to do was turn it over and start again at the beginning. It had a sustaining energy that meant it never flagged. Most of the songs were under three minutes long. One of the Beatles' many graces was their short attention span. They were children of Buddy Holly. They didn't have the patience that's required to make something boring. Most of the *Sgt Pepper* songs were up-tempo and optimistic. Most of the lyrics made little sense. In the hands of these four makers of miracles they slipped the surly bonds of sense and took wing according to their own giddy logic.

The Beatles were a class above. This was doubly impressive since the rest of the class were quite good. You could have given those same songs to another group and the results wouldn't have been anything like as special. *Sgt Pepper* was the apogee of the art form they and George Martin had begun to forge in 1963 when they took the previously discrete crafts of writing, playing, singing and record-making and subdued them into one new form. And here, just four crowded years since that time, was the *Citizen Kane* of that form. And more than that. It was a record which was, if anything, more charismatic than the people who made it. Here, in a shape you could hold in your hand, was the long-playing record as art object, novel substitute, wall hanging, vessel of secret messages and perfect summation of the totality of our consumer desires. We played it again and again like one massive single, gazing upon it all the while, watching the black and yellow pound sign on its Parlophone label revolve. We didn't play it in the background. It was front and centre.

Long-playing records were a social thing, and for many people

8

their first hearing of *Sgt Pepper* took place in the company of others. The engineer on Judy Collins' *Wildflowers*, which was being completed in the wake of *Sgt Pepper*, entertained the whole team at his home in Laurel Canyon, Los Angeles. After everyone had smoked a lot of dope they lay on the floor and listened to Bach's Mass in B Minor followed by *Sgt Pepper* – an indicator of the new expectations that were being set up by this clearly unprecedented LP. 'It was a quintessential California experience and one of the most wonderful evenings I have ever spent,' remembered Collins' arranger Joshua Rifkin. In London the young record company man Joe Boyd drove the singer Sandy Denny back to her parents' place in Wimbledon that June and they sat up all night talking, and then, as dawn was breaking, they listened to a samizdat reel-to-reel recording of the Radio London broadcast. It was as they sat there in what Boyd recalled as the 'stunned aftermath' of listening to *Sgt Pepper* that she decided she needed to join Fairport Convention. It's remarkable how many people's memories of their first encounter with *Sgt Pepper* are set in similarly halcyon summer dawns. The Beatles themselves took an acetate round to the Chelsea apartment where Cass Elliot was staying just as dawn was breaking on a Sunday morning. Her sound system was placed on a window ledge so that her neighbours could be woken by the sound of this new miracle. 'All the windows around us opened and people leaned out, wondering. People were smiling and giving us the thumbs-up,' recalled Beatles assistant Neil Aspinall.

It took *Sgt Pepper* a month to go to number one in the United States where for the next fifteen weeks it was to lord it over the Monkees, Jefferson Airplane's *Surrealistic Pillow*, Bill Cosby's *Revenge* and records by Herb Alpert and Andy Williams. On 1 July the American trade paper *Billboard* reported that some record stores were looking at their sales returns and deciding that in the future they would be stocking stereo records only. In Britain in 1967 most people only had mono record players and therefore *Sgt Pepper* was still overwhelmingly a mono experience. Even the Beatles had little interest in stereo. They were in the studio when the mono mix of the album was done but left the stereo to their producer.

The heavy papers didn't yet cover pop albums so it was similarly unprecedented when both Richard Goldstein in the *New York Times*, who was styling himself the world's first rock critic, and in the UK William Mann, the classical music critic of *The Times*, weighed in on the subject of *Sgt Pepper*. They couldn't help sounding like dons pronouncing on a particularly promising student revue. Both were so busy panning for profundity that they missed the pop genius which was always the Beatles' signal quality. Mann wondered if the pop album, which he said was usually an unconnected anthology, might soon aspire to produce a Tin Pan Alley equivalent of one of Schumann's song cycles.

The Beatles were a wonderful group but they were often a less than benign influence. They had led other groups to assume that since the Beatles could write their own songs they should be able to do so too. *Sgt Pepper*, which raised the long-playing stakes, put further dangerous ideas in the heads of their peers in the months after it came out. The first recorded use of the expression 'concept album' came in a *New York Times* interview in June 1968 during which Pete Townshend of the Who said he felt rock was in danger of becoming too serious. Even from its earliest days the concept album was a form more honoured in the breach than the observance. Very few bands had the discipline it takes to stick to a story. Vestigial elements remained, such as the popularity of segueing from one track into another. This had the additional benefit of being a way to use up the leftovers of songwriting sessions which hadn't quite panned out. Most groups had the good sense to let the concept slip if they felt it was getting in the way of the right material. Only the truly unimaginative doggedly saw it through.

The universal acclaim that had accompanied *Sgt Pepper*'s arrival was particularly galling for those acts that had already embarked on a grand statement of their own. Brian Wilson had been waiting for one of his soothsayers to tell him the most propitious time to release his follow-up single to 'Good Vibrations'. She nominated 11 July 1967, not realizing this would be just a few weeks after *Sgt Pepper*. On that evening Wilson whistled up his retainers and ceremonially delivered an acetate of 'Heroes And Villains' to a Los Angeles radio station, offering them the great honour of being the first people in the world to play it. This offer did not get the reception he expected. In fact he was told they couldn't play anything that wasn't on the playlist. As Wilson biographer Peter Carlin writes, 'in a world still rocked by *Sgt Pepper* it seemed beside the point'.

Wilson didn't seem to realize that he had been outflanked. Other members of the sixties beat generation did. Pete Townshend was on a tour of the USA with the Who at the time and recalled, 'We listened to *Sgt Pepper* and not much else.' David Crosby of the Byrds had visited the *Sgt Pepper* sessions in February and been played 'A Day In The Life'. The Beatles placed him in the studio with coffin-sized speakers either side of him, left him alone and pushed play on the tape. They wanted to see him suffer. 'By the time I got to the end I was a dishrag, I was stunned. I didn't know you could do that.' Graham Nash of the Hollies, who was given a copy by Brian Epstein, admits to the honest response of all fellow musicians, which was unconcealed envy: 'I wish we'd been that smart.'

Songwriter Jimmy Webb and hitmaker Johnny Rivers got an early copy. 'It was a tidal wave of sound, texture on cross texture. Music had never in its entire history said or done quite so much,' recalled the songwriter, who at the time was riding high with hits for the 5th Dimension. *Sgt Pepper's Lonely Hearts Club Band* is a very good record but Webb's reaction may have had as much to do with the acid he and Rivers had taken before listening as the music per se.

However, like every other person in the business of pleasing the ear, he recognized the fact that this one record changed the game.

The cliché 'if you can remember the sixties you weren't there' applies perfectly to the people who were making records at the time. Whether or not all these events unfolded quite as euphorically as their memories insist, the more important fact is that suddenly everybody shared in the feeling that this was a moment for breaking free of the discipline of the hit single and instead going into the studio, preferably with a limitless budget and a friendly producer, and just seeing what happened.

This of course was every bit as likely to lead to misery as vindication. At the time of the Beatles' momentous release engineer Glyn Johns was working with the Rolling Stones, who had already recorded some of the tracks for their next album. Halfway through the sessions they parted company with Andrew Loog Oldham, their producer and manager since the beginning of their careers, and thus Johns was left to make sense of whatever the band came up with. Since they appeared to have booked unlimited time this meant whole days and nights spent waiting for either Keith Richards or inspiration to arrive.

Prior to the summer of 1967 no band in their right mind would have booked a recording session without having some idea of what was to be recorded. From the middle of 1967 for an increasing number of bands an album became something they trusted would magically just happen following a certain period of time in the studio. In Johns' memoirs he recalls the nadir of those 1967 Stones sessions. One day, in a vain effort to put some order on the proceedings without appearing to put some order on the proceedings, Mick Jagger called for as many different percussion instruments as he could. As the band drifted in he invited each member to pick up something to hit or shake. They would then pick a tempo entirely at random, record the resultant racket for up to fifteen minutes, listen back to it and then do the same thing all over again. This explains, says Glyn Johns, why 'Sing This All Together' is 'unadulterated drivel'.

If *Sgt Pepper* was a banquet such as only the Beatles could serve, *Their Satanic Majesties Request*, which came out at the very end of 1967, was an overcooked pot roast such as only the Rolling Stones could have contrived. The two records were fated to be forever yoked together in a comparison that did the Rolling Stones no favours. That was largely because of the cover. For this they hired Michael Cooper, who had photographed Peter Blake's tableau for *Sgt Pepper*, flew everybody to New York, threw on pantomime costumes and arranged themselves in the midst of fruit and flowers before having the resulting image reproduced via a process that aspired to 3D and fell somewhat short. On *Sgt Pepper* there had been a rag doll bearing the legend 'welcome the Rolling Stones'. On *Their Satanic Majesties Request* the heads of the four Beatles peeped out from the undergrowth. Just as the Beatles had children's cardboard cut-outs inside the cover of their album, the Rolling Stones' cover opened to reveal a maze. This being the Rolling Stones, the maze was deliberately designed so that it didn't work.

Lots of the albums in the window of the Record Bar in time for Christmas 1967 were manifestly indebted to *Sgt Pepper* in one way or another. Cream's *Disraeli Gears*, which had been dashed off in just three days in New York in May, appeared in November in a throbbing psychedelic cover designed by Clapton's flatmate Martin Sharp through which he aimed to match what he called their 'warm, electric sound'. This was a compliment unlikely to be extended to the final track 'Mother's Lament', a raucous music-hall singalong otherwise known as 'Your Baby Has Gone Down The Plughole' which had been added to get the record over the thirty-minute mark and also, via the publishing credit 'Traditional Arranged By Cream', to ensure that all the record's revenue remained within the band.

Nobody in the music business has ever acted out of pure motives and that was as true in 1967 as it is true today.

But everybody knew the stakes had been raised and it was no longer acceptable to just turn up with a clutch of new tracks. Everybody was trying to prove they had a narrative spine, that their record was somehow about something more than just a bunch of songs. Released on the same day as the Cream album was *Days Of Future Passed* by the Moody Blues, the story of an everyman's journey through the day, garnished with string arrangements paid for by their record company Deram in order to showcase what they hoped the world would soon be calling 'Deramic' sound. *The Who Sell Out*, which appeared a few weeks later, had a cover featuring Roger Daltrey in a hip bath full of baked beans with Townshend applying an outsized can of deodorant to his armpit. The songs were linked by the kind of jingles that would be used by radio stations and also some leaden 'skits' by members of the band. The songs themselves had little to do with one another apart from the fact that they were on the same LP.

Those who had previously been happy to be regarded as rockers or scream idols hastened to turn their new, more 'woke' face to the world. Eric Burdon's *Winds Of Change* came with dedications to Lyndon Johnson and Ho Chi Minh (who he devoutly hoped would listen to the album together). The sleeve notes to Scott Walker's first solo LP, which also came out that autumn, referenced the actor Montgomery Clift and the poet John Keats. Jimi Hendrix, who had appeared on the cover of his first album only a few months earlier looking as if he was on his way to the Scotch of St James, was transformed into a Hindu god for the cover of *Axis: Bold As Love*. Steve Winwood, who had been a pimply pin-up in his Spencer Davis days, was reborn as a truth seeker on the cover of Traffic's *Mr Fantasy*, gawping at a mystic mannequin by the light of a fire in the grate of a country cottage.

The LP and the psychedelic revolution were made for each other. An LP allowed bands to swiftly place themselves on the right side of this new divide. With an album they could make claims that nobody would bother to challenge. They could pick their own pictures, write their own testimonials, make the most outrageous claims for themselves, and the audience would forgive them because they wanted so desperately to believe in the promises therein. 'He will sing you his ten tales and then wander till spring,' claimed the liner notes of Tim Buckley's *Goodbye And Hello*, which came out in August. This may have been underselling the punishing regime of drinking and fornication with which Buckley preferred to punctuate said wanderings.

The great psychedelia scare of 1967 provided a once-in-a-lifetime chance for all the acts that had prospered in the beat boom to transform themselves. Psychedelia provided a magical wardrobe; they could enter at one side as road-hardened cherubim, throw on the tabards and sashes which that brief puzzling fashion moment seemed to demand, and then be extruded at the other end only a few months later looking older, leaner and oddly wiser.

Musically what everyone aspired to was *Sgt Pepper*'s sense of being more than the sum of its parts. Some felt it must have been achieved according to a great vision. Many were still thinking it the next year. When in 1968 producer Glyn Johns had his first meeting with the San Francisco-based musician Steve Miller prior to producing his second album he was surprised when Miller arrived with a large roll of paper which he had covered with wavy lines. These, Miller hoped, would describe the 'flow' that the resulting album would have. Nobody had ever thought about flow before. Miller wanted the record to be called *Sailor* and was so enamoured of this concept he wanted to change the band's name to the same word. Johns shrewdly headed this off by suggesting they start the album with the sound of a fog horn; the songs that followed could reflect the changes that had taken place while the mariner was away. Immediately satisfied by this hard-headed solution to a fatheaded premise, Miller's band set to work, forgot to change their name, and the concept idea was never spoken of again. Similarly the Rolling Stones never played any of the songs from *Their Satanic Majesties Request* ever again.

With *Sgt Pepper*, the Beatles set a standard even they couldn't maintain. On the day it was released they were in the studio labouring over 'You Know My Name (Look Up The Number)', a future B-side which was firmly on the wrong side of the fine line separating self-expression from self-indulgence. Their next two singles, 'All You Need Is Love' and 'Hello Goodbye', were lacking in spark. At the end of 1967, in the unhappy period following the death of Brian Epstein, they released the soundtrack to *Magical Mystery Tour* as two EPs. Like *Sgt Pepper* this was named after a fictional enterprise, and contained a cosy nostalgic tea-room dance number from Paul, an eastern-influenced meditation from George and a playground primal scream from John. It was good, but it wasn't as good as *Pepper*. It didn't have its pulse. It didn't have its spark. It didn't have its tunes. It didn't have its all-conquering brio. They would make outstanding records in the time they still had together but for the Beatles it would never be glad confident morning again.

1968

'The Rock Machine is a machine with a soul'

Not everyone had bought into the *Sgt Pepper* epiphany. In the autumn of 1967 Bob Dylan flew down to Nashville and in the course of just three sessions recorded the songs that were to make up *John Wesley Harding*. His was a record as austere as the Beatles' masterpiece had been ornate. Dylan's way of working couldn't have been further away from the layered approach everybody else was taking if they got the chance. Most of his tracks were recorded with just a bass player and a drummer, who both played with customary Nashville restraint. His original plan was to then get Robbie Robertson of his erstwhile road band to overdub guitar. When Robertson heard the tracks, which included 'All Along The Watchtower' and 'I Pity The Poor Immigrant', he realized they were perfect as they were and didn't need any further ornamentation. The album was released at the end of 1967 and became a hit. Its cover, which featured an unexplained snapshot of Dylan posing with two musicians visiting Woodstock from south Asia plus a local carpenter, was the antithesis of the grand statements everyone else was spending time on. It didn't seem to matter. In the UK *John Wesley Harding* spent thirteen weeks at number one at the beginning of 1968. This is still a record for a collection of biblical allegories performed country-style.

One day in late 1967 a twenty-six-year-old Welshman called David Howells was working in his office at the recently established London headquarters of Dylan's record company Columbia. A call from reception announced that a Mr Cohen would like to see him. Mr Cohen didn't look like most of the artists David Howells was accustomed to dealing with. Mr Cohen was a striking thirty-three-year-old Canadian who carried himself more like a particularly intense college professor than a member of the Tremeloes, the Love Affair or any of the other groups who were signed to CBS at the time.

Leonard Cohen had already made something of a name for himself as a poet in Canada and was now trying to do the same as a singer. Howells had already learned of Cohen from John Hammond, the aristocratic eminence of Columbia Records in New York. Hammond was the man who had famously recorded Billie Holiday and had the vision or good fortune to sign the young Bob Dylan to the label. Hammond had also signed Cohen for a $2,000 advance and had begun to make an album with him before handing off the job to John Simon, a young staff producer at Columbia. Cohen had two tapes with him in London that day, the results of his work with Simon. Would Howells have the time to listen to them?

Howells threaded the first tape on the Revox at his desk and pushed play. As the music began, Cohen placed his elbows on the desk and fixed the listener with his gaze, watching his face for any trace of a reaction. The first side began with 'Suzanne', which had been a poem and then a song, and finished with 'Sisters Of Mercy', which was about sharing a hotel room with two young women. Cohen's penetrating gaze did not relent as Howells changed the tape. The second side began with 'So Long Marianne', which was about a mature adult break-up, as was 'Hey, That's No Way To Say Goodbye'.

When the last chords faded away, Cohen asked, 'Is it any good?' Howells enthused. He enthused energetically. In doing this he wasn't merely offering the tribute traditionally expected of record company employees in these situations. Many talented new song-writers had come along in the middle years of the decade but most of them couldn't project on to tape what they managed to project in a folk club once they were placed in the clinical surroundings of a recording studio with the clock counting down the company's time and a bored engineer looking on. And if they could, they couldn't sustain it over more than half an hour. For all its dolorous restraint, this record, which was called *Songs Of Leonard Cohen*, had a decided catchiness to it. Furthermore it projected a kind of bruised romanticism few women could resist and all men were convinced they detected in themselves. Whereas the new songs by Bob Dylan were opaque, Leonard Cohen's described situations you liked to feel you could see. And for all the production touches John Simon had managed to lace it with, the girls' chorus and the jew's harp, the record was as foggy and autumnal as *Sgt Pepper* had been summery and pin-sharp.

David Howells was listening to something which didn't seem to concern itself with variety. He was hearing an LP that made a virtue out of sustaining one mood through its duration. That mood seemed to be a dark one. Howells, with the optimism of youth, assured Cohen, who was in bad need of assurance, that they could sell a few copies of his record in Britain. It came out in the United

States at the end of 1967 to generally dismissive reviews. Cohen was so discouraged by the reception he thought he might not bother recording another. But by the time *Songs Of Leonard Cohen* was released in the UK in early 1968, David Howells had done two things which it's possible to argue gave Leonard Cohen his career as a recording artist. The first is that he had, without asking permission, replaced the Mexican cross on the back of the American cover with an essay about Cohen written by a critic he had just happened to be sitting next to at a London dinner party. The second, and more significant, move was to put the track 'Sisters Of Mercy' on another record. This second record was to prove instrumental in the careers of a number of artists that Columbia had recently signed and in the UK would also be responsible for moving the LP record from luxury good to cultural artefact.

'We had all this talent on CBS,' recalls Howells, 'and there was no way of getting people to hear it. In 1968 the music papers were still mainly bothered about singles, the newspapers didn't really cover music and the radio didn't really feature albums.' The launch the previous year of Radio 1, the station designed for young listeners, hadn't been all that revolutionary. In February 1968 Tony Blackburn was still handing over at nine o'clock to dance band singer Sam Costa and the lunchtime slot was still given over to the Johnny Howard band plus featured vocalists presenting cover versions of chart hits. On Saturday, John Peel hosted *Top Gear* for two hours, introducing his guests the Jimi Hendrix Experience, Captain Beefheart and His Magic Band, the Moody Blues and Tyrannosaurus Rex. This bill of fare was the exception rather than the rule.

Howells' way of breaking this log jam and finding a way to put CBS artists like Leonard Cohen, Moby Grape, Spirit and Taj Mahal before the public was based on a cheap sampler of RCA material called *Pop Shopper* which he'd seen ten years before. He took advantage of creative work that had been recently commissioned by the American parent company Columbia. Clive Davis, the company lawyer who'd been suddenly elevated to the senior position at Columbia, had returned from the Monterey Pop Festival in the summer of the previous year an apparently changed man, suddenly affecting Nehru jackets and flashing the sign of peace. He announced the arrival of a musical revolution that would change hearts and minds and he impressed on his staff the urgency of putting his company's brand on it. He didn't want Columbia to be seen any longer as the home of singing duo Steve Lawrence and Eydie Gormé. He wanted to shrug off any lingering association with the policies of Mitch Miller, the sworn enemy of rock and roll who had been the label's head of A&R in the early part of the decade. He wanted Columbia to be seen as hip and he wanted it to happen quickly.

A marketing campaign was called for and a new portmanteau term decided upon. Henceforth anything that Columbia released which couldn't depend on getting traditional airplay – which could mean a folkie like Tim Rose, a repurposed poet like Leonard Cohen, purveyors of landfill folk rock like the Peanut Butter Conspiracy and even a hastily psychedelicized jazz band like the Don Ellis Orchestra – could be presented as the products of something that Columbia had decided to call the Rock Machine. According to the advertising copy, 'The Rock Machine is a machine with a soul. The Rock Machine isn't a grind-you-up. It's a wind-you-up. The sound is driving. The sound is searching. The sound is music. It's your bag. So it's ours. It's the Super Stars. And the Poets. It's the innovators and the Underground. It's the Loners and the Lovers. And it's more. Much more.'

Not since the advent of the Twist had so many grown-ups tried so hard to get down with the kids. In that copy it's possible to detect the authentic sound of the Don Draper of the hour trying on his hippy sandals and seeing if he can spin this burgeoning market as something profound. In London, David Howells took this copy and put it on the cover of an album for the UK market which he called *The Rock Machine Turns You On*. He persuaded his masters to release it at just under fifteen shillings, which was less than half the price of a standard UK album. He backed it up with strong point-of-sale material and made sure that upon release in early 1968 it would be difficult for any record-shopping longhair not to bump into it, and having done so and consulted the track list it would be equally impossible not to buy it.

I found it in the 'Browserie' section at Vallance's on the Headrow in Leeds in June 1968. As usual I was just looking rather than buying. There was no question of my being able to afford *Gris-Gris* by Dr John the Night Tripper, *Song To A Seagull* by Joni Mitchell or *In-A-Gadda-Da-Vida* by Iron Butterfly, all of which had recently arrived in the racks; however at fourteen shillings and a sixpenny piece *The Rock Machine Turns You On* offered the chance to hear Taj Mahal, Bob Dylan, the United States of America, the Electric Flag, Tim Rose and more for a fraction of what it would cost you to buy any of their individual albums. *The Rock Machine Turns You On* was a huge success, so successful that it resulted in a series of Rock Machine albums. It ensured that every college student in the UK became familiar with the sound of Spirit's 'Fresh Garbage', the Zombies' 'Time Of The Season', Taj Mahal's 'Statesboro Blues', Moby Grape's 'Can't Be So Bad' and, most significantly, Leonard Cohen's 'Sisters Of Mercy'.

People who had shelled out their grant money or the proceeds of their Saturday job for one of these new 'sampler' albums (so-called because the first one, which had appeared on Elektra in the USA in 1954, was designed to look like a needlework sampler) listened and listened closely. They paid no less attention to *You Can All Join In*, the sampler of acts on the Island and Chrysalis labels, to *Gutbucket*, the 'underworld eruption' from the Liberty label with a young pig on the cover, and to *Picnic (A Breath Of Fresh Air)*, which tried to interest Pink Floyd fans in Pete Brown and Piblokto!, and the Edgar Broughton Band. In her memoirs the musician Viv Albertine recalls experiencing a Proustian rush on finding a 1969 sampler album in a charity shop in recent years. 'It was like I'd come upon an old and dear friend I hadn't seen for thirty years. Somebody I'd told all my secrets to. The blue cover with the jumbled-up sweets spelling the bands' names was so familiar, it meant more to me than seeing a family photograph.'

The objective of the Rock Machine campaign had been to sell LPs by artists who couldn't be guaranteed radio play or press coverage, and it worked, particularly in the case of the *Songs Of Leonard Cohen*: this sold 150,000 copies in the UK, at the time an unimaginably large number for a record by a previously unknown quantity. This success was an early demonstration of the transformative power of the LP. If you went into a girl's room at college in the year 1968 it seemed inevitable that it would be the first record your eyes fell upon. I began my college career in September that year, just a couple of weeks after it had entered the British LP charts. It felt as if the grown-ups' favourites such as Tom Jones, Engelbert Humperdinck and the soundtrack of *The Sound of Music* were suddenly being jostled by the chosen favourites of an insurgent army of longhairs among whom could be numbered John Mayall's *Bare Wires*, Pink Floyd's *A Saucerful Of Secrets* and Tyrannosaurus Rex's charismatically long-winded *My People Were Fair And Had Sky In Their Hair . . . But Now They're Content To Wear Stars On Their Brows*. Some of those records were fly-by-nights but Cohen's was to spend seventy weeks on the charts, eventually rising as high as number thirteen. It was the rise of his LP in the UK that took him places that book publishing could never have carried him.

The rise of the popularity of the LP closely paralleled the rise of higher education. A good percentage of those 150,000 buyers of Cohen's album were baby boomers who were going away to college and university in the late sixties in unprecedented numbers. They found in Cohen's album something similar to what earlier generations had found in their dog-eared copies of Kerouac. It was a comparable badge of belonging to a community of sensitive types. Like Tim Hardin, whose first two albums had produced songs like 'The Lady Came From Baltimore' and 'Don't Make Promises', Cohen's work suggested a life which appeared to be spent either in bed with beautiful women or at his desk writing about being in bed with beautiful women. His songs also cunningly hinted that all his manoeuvres beneath the eiderdown had not been accomplished without some expense of soul. He had the precious quality, so valuable in the burgeoning LP age, of being able to generate just enough drama to be magnetic while also remaining soft enough to serve as background music.

Van Morrison's *Astral Weeks*, which came out at the end of 1968, in the same week as what history came to call the Beatles' White Album and the somewhat less memorable *Release Of An Oath* from the Electric Prunes, had a similar consistency of mood. *Astral Weeks* had been recorded in just three sessions in September and October. The initial signs were not promising. Morrison was accompanied by jazz musicians he had never met before the recording and didn't communicate with during the session. *Astral Weeks* didn't bother any charts at the time. Its subsequent exaltation enabled Morrison and his record company to seize every opportunity to remind the public of what they had so disgracefully passed up.

In the record business there's no success like failure because it provides executives with that tiny bit of high ground from which they can lecture the public on having passed by on the other side. They rarely apologize for having spent just as much money and energy trying to convince us of the qualities of records that even they now admit are stinkers. Nonetheless *Astral Weeks* got a rave review in *Rolling Stone* from Greil Marcus, who called it 'a profoundly intellectual album', which is the kind of judgement that has dogged it ever since. He also said that while it wasn't strictly a rock record it was the kind of thing that would appeal to people who liked rock. This was bad news for Van Morrison because he had tried above all to make something that wasn't rock. The problem was that while jazz fans or folk fans or fans of so-called serious music were the first to point out what was wrong with music, fans of rock music were far more accepting, often because whatever they were listening to they had never heard before. Even for somebody as determinedly out of step as Van Morrison it appeared there was no escaping the rock machine and its attendant benefits.

Astral Weeks was the first album I remember being regularly referred to as 'underrated'. All the people who bought it considered it their special secret. That was a key part of its appeal. But, like the Masons', this was a secret shared. In the last paragraph of Marcus's review in *Rolling Stone* he talks about turning off 'the phonograph' and then hearing from across the way the sound of Richard Davis's bass and Van Morrison's voice. Apparently he wasn't the only one. I remember hearing John Peel play 'Sweet Thing' one Saturday afternoon in 1968 when I was washing my dad's car. I can't remember what he said about it but I came away with the strong impression that this record was rated, and more importantly rated by the right people. At some point in the next few months I bought it. The first side of *Astral Weeks* was titled 'Part One: In The Beginning'; the second side was 'Part Two: Afterwards'. There was no explanation for what it all meant but that didn't seem to matter to us if we decided we liked the singer. There were other singer-songwriters, such as Donovan, who could never convincingly stretch themselves over two sides of a long-player. Van Morrison clearly could. *Astral Weeks* never sold intensively enough to get in the chart at the time, but it didn't stop selling for the next fifty years. This presumably is some consolation, even for Van Morrison.

The LPs of the singer-songwriters had the happy side-effect of seeming to glamorize the apparently indigent lifestyles of many of the people who bought their records. The artists who made these records seemed to inhabit the same world of rented flats, Nescafé breakfasts and distances covered by hitch-hiking as the rest of us, and their records seemed to have come from the same kind of rooms in which we listened to them. The British singer-songwriter Al Stewart, who had previously shared a flat in the East End with Paul Simon, had laid a marker for this genre with his 1967 debut *Bed-Sitter Images* which, via songs like 'Swiss Cottage Manoeuvres' and 'A Long Way Down From Stephanie', exhaustively catalogued his own blue-fingered fumblings with a succession of Silvikrin madonnas. Stewart scored a further first with his album *Love Chronicles* wherein he recapitulated his entire amatory CV in an eighteen-minute title track which inevitably peaked with the line 'it grew to be less like fucking and more like making love'. This was the first use of that Anglo-Saxon verb in a mainstream album that you could buy on any high street. At the time that was sufficient outrage to get him on the front page of the *Sunday People*. Like the songs of Cohen and Hardin and even Paul Simon, every such song about love gone wrong was actually a brag masquerading as an apology.

True confessions were suddenly at a premium. Those of us who were learning about life couldn't get enough of the apparently valuable experiences of the people who were as many as five years older. Some were persevering with concept albums. Simon & Garfunkel's *Bookends*, which was released in April 1968 to take advantage of the duo's popularity surging on the back of the use of their music in the Mike Nichols film *The Graduate*, had started life as a birth-to-death concept. This conceit just about got them through the first side, which began with the impassioned cry of an anguished mother 'Save The Life Of My Child', included the definitive me-and-my-girl-against-the-world song 'America' and managed to get as far as the closing tune 'Old Friends' thanks to some vox pops Art Garfunkel had recorded at an old people's home. The rest of the album was made up of songs such as 'A Hazy Shade Of Winter' that hadn't made the soundtrack and one that had.

'Mrs Robinson' was a classic illustration that no matter how a concept arises in pop music it's he who pays the piper who calls the tune. This song started life as 'Mrs Roosevelt' and was changed so that it could be profitably applied to the character played by Anne Bancroft in the movie. The exposure in a hit film took Simon & Garfunkel up to another level. According to Columbia Records the *Bookends* album had over a million dollars in advance orders before it even left the warehouse and was already qualified for gold status. Clive Davis, the new boss of Columbia, wanted to put it out at a dollar more than the usual list price of $4.79. This kind of premium pricing of a record that is guaranteed to sell well no matter the price was not yet widespread industry practice. The duo objected on the grounds that it would not make them look good. However, they got over their objections once they had taken the opportunity to renegotiate their deal with Columbia for a longer term and at a higher royalty rate. *Bookends* went into the chart and remained there for the rest of the year. In the UK it was a number one album. The albums gold rush was on its way.

When Simon & Garfunkel had originally signed for Columbia in 1966 they had been seen as a folk act and therefore they had a contract that specified that all the musicians' costs would be paid for by the company. This was standard practice dating from the days when an album would be completed in a couple of days. Once they started making *Bookends* Paul Simon took advantage of this by bringing in strings, percussion and, on 'Save The Life Of My

Child', the first recorded use of Robert Moog's recently invented synthesizer. This was operated by John Simon, the same producer/arranger who had worked on Cohen's record. By the time Cohen's album came out John Simon had been demoted from producer to production assistant. But by then he had left Columbia's employ and been tempted away by Al Kooper, who wanted him to produce and, where necessary, arrange the first album by the new big band he'd put together upon leaving the Blues Project, who were now named Blood, Sweat & Tears. This was the kind of name that people suddenly expected pop groups to come along with. We were no longer in the world of *Thank Your Lucky Stars* and *American Bandstand*. The group's album *Child Is Father To The Man* bore many of the marks of that post-*Pepper* summer. The cover featured each member of the band dandling a dummy of them as a child on their knees, it had not just an overture but also an underture, and to cap it all a track called 'The Modern Adventures of Plato, Diogenes and Freud'. It also had some smart song choices from new writers – 'Just One Smile' by Randy Newman, 'Without Her' by Harry Nilsson and 'Morning Glory' by Tim Buckley – but the quality it led with was heaviosity.

John Simon was an unusual creature in this place and this time. He was a properly trained musician. Like George Martin on the other side of the Atlantic he had been apprenticed to a major record company where he found himself called upon to work on everything from records of hymns to the latest by America's polka king Frankie Yankovic. Simon had perfect pitch. He could instantly identify by ear any note any musician was playing. When working with trained musicians perfect pitch is a blessing. When working with musicians who had difficulty tuning their own instruments this could just as easily become a cross to bear. Simon was only a few years older than the rock musicians he was frequently sent to work with but he couldn't conceal the contempt he felt for many of them. Simon thought most of them were all hair and tight pants. His next clients were much celebrated for both.

Clive Davis had signed Big Brother and the Holding Company on the basis of the widespread enthusiasm for their singer Janis Joplin. Any such signing was largely a matter of faith. It was one thing to see somebody perform for an audience of converts who had probably been taking exactly the same drugs as the people on stage and had been softened up by the word from hip quarters to accept what they were hearing as being the last word in rhythm and blues. It was quite another to take such a group into a studio and make the kind of record that would pass muster on a radio programme or while playing over the PA in a record shop. Only the Rolling Stones had managed to put their stage act on record and have it sound even more exciting than it did in person. Everybody else had failed.

Simon was an interesting choice to get a hit album out of Big Brother. For a start he thought they were terrible. He had an East Coast elitist's disdain for a lot of the music that had come out of San Francisco under the flag of the Summer of Love. He wasn't the only one who felt this way about the folkies and jug band players who seemed to have suddenly plugged in, dropped acid and were making music that no doubt sounded great to initiates but tended to expire on contact with vinyl. Even Joe Smith, who signed the Grateful Dead to Warner Brothers at the same time, said of them 'they did so much acid it was hard to separate reality from make-believe'. It would be another two years before Warner Bros would work out how to sell an album by the Grateful Dead.

Simon thought Janis had star quality but didn't particularly like her, either as a singer or a person. Her act was allegedly spontaneous but in fact was highly contrived. 'She would rehearse her screams,' he later remembered. 'This is my Tina Turner scream. This is my Big Mama Thornton scream. Which one shall I use in this spot?' Furthermore he thought the band were dunderheads who played too loud and couldn't keep time. Since Janis had first made a splash on stage at the Monterey Pop Festival it had been his plan to record them live. Columbia took them to Detroit and taped them in front of an audience in what was then regarded as Rock City USA. The audience in Detroit were simply puzzled. Simon began to suspect that this band's music couldn't survive more than ten miles outside San Francisco because it depended on an audience being every bit as out of it as the band.

Because they weren't good enough live to be able to survive a live recording and they weren't polished enough in the studio to make a traditional record, Simon decided he was going to make an LP that was almost an artist's impression of a night out among the freaks of Haight Ashbury. They recorded it over three months in a studio in New York. Hardly any of it was live but the finished item was tricked out with all kinds of devices to give the listener the impression that they were experiencing it in an atmosphere thick with patchouli oil and body odour. It began with an introduction by the concert promoter Bill Graham – 'four gentlemen and one great, great broad' – which was added in the studio. Tracks were peppered with the sound of breaking glass and extraneous crowd noises supplied not by two thousand rabid hippies but by volunteers from the Columbia Records typing pool. And in case anybody didn't get the point the finished record was put in a jacket drawn by the underground cartoonist Robert Crumb. This was a kind of altar piece among whose panels could be seen the audience at the Fillmore Auditorium pronouncing it all 'sike-ay-delic', Janis Joplin making her way through the desert shackled to a black ball and chain labelled 'Big Mama Thornton', and a cartoon black mama holding a baby evidently traumatized by the sound of Janis shrieking George Gershwin's 'Summertime'. It spelled out the message 'never mind the music, feel the lifestyle'. It worked. It was at number one in the United States throughout the summer of 1968.

John Simon asked for his name to be taken off *Cheap Thrills*. This was an unusual thing to do. It was particularly unusual since with this record he became one of the first record producers to qualify for royalties (the band's manager Albert Grossman had told them 'he's getting two-fifths of your royalties and he'll be worth it'). Simon had no wish to repeat the experience of producing Big Brother. He was eager to move on. By the time Big Brother were riding high on the *Billboard* chart Simon was putting his producer's credit on two further albums that were made in the *Sgt Pepper* aftermath, both of which are more celebrated than either *Cheap Thrills* or *Bookends*. Speaking of the group who made them in later years Simon recalled, 'I thought it was the best music I'd ever heard.'

1969

'Fucking incredible'

On 10 October 1969 the *New York Times* reported that 2,500 members of the National Guard had been called on to the streets of Chicago to deal with rioting. This was in the midst of Days of Rage, an attempt by factions of the anti-Vietnam war movement to 'bring the war to America'. Protests against the war seemed to be moving away from demonstration towards direct action. The trouble in Chicago the previous day had begun with sixty members of a self-declared 'women's militia' gathering in a park intending to destroy a military induction ceremony. It was easy to see they were serious because they had arrived equipped with motorcycle helmets and clubs.

This was the year that climaxed in August with Woodstock and reached its nadir in December with Altamont. It was a year of wild contrasts. The more bucolic side of youth was also on show on the same day with the *Times* report on a special wedding. Here the bride and groom had stood in the middle of a meadow to make their vows. At the climax of the ceremony Judy Collins had stood before them with her guitar and sung Leonard Cohen's 'Suzanne'. The *Times* reported that it was not a traditional wedding, but it approved nonetheless. The couple getting married were Arlo Guthrie and Jackie Hyde. The son of Woody, Arlo had been recently enriched by the success of the film based on his song 'Alice's Restaurant', to the extent that he had been able to buy 200 acres of land and two houses. His new album *Running Down The Road* was out that week, which may have been why he invited the press to his wedding. He knew that he would be going up against the new record from the Beatles, which was named after the address of the studio where it had been recorded. The number one single in the United States that week was 'Sugar, Sugar' by the Archies.

Also on 10 October 1969, *The Times* of London reported that the Conservative Party Conference had voted by a substantial majority to support Britain's entry into what was known as the Common Market. It further reported that dustmen in London were going on strike in support of their claim to be paid £20 a week. *The Times* understandably didn't report that on that same day work began on recording the title song of a a proposed stage musical which was to be called *Jesus Christ Superstar*. Tim Rice and Andrew Lloyd Webber's earlier success with *Joseph and the Amazing Technicolor Dreamcoat* had persuaded them that their new work, about the passion of Christ, would stand more of a chance of being produced in the West End and possibly even on Broadway if they made it as a record first. The single attracted enough attention for the record company MCA, who feared they might be getting left behind in the great long-playing land grab, to pay for the whole thing to be recorded and marketed as a double album before there was any interest in it being performed on a stage. This was a complete reversal of the way these things had traditionally been done but it was also a recognition that the one guaranteed way to get yourself noticed was to have an album in the racks.

Thus Rice and Lloyd Webber got an advance from MCA which was enough to buy them recording time, book the highly prestigious Olympic Studios in Barnes and manage to persuade a cast of rock musicians and actors to contribute to the recording. These were given the choice of being paid a session fee or holding out for a royalty. Some of them, such as the members of Joe Cocker's Grease Band who were providing the rhythm section, decided they would rather have beer money today than pension plan money tomorrow, which may not have been the wisest choice. In the rock category there seemed to be an appetite for things that had never been done before. It was no use trying to interest the press or the radio. Increasingly, it seemed, they would follow what was happening in the shops.

On that same 10 October, Bruce Findlay opened the door to his record shop in Edinburgh. He and his brother, who were both in their twenties at the time, had followed their mother into the record retail business when Bruce had returned from working in shops in London. Bruce had been at Disci in west London on the day *Sgt Pepper* came out and had seen for himself the LP gold rush. He and his brother started out in Falkirk with a tiny shop modelled after the One Stop shop in London's South Molton Street which was, as far as he was concerned, the acme of the fashionable record shop. Within two years they had extended their reach into Edinburgh where a burgeoning student population offered a commercial opportunity.

'We were the first people in Scotland to provide headphones for people to listen to records before they bought,' he recalls. 'Most of the old-style shops had those hardboard listening booths and they didn't like you listening too long if you didn't buy anything. Provided we weren't too busy we didn't mind. People would listen to one side and then ask for it to be turned over and sometimes leave without buying anything. It happened. But when the shop was busy it was very different.'

The 10th of October was one such busy day. On that day Bruce received his shipment of *In The Court Of The Crimson King – An Observation By King Crimson*. This marked a singularly portentous way of talking about the first album by a new pop group. It was one of those releases that drew a dividing line between the old and new worlds of the LP and, in hindsight, inaugurated a whole new category of music that simply would not have had any reason to exist had it not been for the long-playing record. That week a full-page advertisement for the album appeared in *Record Retailer,* the British trade paper. This advert was unusual in that the copy was written by Pete Townshend, who was neither a member of King Crimson nor an Island artist. Nonetheless he had agreed to enthuse about this first album by this group who had been entirely unknown a few months earlier. Island Records, who were at the time positioning themselves as the cognoscenti's record label of choice, had announced that they had sufficient faith in the quality of their output to let others speak on their behalf. Townshend did his part, describing it in the first paragraph of the copy as 'fucking incredible'.

The following week the editors of *Record Retailer* were forced to apologize for allowing this incendiary adjective to slip through. Their letters column carried indignant complaints from the managers of the Music Centre of Cornwall and Hammonds of Hull, saying that while they were ex-army and broadminded they had been compelled to hide the previous week's issue lest some of their staff – who were, let's not forget, female and teenagers – should see this offensive word.

In 1969 it was not easy to predict what might cause offence. The *Blind Faith* album had been released by Polydor that August and there had been little comment about the fact that its cover featured a bare-breasted pubescent girl. Geoffrey Cannon's review in the *Guardian* in September hadn't mentioned it at all. The photographer Bob Seidemann had simply approached a teenage girl on the London Underground who had the perfect pre-Raphaelite look. She declined to pose but her younger sister agreed in exchange for a horse. Eric Clapton remembers that when he was first shown it by the photographer he liked it because it seemed innocent. There was a full-page ad for it in *Record Retailer* which didn't occasion any complaints. There was more push-back in the United States where it was agreed to issue it with an alternative cover featuring a picture of the band.

Nudity was part of the scenery at the time. 1969 was the year when *Hair*, the so-called 'tribal love rock musical', was the hottest ticket on Broadway and the West End, the year when overheated heads at Woodstock took off their clothes and went swimming, the year when almost every page of the young *Rolling Stone* featured somebody in some state of undress: nakedness seemed to be unsexualized and uncontroversial. The people with long hair who had been marching against war and discrimination hadn't yet worked out what, if anything, they were supposed to be offended by.

The first Rod Stewart solo album appeared in the United States in late 1969 with a plain cover. In Britain it came out early in 1970 under the title *An Old Raincoat Won't Ever Let You Down*. To drive the point home its cover featured a picture of an elderly pervert chasing cherubic young children in the park. Nobody batted an eyelid.

Hip young retailers like Bruce Findlay directly profited from the fustiness of a traditional retail sector which was suddenly having to deal with material much of which was deliberately provocative. When *In The Court Of The Crimson King* was sold in by the record company he discovered that the local chain stores who were his competitors were buying only a single copy. Therefore he felt confident that if he ordered a lot then the potential customers, most of whom were students, would buy it from him. He ordered 250, which seemed a great deal for the first album by an unknown group. Halfway through the Saturday of that week he had already sold a hundred and was on the phone to Island to make sure he could get more.

From the start King Crimson had enjoyed the following wind of industry confidence. Le tout Mayfair seemed to have decided that they were the group to be talking about, regardless of whether they had heard them or not. They had made their London debut in front of the Moody Blues, Manfred Mann and Ginger Baker. Jimi Hendrix was said to have called them the best band in the world. They did their first major London show supporting the Rolling Stones at Hyde Park in front of 650,000 people on 5 July in the same week that Brian Jones had died. Following that show Muff Winwood at Island changed his mind about signing them and so they severed their previous ties with Decca and the Moody Blues. This was probably best for them. It's doubtful that Decca, Britain's most conservative record company, would have been as adventurous as Island were when it came to the all-important business of marketing the record. In King Crimson's case it was the cover that put them over the top. This was designed by Barry Godber, a twenty-five-year-old friend of the band who only ever did one record cover. Godber had originally intended to go to art school but decided to become a computer programmer instead. To achieve the striking image on the front Godber simply opened his mouth in a shaving mirror and then painted what he saw. Tragically, Godber died the following year of a heart attack without painting any other album cover.

Greg Lake, who was King Crimson's lead singer at the time, later said 'it's a great cover because it's a great record'. This statement, on the face of it a non sequitur, points to a key truth of the emerging album market. LPs and LP covers had a symbiotic relationship.

There are few criticisms of the cover design of an album once it is accepted as a good album. A powerful record encourages us to give even the cover of *Let It Bleed*, featuring a squashed cake baked by the young Delia Smith, the benefit of the doubt. But once powerful music is combined with powerful image-making a multiplier effect increases its charisma. That certainly applied with *In The Court Of The Crimson King*. It didn't have the name of the artist or the record on the outside. Godber had cropped in tight on his own face which gave his open mouth and oscillating epiglottis the look of a creature dwelling in a cave. Its livid colour scheme added a further comic-book tone. The cover was the only sales tool the record needed. Any record shop that stocked it put it in the front window. The producer Rhett Davies, at the time working in a record shop in east London, filled the entire window of his branch with twenty covers for the record with a joint stuck in one of the mouths. *In The Court Of The Crimson King* eventually went as high as number five in the UK LP chart, which was a significant performance for a new group with no hit single.

The music King Crimson made in 1969 would come to be described as 'art-rock' and even, in the fullness of time, 'progressive', but that would take a while. Praising *In The Court Of The Crimson King*'s steely playing and its head-spinning use of multi-track, the underground paper *International Times* gave up trying to convey the details and simply pronounced it 'the ultimate album'. It was difficult to tell whether people actually liked it or not but they all agreed it was 'amazing' as if the primary job of music was to amaze. It appeared that the album form had been perfected only a few years after being invented.

The market for rock LPs at the time was so febrile and happily immature that King Crimson was just waved in alongside the other significant releases of the year such as *Abbey Road* (described by *Record Retailer* as 'the Beatles' first album this year'), the Who's unprecedented *Tommy*, Pink Floyd's *Ummagumma* (the first double album on the Harvest label, which retailed for a stiff fifty-seven shillings and sixpence), Bob Dylan's blithe *Nashville Skyline*, Joni Mitchell's *Clouds*, *Hot Rats* (the only record Frank Zappa ever made that could appeal to anyone beyond his fan base), Neil Young's genuinely influential *Everybody Knows This Is Nowhere*, and albums by the Stooges and Velvet Underground. Even those records that might be considered deficient in charm were found amusing. We forgave everything, whether it was the punishment by dissonance that was Captain Beefheart's double album *Trout Mask Replica*, the unaccountably three-sided double album *Second Winter* by Johnny Winter, or the fact that Ten Years After decided to give over one track to their percussion version of 'Three Blind Mice' just so their drummer could share in the royalties for allegedly songwriting. Only a fool would have bought an album called *Stonedhenge*. I was that fool.

In 1969 this new market for LPs, all of which could be ushered beneath the welcoming umbrella of rock, seemed so exciting, so full of newcomers (this was the first year of Nick Drake, Boz Scaggs and Santana) as well as new records from established favourites (Fairport Convention, for one, released no fewer than three completely new albums, each with a different line-up, while undergoing a fatal road accident that would have destroyed most bands, all in the space of this single calendar year), that it seemed churlish to decide that any of it was beyond your personal taste. Rock was a broad church and none of us were sectarians. Despite the dramatic difference in their styles and iconography, *In The Court Of The Crimson King* was bought by some of the same people who bought the albums by the group John Simon had been so keen to produce, the one who played what he called the best music he had ever heard. I was one of them.

Just as the Beatles had been putting the finishing touches to *Sgt*

Pepper, Bob Dylan, Robbie Robertson and the rest of the road band which had toured with him up until his motorcycle accident in 1966 had played, for their own amusement, in the basement of a house near Woodstock in upstate New York. Instead of the torrents of vituperation that had proved so popular on Dylan's last album *Blonde On Blonde*, Dylan and his band had started off playing traditional material. Excited by the idea that he could finally record in a place that wasn't owned by a record company, Dylan embarked on a compositional hot streak, turning up every day with new songs of his own to play with the band. Some of these new compositions, such as 'You Ain't Going Nowhere' and 'This Wheel's On Fire', would in the future provide big hit records for acts like the Byrds and Julie Driscoll. At the time home recording was a seductive novelty. Robertson and Garth Hudson, who supervised, ran their tape at a slow speed because they didn't have the budget to afford more of it. Most of the rest of the recordings would not be released for another ten years, by which time the bootleg industry had ensured that 'The Basement Tapes', as they had come to be known, would be legendary.

The four Canadians and one American from Arkansas who made up this band had been variously known as the Crackers and Levon and the Hawks. By 1968 they were referred to by the people who lived near them in the bohemian enclave of Woodstock as 'the band', much as if they'd been the plumbers or the gardeners. Albert Grossman, Dylan's manager, had heard them playing in the basement of Big Pink, the house on Stoll Road, West Saugerties where the musicians had been living that summer, and decided he should get them their own record deal and so they started using their town name as their professional name. Most band names in 1968 were deliberately incongruous shotgun marriages of adjective and noun such as Moby Grape, Iron Butterfly, Black Sabbath, Mighty Baby, Heavy Jelly and Led Zeppelin. By choosing instead to call themselves the

Band these five were not being arch but there was no doubt they were certain of themselves.

They had good reason for this confidence. Between them the five could boast three exceptional singers, three songwriters, two drummers and a combined skill set that meant that unlike Big Brother and the Holding Company they could get a tune out of just about anything. As though to drive home the point, drummer Levon Helm recorded their entire second album using a wooden-rimmed kit he'd picked up in a Los Angeles junk shop.

Their songs, most of which were supplied by Robbie Robertson, didn't sound as though they came from anywhere on the musical map. In fact, although they hinted at much music that had gone before, they were entirely without precedent. Robertson was the obvious leader in the band. He was only twenty-six in 1969 but had left Ontario at the age of sixteen to join Ronnie Hawkins's band in Arkansas. During his ten years with Hawkins and then Dylan he had absorbed a great deal. He was now able to write songs that were inspired by earlier songs but happily didn't wind up sounding like them, and also he could cast the contrasting voices of Rick Danko, Richard Manuel and Levon Helm as the different protagonists of these songs. In the case of 'The Night They Drove Old Dixie Down' he wanted Helm, the group's only Southerner, to sing something about the American Civil War. He researched the subject at the Woodstock Public Library, taking on board Helm's injunction never to mention the name of Abraham Lincoln.

They made some demos of their early songs with John Simon producing. Albert Grossman took them to Capitol, who signed them. Then they went to New York and Los Angeles to make an entire album. In his memoir *Testimony*, Robertson says that the songs weren't inspired by personal experience or a particular era. The Band were simply motivated by the desire to put together songs that worked. In the past their job had been to supply the sound demanded by a particular employer. Now suddenly they had to find their own voice. They had no way of knowing that what had sounded good in the basement would still sound good once it was put through the professional recording machine.

They insisted on playing and recording in a circle so that they could exchange visual cues. Their first engineers warned this was contrary to good recording practice and would result in sound leaking from one microphone to another. They said that was a risk they were prepared to take, but even they were amazed at how well those recordings turned out. It was only at the last moment that they came up with a song that seemed striking enough to have a chance as a single. When 'The Weight' was released in the summer of 1968 it was credited on the label not to the Band but to the five individuals who had played on it. It was only at the last moment, on 13 July, when *Music From Big Pink* was released with a cover fronted by one of Bob Dylan's less sophisticated daubs, that it was finally announced as 'The Band'. It came out the same day as *In-A-Gadda-Da-Vida* by Iron Butterfly, which did rather better.

There must have been people who felt that it would be forgotten as quickly as the other records that came out that week, which included Donovan's *In Concert* and the first records by the Ohio Express and the New York Rock and Roll Ensemble. If so they could not have been more wrong. The record that turned most heads in that time was *Sgt Pepper*. The record that turned the second most heads was *Music From Big Pink*. Among the most fervent admirers of the latter were the men who made the former. Within months of its release George Harrison had beaten a path to Woodstock to find out how they had done it.

The album wasn't a huge hit but John Simon recalls that 'among musicians it was the bomb'. Many of those musicians took *Music From Big Pink* as a repudiation of the excesses of the previous year. This certainly applied to Eric Clapton, who heard an advance tape while he was touring America with Cream on the back of the successful *Disraeli Gears*. 'It stopped me in my tracks,' he recalled. The Band couldn't tour to support *Music From Big Pink* because Rick Danko had crashed his car while drunk and required hospital treatment. The fact that at the moment of their greatest triumph they could only be heard via that one record only increased *Music From Big Pink*'s mystique. Because they couldn't tour they rolled right into making another record, again with John Simon.

Although the first record was named in honour of the Big Pink house where the musicians had been living, the recording itself was actually done far from the country, at a studio in the middle of Manhattan. Producer John Simon was enjoined to make it sound like the demo, which he did, conjuring the same sound picture whether the songs had been recorded within earshot of birdsong, amid the thrum of crosstown traffic or in the same Hollywood studio favoured by Frank Sinatra and Nelson Riddle.

To make the second album, which was released in September 1969 under the name *The Band*, they insisted on getting as far away from the East Coast weather as they could, renting a house in the Hollywood Hills which was owned by Sammy Davis Jr and setting up their instruments and recording console in the swimming pool house. Although the lyrics of Robertson's songs conjured a woodcut world of Civil War veterans and Texas storms, although they sounded like a bar band whiling away the afternoon in a deserted hotel as some ineffably sad Salvation Army band trudged by outside, those recordings were made using exactly the same late sixties amenities as all the other rock bands. But the sound of *The Band* was defined as much by the buttons it refused to press as *Sgt Pepper* had been by its eagerness for sensation. It had a new fingerprint which was as consonant with a new age of disillusion as the Beatles' masterpiece had been with the Summer of Love.

As the casualty count from the war in Vietnam peaked, the

comedown from the Summer of Love was marked by Jimi Hendrix conjuring the rocket's red glare in front of the apparently shell-shocked, blanket-wrapped battalions retreating from Woodstock, and many different bands sought the shelter of established musical traditions. Fleetwood Mac launched themselves playing the blues of Elmore James. The Byrds turned from 'Eight Miles High' to the country gospel songs of the Louvin Brothers. In Britain, Fairport Convention treated their road crash injuries with old English ballads collected by Cecil Sharp.

The Band did something even more audacious than all of them. The Band didn't play the old songs at all. The Band wrote their own old songs. They fashioned a tradition to suit their own tastes. These were Canadians in their mid-twenties singing about their desire to be home in old Virginny. These were sons of Bo Diddley who seemed to be channelling music from the past, in many cases a past that had never actually existed. It was 'cultural appropriation' on a massive scale. It was magnificent.

As is always the case with acts that are hailed as being 'all about the music', the Band were quite happy to project an image which helped promote and also make more sense of the music. They carried themselves like artisans rather than visionaries. They looked like men rather than hippy boys. In the middle of 1969, when so much music seemed to have broken loose of its moorings and America itself seemed riven by conflict over long hair and Vietnam, they seemed refreshingly grounded. While the Doors sang about breaking on through to the other side, the Band, who had appeared on the inside cover of their first album surrounded by members of their families, instead celebrated the ties that bind.

It was vital that the packaging of this second album reflected this. The job was given to Bob Cato, the former art director of snazzy uptown magazines and also, in his capacity at Columbia, the guy who had the idea to get Robert Crumb to do the cover of

Big Brother's *Cheap Thrills*. A lot of the key decisions were already taken for him. Elliott Landy had photographed the five members of the group on a road near Danko's house in Woodstock. During the session it had begun to rain, making them look even more like staff officers in one of Mathew Brady's field photographs from the Civil War. By that time they had begun to consciously shape their own image. They also absorbed one of the key responsibilities of all great bands, which is to begin to resemble each other. Gone were the Nehru collars and studious spectacles of *Music From Big Pink*. At around this time they turned up at someone's house and they were said to suddenly look like a daguerreotype.

Cato listened to the record twenty times before he decided how he was going to design it. He went for sepia brown, an earth tone redolent of agricultural toil or a nineteenth-century *carte de visite*. Whereas the front of the previous album had dodged the idea of what they looked like, this time he put them front, centre and huge. Cato similarly seized on Garth Hudson's idea to put some of the lyrics of 'The Darktown Strutters' Ball' on the back. The final package looked substantial, adult, soulful. When you first glimpsed it in the racks of your local record store you knew what henceforth you wished to look like and the experience of the cover dramatically shaped your expectations of what would happen when you took it home and put it on.

People who heard the Band's music were puzzled and also moved by it, which probably accounted for how successful *The Band* was when it was released. Many years later Bruce Springsteen sagely observed that 'all popular artists get caught between making records and making music. If you're lucky, sometimes it's the same thing. When you learn to craft your music into recordings, there's always something gained and something lost. The ease of an unselfconscious voice gives way to the formality of presentation.' *The Band* is one of the few records of the LP age that seems to have avoided making that compromise. I have a friend who claims he has still never heard the second side since he considers the first side, which begins with 'Across The Great Divide' and finishes with 'Whispering Pines', too perfect to require adding to.

Everything on *The Band* seemed reminiscent of an earlier era yet nothing on it sounded as though it had been actually played before. It wasn't a record that gave itself up easily. It was a record that demanded to be played in its entirety and played repeatedly in order for its emotional punch to land.

The other members of the group did their sterling stuff and then went off drinking and drugging and driving their cars into the many ditches around Woodstock. Robertson and John Simon had greater ambitions for *The Band* and closely supervised each stage of post-production until they held it in their hands. Robertson was a film buff, and his ambitions for the record were almost cinematic. His aim was that it should above all capture a feeling. Film directors Dennis Hopper and Michelangelo Antonioni both dropped in to hear it as it was being recorded and they felt it too. *The Band* was the first LP to carve out a place in the imagination of a generation, a place that was as much visual as musical, and this was achieved without the help of promotional video. *The Band* was as much a work of imagination as *Butch Cassidy and the Sundance Kid*, which came out the same year, and as rich and resonant as *Midnight Cowboy* or *Easy Rider*. In a sense *The Band*, a mere record, is a better movie than any of them.

1970

'The Man can't bust our music'

I may not have used the word out loud but by 1970 my all-consuming interest in long-playing records made me feel qualified to be a paid-up member of the emergent sub-culture of people increasingly referred to as 'heads'. 'Head' was a term originally borrowed from jazz, intended to be a nose-tapping indication of a fondness for soft drugs. For most of us lack of funds, difficulty of access and unwillingness to get involved in anything which seemed to call for so much paper-folding meant our acquaintance with the drug culture didn't go much further than nodding knowingly at anything we didn't understand in a song lyric and assuming it must be something to do with that side of things. The overwhelming majority of the people who bought the records that celebrated drug use didn't use drugs themselves. In every other respect, in the length of our hair, in the way we dressed and in the way we attempted to emulate the faintly arch and apparently bemused way of speaking made popular by the DJ John Peel, we identified strongly with the tribe who did.

It was still possible for heads to live a low-budget life in London in 1970. Although student numbers were rising steeply as the baby boomers left school, higher education was still only available to 8 per cent of the population (today it nudges 50 per cent). This comparatively privileged group had their education financed by a grant from their local authority, money from their parents if they were lucky, and whatever they had managed to save from a holiday job, which usually involved some form of hard physical labour. With a loaf of bread costing 5p (or one shilling – this was the last year of pounds, shillings and pence), a packet of Embassy cigarettes 20p and a Wimpy hamburger 10p, most of their daily requirements could be covered easily. In many respects the world seemed as economically stable as it had done in the fifties. But 1970 was one year before the decision to take America off the gold standard and the subsequent rise in the price of oil ushered in an era when inflation became endemic. In 1960 the rate of inflation had been 1 per cent. By 1975 it was running at 25 per cent.

In 1970, heads sharing a flat in central London would expect to pay around £7 each per week. If they were prepared to settle for cheaper areas like Muswell Hill and Finsbury Park *Time Out's Book of London* predicted they could get a three-room flat for £15. Most of their entertainment was cheap. If they had gone to see *Five Easy Pieces*, which opened in London at the end of September, they might have paid 30p for their cinema seat. Most of the pleasures and diversions London offered to the tourist were too expensive for heads. They didn't eat out. They never took a taxi. The *Time Out* guide to alternative London advised that if you had difficulty getting back to the suburbs after a night at Middle Earth you could hitch a lift on one of the lorries leaving Fleet Street in the early hours to deliver the morning papers to the distributors. Credit cards were strictly for the adult world. Banks didn't open at weekends. When they were open they made it clear that they disapproved of anyone taking out any money. Anyone with as much as five pounds on their person was bent on some sort of blow-out.

The primary sign of belonging to the tribe of heads was length of hair. Hair was not a side-issue. In 1970 hair was the great non-negotiable. Some people left home at the age of eighteen and went to live in faraway cities, not primarily to take advantage of educational opportunities or to learn a new way of life; they did it in order to be able to grow their hair. Hair could not be compromised. Hair was a civil right. Disputes about that right could be as intense as some of the battles which are fought in the twenty-first century around sexual orientation. In 1970 a company making trailers in the Midlands went on strike when a twenty-year-old welder was sent home to have his almost shoulder-length hair cut. In Brittany in the same year, a young man called Albert Lefort refused to comply with his employer's demand that he get his hair cut. He bought two litres of petrol, soaked his clothes and set fire to himself at his place of work. He died rather than cut his hair.

Hair was not funny. Since it took time to grow in the first place the length of the hair was an infallible indicator of how long you had managed to outrun the demands of the straight life. When David Crosby's key contribution to the Crosby, Stills, Nash & Young album *Déjà Vu*, which was released in March after what seemed like an unconscionable delay of an entire year, turned out to be 'Almost Cut My Hair', nobody laughed. When at the end of their period of full-time education they had to choose between the working world and their hair, a significant number of heads chose the hair. They would prefer low-status work with their hands than to take an office job which would have meant parting with the thing that above all defined them. Hair was more than a fashion statement. Hair could get you into a fight. Hair could keep you out of a job. Hair meant everything. It was the hijab of its day.

Apart from the hair, the secondary identifying characteristic of the head was the LP often carried under the arm. Carrying a long-playing record into the outside world was not a task to be undertaken lightly. It required planning. It was not done on the spur of the moment. An LP could only be taken somewhere if the owner had some definite purpose in mind or if it was being returned to its rightful owner. Come the appointed day the person taking the LP would step out of their door with their senses working overtime, eyes filmed over with the peculiar mixture of pride and embarrassment which attends appearing in public holding anything that is such a powerful statement. The bearer would do that in the sure and certain knowledge that at some point in the day they might enter the carriage of a tube train, pass through an open office, arrive in a particular pub or otherwise cross the eyeline of another member of the tribe of heads. That fellow member would be able to recognize at some distance the record you were carrying and, once drawn near, offer the barely perceptible nod of respect which was a fellow believer's due. Those who weren't in on this secret traffic, those poor benighted straights, would look puzzled at why on earth somebody should be on public transport carrying a twelve-inch picture of a Holstein-Friesian cow, a nineteenth-century engraving of a wheat sheaf, a picture of an aesthetic young man reclining on a fainting couch while wearing a woman's gown, or the naked figure of a handsome black woman with a white dove shielding her pudendum. They would not be in a position to recognize Pink Floyd's *Atom Heart Mother*, Traffic's *John Barleycorn Must Die*, David Bowie's *The Man Who Sold The World* or Santana's *Abraxas*. Only the heads would.

In the year 1970 the business that would eventually cater to the leisure needs of this growing tribe of undergraduate baby boomers was just being born. It was still a sub-culture, albeit for a few entrepreneurs who were particularly fast on their feet it was already proving a cash-generative business. Often it happened by accident. Richard Branson was a former public schoolboy who failed to make his fortune publishing a magazine aimed at students but on the way discovered that the readers would buy LPs on mail order through its pages. Although he and his partner Nik Powell had very little interest in music (Branson didn't even own a record player) they were excited by the idea of capitalizing on this market. Thus they began Virgin mail order, selling records that were often difficult to find in Britain's faraway towns and at a discount on the price you would pay in a high-street chain. This did well enough for them to open their first shop, in Notting Hill in 1969. By the following year they had opened another above a shoe shop in Oxford Street.

Steve Lewis, a teenage record fan who was originally brought in to tell the founders things they didn't know, such as what company the Beatles recorded for, remembers what made that Oxford Street shop such a revolutionary outlet at the time. 'I'd grown up in Hendon, north London, and I used to go to a record shop where the bloke behind the counter would just glower at me. My ambition was to have a shop that wasn't like that. The Virgin shop on Oxford Street had a load of floor cushions placed round a pole from which ran different pairs of headphones. People would ask to hear a record at the counter, I'd put it on and then refer them to a particular pair of headphones. Then they would lie on the cushion and listen. At the end of side one they'd ask for it to be turned over and we would. We didn't really care if they were there all day, so long as they were the right kind of people. I'm not proud when I think about it now but if people came up and asked if they could order a Perry Como record I would say no, just because I didn't want those kind of people in the shop. I wanted people who wanted the new Bob Weir album.'

There were two reasons visitors to London might seek out this new shop, which they might have read about in the underground press or the recently launched listings magazine *Time Out*. The first was they knew it was the place they could find records that would be hard to find in their local high street. But the even more powerful pull of the place was its attraction as somewhere to hang out, to overhear conversations between heads who may even have been slightly more in the know than you were, to puzzle over the precise use of the various items of drug accessories which would be marketed under the catch-all term 'paraphernalia', to wonder whether the long-haired madonna behind the counter was wearing anything under her leotard, to savour the tang of disrepute that hung in the air like patchouli, to hang out, to browse, to flick, to sort, to simply be near records. In the days when the majority of retail environments were more utilitarian than seductive the new breed of record shop represented by Virgin aspired to the condition of some sort of church.

Much as you might slip into a church in the middle of the day to think about higher things or recover from one of life's reverses, so you could disappear for hours into these new shops. Here for the first time you might run your hands over the thicker card or feel the heft of the denser vinyl that could only be found in the imports section. These would be made by American acts whose names seemed more charismatic the more you rolled them around your tongue. The Flying Burrito Brothers. Quicksilver Messenger Service. The Holy Modal Rounders. The Amboy Dukes. The Nitty Gritty Dirt Band. Pacific Gas and Electric. Area Code 615. NRBQ. The Hampton Grease Band. Most of these groups turned out to be not quite as good as they promised to be, but that mattered less than the part they played in building a mosaic of this expanding religion, of mapping out another square in the emerging tapestry of rock. Radio and press couldn't hope to match what you could intuit after spending an hour or two in these high-street temples. The shop was where you learned things.

The early Virgin operation skirted the law, much as you might expect of a business whose oldest principal was twenty and blessed with a public schoolboy's confidence that he could talk his way out of any trouble he got himself into. Branson would fabricate the paperwork he needed to prove that the records he was buying were for export, thereby avoiding purchase tax, and then repatriate them and sell them in his shops. Nobody dreamed that he might ultimately have a knighthood. At the time the legitimate LP business was rarely that far from its illegal cousin. Steve Lewis was Virgin's de facto 'buyer' of bootlegs. 'I used to go down to a bloke who had a place off the beaten track east of the West End to buy records. Ostensibly these were overstocks but then there would be an area where you'd get these plain-covered live recordings of people like Bob Dylan and the Stones. I would buy a load of these and take them back to the store to sell them.'

The first rock bootleg LP had appeared in the summer of 1969. It was known as *Great White Wonder* and was made up of unreleased Bob Dylan material, much of which had been recorded in the basement of Woodstock's Big Pink. Public demand for this material grew after the release in 1969 of *Nashville Skyline*, in which Dylan seemed to disavow his formerly acrid style for a country gentleman approach that for many rock fans was only just this side of soupy. At the same time the Beatles seemed unsure what to do next. After 1968's White Album, in which they had largely acted as each other's backing band, Paul McCartney promoted the idea of doing an album of music made in the way they used to make their music in their early days. Having done so, they shelved the results. Those recordings inevitably leaked and found their way on to the market as bootlegs. At the same time the Rolling Stones had spent a lot of 1969 touring in the United States and it was felt that they had still not made the record that reproduced what they were capable of doing on stage. All this fed into the belief that the LPs you couldn't hear had to be better than the ones you could and were only being kept from you by The Man. In most cases it was The Artist who was keeping them off the market but, as was already traditional, heads preferred to see The Man taking the blame.

There was a feeling among the heads at the time that the standard channels of the so-called 'straight' world were never going to adequately provide for them. It was widely felt that only their own kind could do that. They knew they were part of a movement but they didn't yet realize that they were also a market, a market from which fortunes and reputations would be made. The heads didn't watch television, and even most of the weekly music publications of the time, which were still in thrall to the singles charts, were of little interest to them. On the other hand, shops like Virgin presented themselves like caves wherein something attractively illicit was going on. Here you could buy posters of *Easy Rider* or Robert Crumb's *Keep On Truckin'*. Here you could get underground papers and magazines like *Oz* and *IT*, and even comparatively professional-looking imported American titles like *Rolling Stone*.

A standard issue of *Rolling Stone* in the year 1970 would have a cover that seemed to be ripped from the headlines; an extended Random Notes section which was the only place in the world where you might learn what, say, Dave Mason was planning to do next; newsy features about how British DJ John Peel's record label Dandelion was making a loss and was proud to do so; sidelines on the Charles Manson case, which as far as the longhairs were concerned was far from an open-and-shut one; long, rambling interviews with anyone from film-makers to elderly bluesmen; and finally, the thing the whole issue seemed to be building towards, the section called Reviews.

The lead review slot in the issue of 3 February 1970 was devoted to bootlegs. 1970 was the year when the bootleg was still an exciting novelty. Millions had read about them but only a few had actually heard them. Hence some readers felt they had a right to know more about what was allegedly being kept from them. Greil Marcus was articulating some of this indignation in his *Rolling Stone* review, in which he seemed to be promoting the public's right to know. 'The public is starved for music from The Big Three of rock and roll – an album and maybe a single a year isn't enough, and the rest of the musicians on both sides of the Atlantic are not providing enough excitement on their own to let us take what we get from Dylan, the Stones and the Beatles and be satisfied. We want more, and as the slogan goes "find a hole and fill it" and thus it's being filled up fast.'

He went on to review two unsanctioned albums of Dylan material, one illicit recording of John Lennon's appearance with the Plastic Ono Band at a festival in Toronto the previous year, and then a recording of the Rolling Stones during the previous year's tour of America which had been given the title *LIVE-r Than You'll Ever Be*. No doubt reasoning that most of his readers would never get the chance to find out for themselves, Marcus airily pronounced the Lennon as having more vitality than *Abbey Road* while the Stones live recording, which he speculated must have been done using a tape recorder placed in somebody's lap, is 'the ultimate Stones album'. He finished by challenging the Rolling Stones to 'show the guts' to issue an uncut live recording of their tragic concert at Altamont.

Here we are, at the very beginning of the rock LP era, and already there appears to be a vocal minority who seem to feel there's a conspiracy to keep recordings from them that they have a right to hear. Novelists and film-makers don't come under the same pressure to release material. Our relationship with recorded music, particularly music from Marcus's Big Three, is very different: here we're prone to thinking we know better than the artist what is good for them and us. It didn't happen in 1970 but far away in the future every 'previously unreleased version', every last alternative mix, even the most obscure live recording would eventually find its way on to the legitimate market and still these people, older if not wiser, would be haunted by the idea that something was being held back.

Making an LP of any kind was still ringed around with so many difficulties, in terms of technology, materials, finance and distribution, that the 1970 fan was inclined to consider it a minor miracle that one got through at all. They could no more imagine making a record without a record company than they could imagine making a movie without the help of a studio. Therefore the people who had managed to do this – regardless of whether they were purveying unmixed tapes pressed on vinyl ordinarily used for the speeches of East European dictators, even though they expected their consumers to travel to the seediest parts of town and do cash transactions with people whose company they would not normally seek, and irrespective of the fact there was no money back if you decided you'd been sold a pup – still tended to be viewed as warriors fighting the good fight against the armies of the night rather than the spivs and chancers that in many cases they actually were.

But at least they weren't The Man. That was the important thing. 'The Man can't bust our music' had been the copy line of one memorable ad taken out by Columbia Records back in 1968 to promote the more avant-garde elements of their catalogue. In 1969 their big breakthrough act was Chicago Transit Authority, who made sure that they included audio of the crowd chanting 'the whole world's watching' as they faced Mayor Daley's police outside the Democratic Party convention. They were not above cashing in on the national anguish over Vietnam. In early 1970 the copy on the ad for their second album in *Rolling Stone* straight-facedly intoned 'with this album, we dedicate ourselves, our futures and our energies to the people of the revolution'. The new record, another double, finished with a composition called 'It Better End Soon', which seemed to go on longer than the war.

At Columbia, Don Draper was overplaying his hand by expecting anyone to believe that a record company was essentially different from a shoe company. By contrast Stan Cornyn, who oversaw the marketing for Warner Brothers, was nothing like as tin-eared. Cornyn was the master of the honeyed sell. The long copy of his *Rolling Stone* ad for Joni Mitchell's *Ladies Of The Canyon*, which came out in March 1970, spun the fictional tale of twenty-three-year-old Amy Foster, who we discover sitting in her place in the Canyon waiting for the young man from the country store to turn up with her groceries and the supplies she needed for an evening's tie-dyeing. When he comes she's just finished playing Neil Young's second album. He stays, they play *Déjà Vu*, he compliments her on her 'far-out system', offers her a hit of his joint and then says how he's just bought Joni Mitchell's new album and why don't they sit and listen to it? Even though they knew they could never aspire to live in 'the Canyon' the majority of *Rolling Stone*'s readers would nonetheless have been utterly sold on the lifestyle thus glimpsed and responded to the absolutely central part played in it by the one thing which was within their reach, a copy of Joni Mitchell's new album. As is so often the case, it's the advertisers who are the first to tune into the relationship between a magazine and its readers.

Rolling Stone's championing of the bootleg stung the record companies and the acts into a response, which was the point. By the end of 1970 the Rolling Stones had countered their bootleggers with the release of *Get Yer Ya-Ya's Out!*, their own document of their 1969 tour of the United States. The jokey cover picture of Charlie Watts with a mule, the faux verité beginning of the record with its slurred tape and overlapping stage announcements, and the prominence given to fragments of banter like 'Charlie's good tonight, inne?' all suggested they were trying to borrow some of the illicit crackle of the bootleg for themselves. John Lennon also released a recording of his show in Toronto in the same Christmas period. The market wasn't quite as enthusiastic about it as Greil Marcus had been when it was a bootleg. In May, the Who had put out *Live At Leeds*, which they painstakingly packaged in a sleeve intended to look like something that had been acquired through unofficial channels. It was the first of hundreds of live albums that dressed themselves up as illegal releases in the hope that fans would be doubly excited about the prospect of something which had apparently found its way out without the blessing of The Man. It was a fiction we have been colluding in ever since.

Presumably tired of being the most bootlegged artist, or possibly just tired of trying to keep up with the demands of his contract, Bob Dylan decided to take a load of tracks that he had left over from Nashville recording dates, many of them covers of songs such as 'The Boxer' and 'Blue Moon', plus some live recordings from the Isle of Wight Festival, and put out what amounted to his own bootleg. This backfired spectacularly. Greil Marcus, who had only recently written in praise of the riches of Bob Dylan's bootlegs, opened his *Rolling Stone* review with the words 'What is this shit?' as he set out to explain how come, a mere four years after 'Sad Eyed Lady Of The Lowlands', the spokesman for a generation had wound up covering Gordon Lightfoot ballads, employing backing singers who crooned like your aunties singing along with the old-time radio, and altogether conducting himself with the complacency of a latter-day Bing Crosby. The market seemed to share his puzzlement. This certainly wasn't the Bob Dylan they ordered. And since, unlike the bootlegs, this was Dylan's official release rather than something a third party had rescued from his bin, he had to spend the rest of his career justifying it.

In truth the rock audience were nothing like as liberal as they pretended to be. The contrasting reception given to the bootlegs as opposed to the bootleg-style *Self Portrait* crystallized many aspects of what people were already coming to expect from an LP. Despite the 'it's all in the grooves' rhetoric so beloved of the advertising copywriter, the perception of the value of music was already intimately connected with how it had found its way to them and how it was packaged. If *Self Portrait* had a message it was that Bob Dylan was tired of having to live up to the expectations of the people who believed in him and was quite happy to open up his sketch books to demonstrate that there was nothing in his head but a load of old songs and nothing up his sleeve beyond the standard musician's belief in trying it again in a different key. Everything about *Self Portrait*, from the way it started with a track that didn't actually feature the artist to the child-like painting on the cover, seemed to be shrugging, 'It's only music, you know.'

This was not what LP reviewers wished to hear, certainly not at the point where their own inky racket was trying to present itself as a profession. The new generation of reviewers were starting to flex their muscles as the John the Baptists of the rock revolution. It had not always been that way. LP reviews had previously been written by newspaper reporters who were above all in a hurry. They might be given access to an acetate or a white label and would have a matter of hours to rattle out some kind of track-by-track report. This would give the reader an idea of where the major novelty value lay in the record, where the singles were likely to come from, which tunes you could dance to and where, if anywhere, the act appeared to be setting its cap at some new direction. It was more like a report than a review. Even as late as 1967 the *NME* review of *Sgt Pepper* jauntily pointed out that 'Lovely Rita' has 'a jog beat which will get your toes moving'. Norman Jopling's review of Bob Dylan's *Blonde On Blonde* in *Record Mirror* in 1966 had a strong value-for-money angle, berating the record company for devoting the final side to just one track.

Rolling Stone's major contribution to the story of the LP is that it was the one place where the record review turned into something more akin to a book review. *Rolling Stone* reviews promoted the idea that new albums were more than merely a way to make as much money as possible out of two hits and some filler, or merely a means to bolster the self-image of a guitar player or get back at the former lovers of a songwriter; instead they were messages from the commanding heights of the culture. In a *Rolling Stone* review you would get three things: a description of what the music was like; some stab at assessing how successful the act had been at achieving their own objectives; and finally and most importantly, there would be a section devoted to telling us What It All Meant. In time the portentousness of some of the statements in this third category, particularly when they applied to the Big Three that Marcus had been provoking in his bootlegs piece, would come to be hilarious. Such as when they called *It's Only Rock 'n' Roll* 'one of the most mysterious, as well as the darkest of Rolling Stones records', or said that Bob Dylan's *Slow Train Coming* was 'pure, true Dylan, probably the purest and truest Dylan ever'. That would come later, when they began to realize that there was no guarantee these artists were going to remain inspired for ever. For the moment, though, a useful purpose was being served.

A more reliable guide to where the LP and the LP review might be heading appeared in *Rolling Stone* in mid-March 1970. For some reason it took two people to review this particular album. One was Greil Marcus and the other was Lester Bangs. The joint byline may mean they sat down together and carefully pooled their thoughts. Knowing what one knows about rock critics of this generation it might as well mean that one nodded off while writing it and the other removed the typewriter from beneath his slumped body, hammered out a last-paragraph wrap-up and then made his way to the typesetters triumphantly bearing the script aloft.

This particular review speaks of the artist's previous, much-praised record and predicts that this one will do better in that it will actually be popular as well as acclaimed. This time the artist's picture is in all the record shop windows and he's all over the FM radio. But very often the conditions are all good and still the record fails to deliver. Making records is an art not a science and the things that make one work while another doesn't are often no more than minute differences of degree, infinitesimal increases in temperature, barely perceptible alterations in mood. In this case they point out that although he's been around for a while his style is different and that he 'now sings with a magnetically full electric band. The band's performance has a stately brilliance and if it recaptures some of the feeling of the earlier music, the past is serving as a rite of passage towards the celebrations of this album.' Magnetically full. Stately brilliance. Rite of passage. Writing about pop music here seemed to be asking to be taken seriously in the same way it took the music seriously.

Both the record and the review hinted for the first time that both music and medium might be able to grow up in their own parallel ways and that if there was any justice this LP and also this kind of writing might even outlast the present moment. The review, which was the lead and took up an entire page, finished as follows: ' "Moondance" is an album of musical invention and lyrical confidence, the strong moods of "Into The Mystic" and the fine, epic brilliance of "Caravan" will carry it past many good records we'll forget in the next few years. Van Morrison plays on.'

And they were right about that.

1971

'The annus mirabilis of the rock album'

Woodstock didn't happen at Woodstock. Most of the people who tried to attend the festival, which actually took place at Bethel, New York in August 1969, never got close enough to hear any music. Woodstock really happened in the cinema. It was only when the official film of the festival came out in the spring of the following year that people saw what had been impossible to see at the time. The movie was a huge box office hit. It did for post-San Francisco rock what *A Hard Day's Night* had done for the beat boom. It brought it close enough for people to see what the excitement was about. Being included in the film made the careers of Santana, Joe Cocker and Ten Years After. Refusal to allow their performances to be part of the film probably didn't help the Band, Creedence Clearwater Revival and Mountain.

In the film's wake came an entire triple album of performances from the event, something nobody had seen before. Listening to the album allowed everyone to import the experience of Woodstock into their living rooms. It turned out that even the couple pictured huddled under a quilt on the album's cover stayed just the one night and never got close enough to the stage to hear the music; however, thanks to the film and the film's soundtrack we could all feel that we had somehow participated in something we had in fact been nowhere near. Our favourite tracks weren't the musical performances. Our favourites were actually the stage announcements: the handsome voice of Chip Monck warning, 'The brown acid that is circulating around is not specifically too good,' Wavy Gravy croaking, 'What we have in mind is breakfast in bed for four hundred thousand,' Arlo Guthrie declaring, 'The New York State Thruway is closed, man' as if it were the best possible news. In the end the film and the record overwhelmed what had actually happened in August 1969. The legend wasn't merely printed. It was enshrined on film and made permanently accessible on six sides of vinyl. In time, the triple album took over from the truth.

Woodstock wasn't the only major triple album to come out in 1970. At the end of November the Beatles' fledgling Apple label crowned a year which had seen them put out a bewildering range of records, from Ringo's album of pub singalongs to John Tavener's cantata about Jonah, with a three-record boxed set by George Harrison, largely devoted to matters of spirituality.

This was the first time a former pop star had produced a box set. Box sets were usually reserved for the recordings of classical musicians. Since the third disc was entirely devoted to jams with names like 'Thanks For The Pepperoni', which was some measure of how seriously the musicians had taken them, there seemed even less reason for this extravagance. The cover showed the twenty-seven-year-old Harrison on the lawn of his Henley home surrounded by reclining gnomes. It was black and white. It appeared to be a cold day. He wasn't looking at the camera. The record was named *All*

Things Must Pass. If you were in the EMI sales force and your job was getting it into the trade your Christmas bonus didn't look promising.

By the beginning of 1971, by which time Paul McCartney had started the action that would finally wind up the Beatles, *All Things Must Pass* was at the top of charts all over the world and on its way to being the most successful of all the solo projects any of the individual members of the Beatles would be responsible for. It achieved this signal distinction because Harrison had held back some of his best songs for his solo debut, because it answered the need for something big and spiritual (*Rolling Stone* declared it 'the War and Peace of rock and roll'), and it was trailed by 'My Sweet Lord', a hit single that could be sung by anyone from a Krishna devotee to a window cleaner, a song that combined a roll call of deities with a tune that seemed naggingly familiar because, well, it was. In January 1971, before he was hit by a lawsuit for unconscious plagiarism over the inspiration for 'My Sweet Lord', Harrison's stock was higher than all the rest of the Beatles put together.

In that same month the first albums by Little Feat and ZZ Top were released. Valentine's Day in the following month saw the unveiling of *Tapestry* by Carole King. By the summer this would be selling 100,000 copies a week. In March her friend James Taylor released *Mud Slide Slim And the Blue Horizon*. Both records featured the song of the year, King's 'You've Got A Friend'. April saw the release of the Doors' *L.A. Woman*, the Rolling Stones' *Sticky Fingers* and the first album by War. In May, Marvin Gaye's *What's Going On* vied for attention with Paul McCartney's *Ram*, Rod Stewart's *Every Picture Tells A Story* and the first record by Bill Withers. In the summer, Joni Mitchell released *Blue*, the Allman Brothers Band put out their live album *At Fillmore East*, Black Sabbath *Master of Reality*, the Who *Who's Next* and the Beach Boys *Surf's Up*. In the autumn of that year came John Lennon's *Imagine*,

T. Rex's *Electric Warrior*, Cat Stevens' *Teaser And The Firecat*, Don McLean's *American Pie*, Elton John's *Madman Across The Water*, *Led Zeppelin IV* and David Bowie's *Hunky Dory*. At Christmas the number one LP in the United States of America was Sly & the Family Stone's strange, challenging *There's A Riot Goin' On*. In terms of the number of albums made in a year that we still play today without needing to make any special allowances for their antiquity, 1971 is unquestionably the annus mirabilis of the rock album.

There was never a dull moment in the record shop that year. The above records were only the successes. There were an equal number of albums released in 1971 which over forty years later are regarded as cult favourites but at the time were passed over by most people. There were, for instance, the first records by John Prine, Gil Scott-Heron, Judee Sill and the Electric Light Orchestra; and records by Nick Drake, John Martyn, Ry Cooder, Shuggie Otis, Loudon Wainwright III and Can that are still revered.

Was anyone drawing attention to the riches that were being passed over with so little apparent thought? At no stage in the year 1971 did anyone rush into print with a feature called anything like 'Fifty Records Made This Year You Must Hear Before You Die'. There was no such anxiety about missing things. The reason Nick Drake's *Bryter Layter* at one end of the spectrum and the Velvet Underground's *Loaded* at the other failed to prosper at the time was there was no specialist sub-culture to nourish them and altogether too much competition that was far more appealing, and the market, although it was growing, was still confined to people between the ages of sixteen and thirty. Records like these would go on to find their market years later, primarily among generations of nostalgists as yet unborn. At the time these records first came out there was simply too much that was going on in the moment and the media couldn't keep up.

Much as during 1965, which was arguably the annus mirabilis of the hit single, needle time agreements between the broadcasters and the rights holders meant very few of these great records were actually played on British radio; in 1971 there were not enough channels to make all this music available to hear. The fact that the business wasn't on top of this explosion of interest was a net plus. The degree of difficulty involved in getting to hear and, where possible, buy these 1971 albums gave them a lustre which the passing of time has yet to dull. Records were hard to find, not easy to afford and easily damaged. Small wonder that LP records were seen as precious in those days in a way they never would be again. There was also the fact that, much as you would learn from the most cursory reading of the Book of Love, the pursuit of them was very nearly as exciting as the possession. Everything needed chasing down, not simply the rare and old. In 1971 there was very little interest in the rare and old. The only reissues were the ones that were sold at a knockdown price on budget labels such as EMI's Music for Pleasure, which put out compilations of Pink Floyd and the Beach Boys, or Pye's Marble Arch, which specialized in low-rent repackages of the Kinks and Status Quo.

Shopping for records in 1971 was like going to football in 1971. It was an activity that called for time, know-how, transport, diplomacy, the ability to read your surroundings and the perseverance to keep pushing when most sane people would have given up. Finding out about records, holding them in your hand, getting to hear them and even, on occasions when finances allowed, buying them and taking them home to make them yours was something that required you to step out of your door and deal with the world.

Today I live in a part of London not far from where I lived in the early 1970s. Right now, if I wanted to go and buy a new CD it would probably involve a journey of around four miles. Back in 1971 even the shortest walk from the door of my flat would have taken me to somewhere that did at least an adequate job of selling records. This might be a newsagent, confectioner or general store that had made room for a rusty spinner rack which might creakily twirl to display a sun-bleached Andy Williams album, a best of the Singing Postman, a cheap compilation featuring a hearty girl in hot pants on its cover and, one hoped against hope, a stray copy of some mysterious obscurity like *Records Are Like Life* by Andy Pratt or *Total Destruction To Your Mind* by Swamp Dogg. This was not as unlikely as it would be now. In 1971 the business of record distribution was innocent of science and therefore there was as much chance of finding a copy of Dave Mason's *Alone Together* with its unfeasibly expensive cover in Mrs Miggins' Pie Shop as in Virgin at Notting Hill Gate.

Ranging beyond my immediate locality a 1971 bus journey would have delivered me to one of those medium-sized shops which existed in every London suburb in those days. These were often long-established family businesses that had been given a new direction by the long-haired son of the family. This son would be desirous of a lifestyle that didn't demand too much in the way of effort and allowed him to while away his days smoking, joshing with his mates and listening to the latest record by Blodwyn Pig. These outlets would previously have been called something ending with the word 'Electrical' until a transformation had excised all those jaunty illustrations of spinning discs, replacing them with a naked hippy girl drawn à la Beardsley and a new name cribbed from a favourite album. Few of these shops actually made much money but the rent and rates were low and they could just about get enough from the till to subsidize their lifestyle, which was the main point.

On high days and holidays an Underground train would have taken me to Oxford Circus tube station in the heart of London's swinging West End where I could take my pick between the big retailers (who were not yet calling themselves megastores), the hip head shops of Soho and the mysterious retailers who flew their flags for folk, jazz, reggae, classical or even something called 'international' music and would not have had a great deal to say to the average customer asking for Elton John's *Madman Across The Water*. In the same way that London alcoholics give directions to visitors entirely in terms of pubs, so I still have a mental map of London where whole districts and entire thoroughfares remain memorable purely because they were once the home of an interesting record shop. Virgin was above Shelly's shoe shop in the shadow of Centrepoint on Oxford Street; One Stop was right among the fancy fashion boutiques of South Molton Street; the specialist jazz shop Dobell's was cheek by jowl with the antiquarian bookshops of Charing Cross Road, around the corner from Collet's in New Oxford Street which specialized in folk music; while the market for deletions and ex-promo copies was beginning to spring up among the strip clubs and clip joints of Soho's Rupert Street.

Then there were the range retailers like HMV and Chappell where you could happily spend time laughing at the fact that there were LPs you weren't interested in but which were nonetheless strangely fascinating largely because they existed as records. Here were records of sound effects, records of train noises, records of the soundtracks of forgettable adventure films, records of classical music, records of light music, records of speeches, records of bird sounds, records for children, records for Jewish people, records for particularly devout Protestants, records for the homesick, records of the masses of the Pope, records for country dancing, records to test your stereo with, records through which you could learn to hypnotize yourself, records to make your family party go with a swing, records by Mrs Mills or Joe 'Mr Piano' Henderson or Jimmy Shand and His Band or Manuel and His Music of the Mountains; and finally, when every other avenue of interest had been exhausted, you would almost invariably find yourself pondering one of the live recordings of a man called Blaster Bates, an explosives expert who made quite a good living telling stories about the funny things that happened when he blew things up.

There was a certain etiquette about record shopping. You couldn't just rush into it. The last thing you wanted was to say the wrong thing, or the right thing in the wrong place. It might take a number of trips to a new shop to work out where this particular place was coming from and consequently what it might be reasonable to ask of them. For instance, in December 1971, a year that was not slow to name things after this planet, a shop called Earth Records opened in the Buckinghamshire market town of Aylesbury. The advert in the local paper announcing the fact that it was open for business was at pains to put over the point that it was only open for certain kinds of business. The management wished potential patrons to know that it sold neither singles nor classical records. Presumably if you required a full explanation of the further injunction 'no straights' you were not the kind of customer they were seeking to attract anyway.

When you enquired after a record that wasn't in the racks the answer would be it wasn't released yet, it had recently been deleted from the catalogue, or it didn't actually exist. To save face in these circumstances you needed to establish that you were not asking the question out of sheer ignorance. If, as was perfectly possible, you had more information than they did, the shop's staff would still never drop their front enough to say, 'That's interesting, we didn't know that.' People on the privileged side of record shop counters generally affected not to remember any of their customers. In fact the memory of every single last one of them was scored into their cerebellum, the knowledgeable ones most of all. They just didn't like to admit it.

At the time there were no short cuts to knowledge. Knowledge had to be hard-won over the long haul. Often the people behind the counter knew no more than you did because they simply didn't have the sources of information. Record catalogues were published in book form once a year and they could only be supplemented by back copies of the trade papers which kept weekly lists of the latest releases. The question you were most likely to be asked in a shop was 'What label is it on?' This was not asked out of snobbish interest. Very often it was the only way the dealer had of deciding whether the record somebody was asking about was real or a figment of their imagination. Then they would ask about it the next time the distributors called to take their order. Some records were rumoured for what seemed like ages before they appeared. Some never appeared at all. Jeff Beck recorded an album at Motown in 1970. People would ask for that all the time. It never appeared. There was more enjoyment to be had from thinking about what it might be like than there would have been in actually hearing it.

In the mid-seventies I worked at HMV in London's Oxford Street in what was then the largest and best record shop in the world, a shop that took pride in the fact that it was where people came when they had tried everywhere else and come up empty. The entire prestige operation of this huge store rested on a card index that was filled in by hand by members of staff when new releases arrived and struck through when albums were deleted from the catalogue. This was far from ideal and therefore the shop relied on having the kind of staff who contained among their number experts in most areas of the catalogue. Until Google came along and all information about records became accessible to anyone who could use a search box, the vast majority of knowledge about records was carried in the heads of the people who worked for the record companies or worked in the shops. These were often the kind of people in whom love of music coincided with an anorak's respect for its attendant bureaucracy, the kind of people who would instantly know that ILPS 9135 was Cat Stevens' *Tea For The Tillerman* and that SD 51051 was an American copy of the first album by Jackson Browne.

The hunt for records was made significantly more exciting by the fact that it was conducted amid such an information blackout. The music papers would carry news stories about forthcoming album releases weeks in advance. The only way to find out when an LP was actually available to buy was by returning to the shop, on some occasions more than once on the same day, and asking at the counter whether 'it was in yet'. And if the person behind the counter didn't give you the answer you wanted you would conclude that they didn't know what they were talking about and therefore their response could be safely ignored. Hence you would pass on to another shop and ask again there. And then another. There was no way of finding out for certain and therefore you kept on travelling in expectation. The street date of, say, the second Little Feat album *Sailin' Shoes* was not something you could establish empirically. It was certainly not a piece of intelligence that would ever find its way to you. It was something you could only bottom out by pounding the pavements. It was something that was only properly established when you finally had the record in your hand. Thus our investment in recorded music was made in shoe leather and hope.

The fashionable record shops of Soho, places like Musicland, One Stop and Harlequin, like much of the environment of the early seventies, reeked of Embassy cigarettes, body odour and male anxiety. Long-playing records may have been at the more affordable end of the luxury category but they were still not purchases entered into lightly. A new album cost between two and three pounds. This was almost ten times more than it would cost to get into the ground to watch a game of top-level football. Nobody ever bought anything on a whim. Buying an album meant you wouldn't be able to afford to go out that night. 'Give it a try' was the entirely unrealistic advice offered by the reviewer, which only served to illustrate the massive gulf between the fan who is paying for a record and somebody who is getting it for free.

In the early seventies nobody ever bought a long-playing record without first spending half an hour hovering over the bins where we browsed. Very often you would end up making a choice between something that you were confident you would enjoy, possibly because you had heard a friend's copy, and the left-field comer that you might be tempted to take a flier on. The good thing about going for the new thing was that it would increase your standing among your friends because they would get to hear it as well. You were not just buying for yourself. You were also buying for your social circle.

Around this time Chris Topham was at an English boarding school, where long-playing records were a channel of communication to a world richer and less mundane than the one the boys were forced to live in. He remembers how he and his fellow pupils would pore over the Virgin mail order advertisements in the music weeklies and, in order to avoid duplication, decide who was going to order what. 'I got Brinsley Schwarz's *Silver Pistol* and Pete Dawson got *Fragile* by Yes,' he recalls. 'We would all listen to each other's records. We knew what each other had. I remember cycling fifteen miles each way to a friend's house in the holidays just so that we could listen to *In The Land Of Grey And Pink* by Caravan and *It'll All Work Out In Boomland* by T2.'

In the light of this new-found sense of responsibility we always seemed to be weighing something familiar we were confident we already liked against something flashy and new that we just hoped we might like. Very often you would go browsing with a friend but when you were intending to buy you did it on your own, away from peer pressure. At some point at the end of 1971 I bought David Bowie's album *Hunky Dory*. It wasn't on the day of release. I couldn't afford to be that impulsive. I had to work myself up to making the purchase via a few weeks of browsing the racks of the shops near where I lived at the time in a shabby area of north London. Like any other twenty-one-year-old long-haired student in London in the early seventies I was accustomed to making all financial calculations based on how a sum could be converted into records. Whatever money I had – either from a modest student grant or from holiday jobs – would, once the bare minimum had been shaved from it to put a roof over my head and clothe my body, be spent on records.

Because it was cash which was instantly deducted from my worldly wealth there was a good deal riding on whatever I chose to exchange it for. The year before I had gone one Saturday afternoon to the usual small shop near my parents' home in the north of England and, momentarily swayed by a twenty-year-old's need to feel that he liked the same things all his friends and all the smart people appeared to like, paid cash for Pink Floyd's *Ummagumma*.

I took it home. There was nobody else in the house that day and therefore I wasn't compelled to go through the theatrics that usually accompanied the introduction of a new LP. Had my parents been there, even they, who had no interest in what I bought, would have felt compelled to ask what I'd bought and I would have been forced to assure them I'd purchased something really great. This was always a tricky part of the record-buying process. Taking a new record home was much like introducing your family to a new friend, somebody they might be hearing a lot from in the future, somebody you hoped that both you and they would be able to get along with. But you couldn't be sure. Therefore you had to demonstrate a certainty that you didn't feel. Once you had made the introductions you couldn't then back away, muttering, 'I wasn't sure but I thought I'd give it a try,' any more than you could say the same thing about a girlfriend.

Most LPs are not as good as people say they are. It is true today and it was certainly true then. The desire to embrace whatever seems like the right thing very often gets the better of the young, half-educated male, the key demographic for long-players then and now. If these young males don't like something, that will not stand in their way. They are perfectly capable of lying to others about how they feel about it. More importantly, they are perfectly capable of lying to themselves about it.

I wasn't fully aware of this then. It was a number of years before I was to realize the great truth about men and music – that they like the things they think they ought to like rather than the things they do like. At the time, Pink Floyd were in the category of things I thought I ought to like. Thus, after playing all four sides through, I sat looking at that copy of *Ummagumma*, wondering why it refused to live up to the grandeur of its packaging, to the promise of the picture-within-pictures device on the front and the shot on the back of all their gear lined up on the tarmac at Biggin Hill.

If only I had known then what I know now, after nearly half a century of exchanging cash for records, which is that *Ummagumma* was the perfect embodiment of the 'will this do?' school of album making. In this school, a band seek to mollify their record company by giving them live recordings of tunes they have already recorded plus a second record made up of things they have done individually, the nadir of which in this particular case was 'Several Species Of Small Furry Animals Gathered Together In A Cave And Grooving With A Pict'.

Something remarkable happened that afternoon in my parents' home. For the first time I admitted to myself I didn't like a record I was supposed to like. I may even have looked at myself in the mirror and spoken those words out loud. I don't like this. I never will like this. I am not the kind of person who will ever like this. That is not a failing of mine. I should exchange it for something I do like.

I rang the record shop and threw myself on their mercy. Could I bring the record back? Ken and Betty said yes. I got on the bus, took

Ummagumma back and exchanged it for Fairport Convention's *Liege & Lief*. This was not the LP the hipsters were enthusing about and its cover didn't depict the band via a Droste effect. It was, however, wonderful. It still is.

I would like to say this was the last time I lied to myself about a record. If I did, I would be lying. In later years I even wondered if the traditional male fear of commitment could be traced back to the male awareness of the many records he had bought in haste and then repented at leisure. How many men of the album-buying generation have stood at the altar wondering if the girl coming up the aisle would turn out to be Van Morrison's *Moondance* or John Entwistle's *Smash Your Head Against The Wall*? Over the years I've watched thousands of men – and for much of that time they have been mainly men – standing over the racks in different record shops, for all the world enjoying the simple pleasure of guilt-free consumption, apparently making a finely poised choice based on long consideration, but really, deep down, in the pit of their stomachs, in the dark places where they kept their inner selves, these men were actually engaged in the latest bout of what seemed to be a never-ending struggle between doubt and certainty, between that which is allegedly adventurous and that which is allegedly traditional – between, in my case, Pink Floyd and Fairport Convention, but you could supply your own examples from your own experience. The point is, it's no wonder these men agonize so long. They're trying to make a choice between who they think they ought to be and who they really are.

1972

'There's a new sensation, a fabulous creation'

Brian Cooke was working as a teacher at Middlesbrough Art College in 1970 when Chris Blackwell offered him the job of company art director at Island Records. At first he wasn't sure because he didn't quite know what an art director did. 'You're the third person to turn me down,' said Blackwell. Cooke and his wife came down to London at Easter 1971 and moved into a flat above the studio in Notting Hill, taking pictures of acts signed to the label and designing and building album covers for artists like Mott the Hoople, Head, Hands and Feet, and John Martyn.

The total budget for the design of an album would be between three and four hundred pounds and they would be given a free hand. 'We would go and visit the bands in the studio, listen to the music and talk to them about what might do for the album cover. They would leave it to us. What we were trying to do was illustrate the feeling of the music. An American review of *Inside Out* by John Martyn said that my design was the best reflection of the music he'd seen. I was pleased about that.'

At the time, he remembers, the cover was seen as something that arose out of the creative process itself. It wasn't merely the container that carried the thing that was of interest. It was almost on an equal footing. Designers and photographers were employed because they knew how to do things that nobody else knew how to do, such as take the most rudimentary picture. In many cases even the designers were doing things they had never done before. Cooke remembers holding his breath when album covers came back from the printer because he had no real idea of how they were going to come out. There were no proofs. There were loose conversations, the pictures would be taken, the instructions would go forth, you would wait a few weeks, and then a package would arrive from Tinsley Robor or Garrod and Lofthouse, you'd open it with trembling hands, and you would instantly know whether or not you had one of those rare covers that could make a difference to the success of the project, the kind that made everything that had gone before make sense, the kind that would give some permanence to the fragile record inside.

Today we live surrounded by objects it's difficult to damage. The worst risk most people run is they drop their smartphone and shatter its screen. Even when this happens the phone keeps working, the music keeps playing and nothing is lost that can't be easily retrieved. Our houses are full of inscrutable electronic boxes inside which some invisible process is occurring. If a car goes wrong it goes to a technician who connects it with his computer to work out where the problem is. Most children will grow up without ever seeing anything being repaired. Nobody knows how but they accept that things work.

The one thing everyone knew about long-playing records is they were among the most delicate things that they ever came into contact with. Long-playing records were easily damaged. Everybody knew that. Fathers would teach their offspring how to get them out, how to handle them, how to clean them, how to put them away and how to stack them. It was almost as though they were prize porcelain. Once they became damaged it was difficult to look at them in quite the same way again. A damaged record was a profound disappointment, like a minor bruise to the heart. All the Emitex in the world could not buff that bruise.

A newly purchased LP would only retain its sheen of infinite promise for so long. Even quite early in its life it might acquire a nick in track two side two where an unsteady hand had attempted to cue up a favourite song, lost control of the tone arm at the last moment and allowed the stylus to skate across the surface of the record, digging a shallow gulley across the grooves as it went, a gulley that would be evident on hearing the favourite song for ever more. It might not be apparent to the casual listener but to the owner it would be inescapably present, announcing itself thirty-three times a minute throughout all eternity. You could no more protect a record from ageing and weathering than you could hold back the signs of wear and tear on favourite items of clothing. Scratches, even jumps, became flaws you somehow learned to live with. My copy of the second Band album has been jumping at the end of the intro to 'Across The Great Divide' since Richard Nixon was in the White House. On the occasions I find myself listening to somebody's recently purchased copy, most likely one that has been pressed on 180-gram vinyl, apparently remastered from a 24-bit source recording and which may well have cost as much as the deck on which I played my original copy in 1969, I'm slightly disappointed when it doesn't.

It was one thing to live with a scratch that you had been responsible for. It was quite another to put up with damage that had been inflicted by another hand. Therefore one was very careful who one lent records to, and for how long. People wrote their names on the covers of long-playing records in order to be able to claim their copies back from people who might have been loaned them by other people to whom they had been passed without permission. Once you were satisfied that somebody was a sufficiently close friend to be able to entrust them with temporary stewardship of one of your records, you had to plan how you would get the record to them. This meant removing your prized possession from the domestic sphere, where it usually belonged, and taking it out into the open air, on to the streets and in unfamiliar company. Here, in the unaccustomed outdoors, the LP attained a completely new form of life.

Since the covers were twelve inches square and their contents could not be bent they couldn't be secreted in attaché cases or school bags as might have been most convenient. Instead they had to be carried under the arm. Because they were carried under the arm they would inevitably attract the attention of anyone you passed in the street, on the bus or train, in the schoolyard, or anywhere else you chose to take them.

The worldwide branding business was in its infancy in the sixties. T-shirts with cool logos were not available to the average person. The baseball cap had yet to invade the United Kingdom. Training shoes were for people who trained. In the midst of this iconographic desert the cover of the twelve-inch long-playing record stood alone. It wasn't merely cool. It was the pure concentrate of cool. It throbbed with the stuff. It licensed the carrier to walk the streets flaunting what amounted to the most powerful advertisement not just of who he was but also of who he would like to be.

It opened conversational avenues. When Mick Jagger walked on to Platform 2 of Dartford Railway Station in October 1961 the fact that he was carrying an import copy of *Rockin' At The Hops* with

Chuck Berry's silhouette cut out on the cover was what attracted the eye of Keith Richards. This inevitably led to a conversation. The conversation resulted in the Rolling Stones. Fourteen years later on the other side of the world, during his first week at university in Brisbane, Australia, Robert Forster spotted Grant McLennan carrying around Ry Cooder's *Paradise And Lunch*, Jackson Browne's *Late For The Sky* and the first Ian Hunter solo record. This led to the Go-Betweens. It also started a lifelong friendship between the two of them in which their preferred greeting remained the ''allo' with which Hunter started the record McLennan was carrying at the time.

Forster was impressed with the ease with which McLennan was prepared to face the attention that inevitably came with carrying records around in public. He was too shy to do so. Carrying a record in public required a person to be outwardly insouciant while inwardly hollering for attention. Entering a public space such as a school playground or coffee bar with a cool LP under one's arm made the heart beat faster. It could also be a cry for help. One person I spoke to for this book remembers as a teenager in the early sixties taking a Fabian album down to the local park in the faint hope of crossing the path of a girl he had designs on, and the more distant hope that his happening to be carrying this record might just open up the chance of some kind of conversation with her. On the happy day when he did finally see her he decided to increase the stakes by deliberately sprinting past her with the record, thus presumably demonstrating not just his cool taste in music but also his athletic prowess.

It was the fact that it was impossible to carry an LP without doing so mindfully that meant it was always on display. The photographs, the slogans, the illustrations and the ideas on the covers of long-playing records were the most arresting and provocative pieces of graphic art in the public space at the time. That meant that the images on display were like highly mobile posters taking messages into the public realm, messages that would be unlikely to have got out there any other way. Everything from antique pornography to the exhortatory posters of totalitarian propaganda; everything from the masterpieces of fine art to the work-of-a-moment daubs of friends of the band; everything from idealized celebrations of beauty to the words on a lavatory wall; everything from a rock-jawed forties superman shaving with the help of a rat to the wobbly dependents of Mr and Mrs Ono Lennon; everything from die-cut paper engineering with pop-up figures to records that had to be hand-packaged inside a pair of girl's briefs by teams of tightly permed middle-aged ladies – it seemed that everything was fair game when it came to a way of packaging and presenting a long-playing record.

Tim Milne works in design today where his speciality is the relationship between actual and digital design, and he has some thoughts about what made the album cover so powerful for so many people. 'For a start the cover is twelve inches square. That's an imperial measurement. All imperial measurements are based on the human body. A foot is the length of a foot. An inch is the length of the thumb. Metric measurements, on the other hand, are earth-based. The cover of an album is the perfect size for the human body. An album cover is approximately the area that a T-shirt slogan would take up on your chest. It fits perfectly into the picture of a human.'

For those in the business of the visual arts, rock acts were dream clients. They were prepared to try things no ordinary client would and they seemed to have no fear. Designer John Van Hamersveld had the idea of putting together a montage of pictures of carnival freaks which had been taken by art photographer Robert Frank in the course of putting together his book *The Americans* for the cover of the new Rolling Stones album *Exile On Main St*, released in May 1972. He then matched the tone and texture of Frank's pictures with shots of the band recording in the basement at Nellcôte. Mick and Keith recognized that this would at a stroke make them look both contemporary and retro, and signed it off.

Designers and sleeve manufacturers were allowed to break the budget if that was the cost of innovation. This innovation was often covered by making sure the overspend came out of the artist's cut. The cover of Stevie Wonder's album *Talking Book*, released in October 1972, carried a message from the artist in Braille. Even a beginner like Jackson Browne could have his first album, which came out in the first month of the year, made to imitate the shape and texture of a water carrier such as a driver might suspend from his car's radiator while driving through the California desert. The record was named after the artist but was known to its friends and eventually to the record company as 'Saturate Before Using', after the carrier's original instructions. Browne understood that a cover was more than just a container. 'I always thought of album covers as being like Indians' shields. They would literally dream up the thing they thought represented them and put it on their shield.'

There was a brief vogue for covers that behaved like other objects. *Striking It Rich* by Dan Hicks and the Hot Licks was particularly covetable because it was fashioned to look and feel like a book of matches, striking pad and all. When it was released in September, *Bandstand* by Family mimicked the shape of an early era television receiver with the band seen through a clear plastic screen which had to be inserted into the front of the fold-out. The picture of the artist on Tim Buckley's autumn release *Greetings From L.A.* could be pushed out from the cover and sent as a postcard. All these were zany, almost comic-book ideas that were executed on fine art budgets. The people who bought these records at the time were as likely to take them apart and display them on their walls as they were to preserve them for posterity. Tim Buckley postcards were sent much as Sgt Pepper moustaches had been worn. Nobody put anything away for posterity because there was no sense that posterity would have any interest.

A lot of these ideas came directly from the artists. No longer constrained by elders in senior positions, acts rushed to do things that had previously been considered risqué, simply because they could. Joni Mitchell was photographed naked on a rock in front of the Pacific Ocean for her November album *For The Roses*. This picture was intended to be on the outside of the cover until somebody pointed out to Joni the potential indignity of having a $6.98 sticker on her bare backside. It was promptly relegated to the fold-out. Alice Cooper's manager Shep Gordon decreed that his artist's June 1972 release *School's Out* must be wrapped in a pair of school girl's paper briefs and then arranged to get the story of US Customs sequestering 200,000 imported Canadian pairs on the grounds they were insufficiently flame-retardant on to the front pages of the *Washington Post*.

Most of these covers never managed to fan the flames of outrage into useful publicity for the album. The first album by guitarist Peter Banks, after he left Yes, was called *Flash*. The cover featured a shot of a girl's underwear glimpsed beneath the hem of a flaring skirt. Like the first album by Mom's Apple Pie, on the cover of which a frontier housewife advanced on the viewer proffering a slice of female genitalia, the record was notable for being looked at rather than bought.

Some acts commissioned original works of art in new media. An example was Ron Pekar's neon sculpture which announced the first album by Big Star, released in August. Or they repurposed old art. The cowboy on the cover of the Pure Prairie League's first album, released in March 1972, was originally painted by Norman Rockwell for a *Saturday Evening Post* cover in 1927. This quickly became such a powerful visual signifier for a band who were in every other respect anonymous that they were forced to get other artists to copy the style for future albums.

There were no rules: while some bands such as Chicago and Yes rarely put their pictures on the cover and worked closely with their own artists like John Berg and Roger Dean to ensure brand recognition above all things, others such as Jethro Tull seemed to start afresh with each new album, wrapping their March 1972 offering *Thick As A Brick* in a spoof newspaper front page with actors playing the characters referenced in the songs.

In some cases the artists simply made it up themselves. Wandering around the old Warner Brothers studio lot, which at the time was adjacent to his record company HQ, Ry Cooder found a collection of beautiful old painted movie backgrounds. He and his wife were photographed against them, thus giving his January 1972 album *Into The Purple Valley* the ideal antique vibe.

There were allusions that only a few people got. Martin Muller, who designed the album covers for Little Feat under the pen name Neon Park, was paying tribute to the nineteenth-century French painter Fragonard in depicting a piece of cake on a swing on the cover of their May 1972 release *Sailin' Shoes*. There was the infinite capacity for taking pains of W. David Powell, who took a drugstore postcard of a truck bearing a cargo of one giant peach, hand-lettered the name of the Allman Brothers Band on the side, photographed the logo with a tiny Kodak, had the pictures processed at the same drugstore, and then cut and pasted the letters on to the enlarged image of the truck to achieve the effect he wanted for their *Eat A Peach*, which was released in February 1972.

Some covers seemed to be insuring themselves against the danger of success: the first album by Steely Dan, *Can't Buy A Thrill*, which came out in November, was later described by Walter Becker and Donald Fagen, with some justification, as 'the most hideous album cover of the seventies'. The Doobie Brothers, one of the least toned bands of the era, had themselves photographed naked in a New Orleans whorehouse set for the inner sleeve of their album *Toulouse Street*. After five notably unpopular solo albums the former Monkee Michael Nesmith put out another one in the summer of 1972 which was even less likely to be played on the radio. He called it, hilariously, *And The Hits Keep On Coming*. The gatefold featured him in a luxurious living room surrounded by adoring and remarkably beautiful women. Nesmith was fortunate enough to have independent means (his mother had invented liquid correction paper) and therefore he could afford his records to be, as he helpfully pointed out in his liner note, 'messages to myself'.

Some of the covers which turned out to be most memorable were shot the way they were for no particular reason. The cover of the Van Morrison album *St Dominic's Preview* was photographed on the steps of a church in San Anselmo, California. The image of a young woman swivelling for the camera in Stanley Gardens in Notting Hill in order to show both her hat and her nipples to greater advantage made the career of Carly Simon when *No Secrets* came out at the end of 1972.

In the same year David Bowie released what was his second album in six months. *Hunky Dory*, which came out just before Christmas 1971, had led with a picture of the artist looking like a goddess of the silver screen. For Bowie's next album, *The Rise And Fall Of Ziggy Stardust And The Spiders From Mars*, the cover depicted him as a rock star who has been beamed down from a passing spaceship and landed among the detritus of a back street in the West End of London. In later years some fans interpreted the fact that he was posing outside the premises of a furrier called K. West to mean he was signalling that he was on a quest. (This probably arose from the same quarter as the story that Paul McCartney was dead because he was barefoot on the cover of *Abbey Road*, that you could see the inverted faces of the Beatles in the tree on the cover of *John Wesley Harding*, and that if the centrefold of *Led Zeppelin IV* was viewed through a mirror a horned beast is not so clearly visible.)

Most of these records which came out in 1972 are still remembered today partly because they had the quality of charisma which was lent by the right cover. The right cover is not the same as the award-winning cover, the kind that is revered by art directors. The right cover is the one that grows on the viewer at the same rate that the music grows on the listener until it is fused in the public imagination with the sounds within. The design of *Ziggy Stardust*, by Terry Pastor, would not win any awards but it filled in any blanks the music might have left, and almost fifty years later it remains the wellspring of David Bowie's enduring mystique. Success in pop music is usually achieved by the right sound delivered along with the right optics. The latter may come from the artist's look or from the visuals with which they choose to surround themselves. When people saw the Beatles they were satisfied that they appeared to look the way they sounded. In the future, when pop music became a branch of the TV business, people would increasingly listen with their eyes. The first shot in that war was fired on 16 June 1972.

Roxy Music, whose first album came out in the UK in the same month as *Ziggy Stardust*, were the first and probably the only band to be made by the cover of an LP. This should not have been surprising. The members of the band were already conversant with the language of visuals. They all came from university and art school backgrounds, were more educated than pop stars traditionally needed to be and belonged to a west London coterie of photographers, fashion people and critics who tended to look down on rock while at the same time envying its power in the marketplace. They were slightly older than most bands starting out. They were well connected. They signed to the same management company as King Crimson and, just like King Crimson, managed to get themselves praised in the music press before they had a record deal. Their music sounded like progressive rock without the panache but it was intriguingly crossed with the vocal stylings of Billy Fury. They fashioned their own costumes which were big on high collars and festooned with feather boas. They threw shapes which seemed to have come from comic books or the pre-Beatles era of Elvis Presley movies, either that or the future. They were clearly something different.

Their first album was recorded in a two-week period in the spring of 1972 in a studio above Piccadilly Circus in London. Their management shopped them around the various record companies. One of the firms in the bidding was Island Records, which was still owned at the time by Chris Blackwell. Like most bosses Blackwell didn't like to say yes but he didn't like to say no either. Although his reputation was as 'a music man', Blackwell had never been one to underestimate the importance of surfaces. The thing that tipped him over the edge about Roxy Music was not anything they had written, recorded or done in the traditional sense but it was certainly something they had brought into being. It was only when Blackwell saw the cover that Roxy Music were proposing for their first album that he turned to his lieutenants and said, 'Have we signed them then?'

It really is no exaggeration to say that the cover of the first Roxy Music album made them. In the picture that was chosen to occupy the entirety of the gatefold sleeve the model Kari-Ann was shown from above reclining on a bed of satin. She was wearing one of those swimsuits such as Betty Grable might have favoured, the kind that was unlikely to see much water. The image seemed to belong to the golden age of Hollywood. The name 'Roxy Music' could be the name of the group. It could be the quality the record was offering.

Although Bryan Ferry was credited with the 'cover concept' it took a small army of other people to make it happen. The key person was the fashion designer Antony Price, who designed the costume, booked the model, got the right hairdresser and hired the photographer. As many people were listed on the sleeve as being involved in the design of the outside of the package as had been involved in making the music. This was only fair because the cover had, if anything, more impact than the music.

One of the reasons it made such an impact was that this was still a black and white world. There wasn't ready access to the good life in the UK in 1972, even for the young. *Time Out's Book of London*, published for the benefit of twenty-somethings visiting the city, introduced its apparently provincial readers to culinary terms with which they might not be familiar, such as 'kebab', 'tandoori' and 'pizza', and suggested this was what the more adventurous Londoners were starting to eat. London was open all night but only for the porters at the fruit and vegetable market in Covent Garden or the men working in the print around Fleet Street. The most affordable form of entertainment was the pub. These opened for three hours around lunchtime and then for five hours in the evening. A pint of lager was 16p. The editors advised that the cheapest way to eat in London was to ask for a steak pie and chips which should cost no more than 15p. By restricting yourself to this one dish it was theoretically possible to eat for a week for the price of the first Roxy Music album.

Although 1972 was also the year Alex Comfort published the best-selling *Joy of Sex*, with its message that copulation was something even serious people with beards engaged in, sex appeal tended to be downmarket. The *Sun* began publishing daily pictures of topless models in 1972. The most prominent colour magazines were the top-shelf titles *Men Only* and *Mayfair*, which sold millions despite nobody actually witnessing them being bought. The British film industry was kept afloat by the latest releases in the *Confessions of* series and TV spin-offs such as Frankie Howerd's *Up the Front* and *Our Miss Fred* with Danny La Rue. You could get away with things at the cinema that would have been impossible on the small screen. Here double entendre remained the lingua franca. The big weapons of the two TV channels in 1972 were Larry Grayson and his *Shut That Door* up against John Inman of *Are You Being Served?*

When *Roxy Music* was released on 16 June 1972 Island Records took out full-page ads in the UK music press, all of which led with the cover. It was the kind of cover that, with just a few staples, anyone could turn into an arresting shop window display. It landed in the shops much as King Crimson had done three years earlier with the same kind of visual presence that demanded a similar response. A few took against what seemed to be its bold superficiality but more were immediately enchanted by its promise of luxury. It entered the chart just a week after release and stayed there until November.

Once the album had established them, Island called for a single to build on its promise. It often occurs that when a band feel they have been properly appreciated for doing the heavy lifting involved in 'making the album' they are then happy to come up with the light, appealing single they probably should have done in the first place. 'Virginia Plain' was certainly this. It was a zippy, direct pop record which made it clear that this group were not going to go the King Crimson way and if there was to be any conflict between their arty side and Ferry's instinctive desire to please the crowd the latter was likely to win out. It was included on later versions of the album. Glamour may have been only one weapon in their post-modern armoury but it was undoubtedly the one that felt most comfortable in their hands.

The glamour girl on the cover might have started as an emblem of a life out of their reach. Glamorous women remained Roxy Music's calling card for the next four albums. In ensuring that the first time anyone came into contact with his group it was via such an opulent image, Ferry could be confident that Roxy Music would be the first upmarket group in rock. While their fans would ultimately come from all kinds of backgrounds, from the leafy shires to the coal mining towns of the north of England, Roxy Music always stood for that peculiarly English idea that he who carries himself like a lord deserves to be treated like a lord. In Ferry's case he would eventually wish himself into a marriage into the aristocracy. It all began with that cover. The arty crowd could call it conceptual art if that made them happy. For most people it just looked like a group of blokes having a ball.

Ferry says he never intended Roxy Music to be a singles band. However, once singles success is achieved, once an act has tasted the thrill of being on *Top of the Pops* and being recognized in the street, only a very perverse soul turns his back. The next four Roxy Music albums all followed the same template as the first when it came to the covers. The second one, *For Your Pleasure*, which came out in 1973, featured Amanda Lear with a panther on a lead. Later that year there was *Stranded*, which had Playboy model Marilyn Cole laid out and glistening on the floor of a forest. The following year's *Country Life* was the most startling yet, featuring two German fans of the band posing against foliage with pubic hair showing through their underwear. By 1975's *Siren*, supermodel Jerry Hall was draped across the rocks calling sailors to their doom. She was presumably paid much more for this than the £20 Kari-Ann got for being the best-known cover girl in the history of the LP.

By then all sorts of things had changed. The LP boom had made posh designers and photographers want to work with the music business. Brian Cooke saw things change from the experimental ways of the early seventies. 'They were using fashion and advertising photographers and so eventually people began spending more and more money. But the thing that really changed things was when the marketing people came along and they started treating the cover as a component of the marketing campaign. Before that they were regarded as being part of the creative work.' A lot had changed between the first and fifth Roxy Music albums. By then Ferry was sleeping with the model on the cover for a start. Such was Bryan Ferry's great achievement. He invented a dream, turned that dream into a cover and eventually disappeared inside it.

1973

'There is no dark side of the moon – it's all dark'

In February 1973, just a few weeks after the United Kingdom and Ireland had joined the European Economic Community, the members of Pink Floyd were rehearsing in the Rainbow Theatre in north London prior to their imminent tour of the United States. At the time friends of mine were sharing a rented house just round the corner. This was in Finsbury Park, a district of London which in 1973 was occupied primarily by people who couldn't afford to live anywhere more pleasant. This house was a large one which meant there was room for three couples. On the first floor was a big room running the full width of the house with two windows looking out on to a busy road. This room was sparsely furnished. There were a couple of battered easy chairs and, strewn across the floor, some bulky and somewhat uncomfortable scatter cushions. What furniture was in the room had been carefully arranged so that it pointed in the direction of the most important piece of equipment in the room, the item that gave all the other items a reason to be there. The stereo.

When they had moved into the house the occupants had, just as anyone with longish hair and the habits that went with it would have done at the time, first established a site for the stereo and then arranged everything else around it, much as early settlers might have identified a source of water before establishing their camp. Everyone who lived in, passed through or visited this house for any reason would refer to this room, without the remotest hint of levity or sarcasm, as 'the sounds room'. It was not a room used for general entertaining. In all the time they were there I don't recall it ever being employed for a party or the stereo being used to provide background music. It was a room that was devoted to active listening to music, which was considered the best way to spend any spare time in the house.

The record deck in the sounds room was a Pioneer PL 12D, which had been purchased at one of the scores of hi-fi shops on the Tottenham Court Road for around £40. There was a Rotel RX150 amplifier and a pair of Wharfedale Denton speakers. In 1973, having a system of so-called 'separates' such as this, rather than one of the off-the-shelf music centres with which most people were satisfied, marked the owner out as a person of taste and discrimination. The shops in Tottenham Court Road were all outlets for the same wholesaler and therefore there wasn't much chance of finding a bargain. Nonetheless heads would spend hours with their noses pressed to the windows of these shops, weighing first the wisdom of upgrading their deck rather than their amplifier, their cartridge rather than their speakers, of spending on heavy-gauge speaker lead or an unusually stable piece of masonry on which to position their deck; then they would talk to friends about the relative merits of the scores of brands – Harman Kardon, Thorens, Kenwood,

Garrard, Akai, Dual, Technics, TEAC, Marantz, Denon, Acoustic Research, JBL, Altec, Bose and Wharfedale – names with which everyone who was serious was already familiar.

Getting a better sound system was a Sisyphean task. An improvement in one element of the system would invariably throw light on a weakness in another. Every few months it seemed you would notice something about your 'set-up' that wasn't as it should be. An inadequately earthed deck that was sending out a distracting boom. Was the turntable revolving at the right speed? Where was that distant crackle coming from? Was the record pressed off-centre? One hoped against hope that it wasn't a deficient stylus because replacing one of those could cost you a month's disposable income.

The people who lived in this particular house in Finsbury Park worked in record shops, as social workers or in the book trade. Given these occupations it naturally followed that they invested in a record player long before they thought of buying – or more likely renting – a television. The record player was, by some distance, their most precious possession. The occupants of this house were 50/50 male and female. Despite this it was the males who saw the care and maintenance of the record player as being part of their duty.

In this they were, probably unconsciously, following in the footsteps of their fathers. The hi-fidelity boom of the 1950s had been driven by a generation of middle-aged men, many of whom had learned something about electronics in the forces. While their sons had college degrees, long hair and preferred to feel that they had utterly cut the cord between their parents' world and their own, they nonetheless brought to the business of listening to music in the home the same mixture of pride and anxiety their fathers might have exhibited on buying their first radiogram in the days of Ray Conniff.

The duty of worrying about the stereo, of protecting it against the elements or clumsy visitors who might not fully appreciate its delicacy, and deciding when it might be advisable to upgrade the stylus or the cartridge, these tasks belonged firmly in the male domain. Few even commented on the fact that it was men who put the records on and women who listened to them. The more sophisticated the set-up the more it seemed to require the male to perform the priestly rites at this audio altar. He it was who would ensure that the record was removed from its inner bag in the correct manner, its surface gently wiped with the anti-static cloth or even, as Chris Topham recalls, with a Zerostat, a gun-shaped piece of moulded plastic which removed the static charge on the record so that dust was less attracted to it and ensured that in future the inner bag would yield it more easily.

Finally the disc, suspended between the flattened palms of that evening's priest, would be sacerdotally lowered to the platter of the deck. The correct speed would be identified. The tone arm would be carefully swung into position, then gently lowered to the playing surface with the appropriate care. The room would then hold its breath, waiting one second for the warm bump of the stylus slipping into the lead-in spiral, and then the expectant shush which preceded the opening notes.

Record players were often inscrutable machines. Sometimes it seemed that the more that had been paid for them the less obvious it would be how to get them working. There might be a pre-amp which needed to be turned on before any sound could be heard. The tone arm might have to be lifted by a cueing lever and then, when it was safely raised above the playing surface, delicately moved to the right position on the playing surface, which was long enough before the music started to allow you time to resume your seat before it began. Anyone who wasn't entirely sure what they were doing with a particular record player would stay clear for fear they might damage the mechanism or mark somebody's much-prized LP. Playing a record, particularly a new record, was not something that could be done lightly. It was a ceremony and so it called for records that seemed worth having a ceremony about.

On 27 February 1973 the new Pink Floyd album, *The Dark Side Of The Moon*, was due to be launched to the press and trade at the Planetarium in London. When the launch began at eight that evening only one member of Pink Floyd, Rick Wright, was present. The others weren't there because the quadraphonic sound system they had been promised for the evening had not turned up. Few were particularly surprised that this event hadn't taken place as smoothly as had been envisaged because in 1973 few things turned out the way they were planned. On that very day 300,000 British civil servants, ranging from air traffic controllers to clerks at the DHSS, came out on a one-day strike to protest the government's attempt to restrain inflation by imposing controls on pay and prices. The following day 29,000 train drivers were due to come out in support of their claim for a basic wage of £40 a week. The fact that they wanted this to rise to £50 within a year indicates the grip inflation was already taking.

By the end of 1973 the rate of inflation was 10 per cent. To most people this seemed unsustainable. It proved to be only the beginning. Inflation was to increase to 19 per cent the following year and exceed 25 per cent in 1975. The selling price of *Dark Side Of The Moon* on its UK release was £2.38. The odd figure was because Valued Added Tax had just been introduced to replace the old Purchase Tax. Through the next few years it was to rise along with the rest of the market in what seemed like dramatic jumps until it was over three pounds.

The record came out in the United States in late February to coincide with the band's American tour dates. It didn't appear in Britain until 23 March. (On that same night the Electric Light Orchestra were the guests on *Crackerjack* and the big movie on BBC2's *Film Night* was Maggie Smith starring in an adaptation of Graham Greene's *Travels With My Aunt*.) Throughout the 1970s it was not unusual to have a lag between release dates on either side of the Atlantic, sometimes for as long as months. To take advantage of this gap specialist record importers sprang into being. They competed to see who could be the first to clear a few boxes of *Dark Side Of The Moon* through customs at Heathrow and drive them hell for leather into the West End. Here they would park illegally and open up the back to allow over-excited shop managers to taste and try their new stock. This was a heady experience. Flicking through box-fresh new releases in an import van in the West End of London in 1973 was the record maniac's equivalent of gaining entry to the VIP lounge of some Las Vegas club.

The import market introduced an additional layer of irrational exuberance into a market already capable of getting beside itself with excitement over the arrival of a new album. Eager customers would run across town when it was rumoured that there was something new, something like the lavishly packaged three-record quadraphonic set of live Santana recordings which had been imported from Japan.

Once a new album was mentioned in the columns of the music press unusually committed fans would make a habit of searching for it on a daily basis in every record store they passed. Just as Soviet citizens would carry a 'what-if?' bag with them at all times on the off-chance that the shops might suddenly be full of some rare and unexpected item, so record shoppers might comb through every item in a well-stocked shop in the hope that they would find something they had never seen before.

In March 1973 the fifteen-year-old Danny Baker turned up for his first job at One Stop Records in London's South Molton Street. His first task was to go along the line of Pink Floyd fans waiting outside the shop to tell them that since the shops were expecting no more than a hundred import copies of *Dark Side Of The Moon* that day the people at the back of the line might as well go home.

Dark Side Of The Moon was Pink Floyd's eighth album. With this record the flighty psychedelic band which had previously been the vehicle for Syd Barrett's songs about the outer reaches of consciousness was replaced by a group who were now the medium for Roger Waters' lugubrious laments for the human condition.

The album was made in a very old-fashioned way. Although they had broken in some of the songs in live performance, the band still made a number of key decisions in EMI's studio at Abbey Road. Although they were recording on the latest sixteen-track desk – an enhancement which, as they were discovering, offered fifteen additional ways of avoiding making up their mind – most of the effects that give the record its characteristic sense of inner space had to be added the most old-fashioned way, almost by hand. It was Alan Parsons, the young engineer who was the de facto producer of the record, who went to the clock shop round the corner from the studio to record the various mechanisms that begin 'Time'. The sound of footsteps on 'On The Run' was made by a tape operator running round the parquet floor of Studio Two. The voice at the end saying, 'There is no dark side of the moon' belonged to Abbey Road commissionaire Gerry O'Driscoll. Many of the record's most memorable touches were supplied by guest artists. Clare Torry, an unknown session singer, was brought in to improvise over Rick Wright's 'The Great Gig In The Sky'. 'Just sing,' they exhorted her. Then they stepped in as soon as she sang the word 'baby'. The word 'baby' was an anathema to Pink Floyd.

The final mix was done by Chris Thomas, who was brought in as an honest broker to stop the four band members simply turning up the volume on their individual contributions. It was left to Thomas to choose which of the hundreds of different inputs that had gone into the recording should be audible to the listener and in precisely what proportions. In Thomas's version it's the extraneous elements that provide the record's fingerprint. His mix accentuates the continuity between one track and the next and ensures that, more than any record made in the middle of the 1970s, *Dark Side Of The Moon* was something you played from the beginning to the end or you didn't play it at all.

It started, like a very superior student play, with that internationally recognized sign of serious business, the sound of a heartbeat. This called the room to order like the ghost of Hamlet's father. At no stage over the next forty-two minutes did any occupant of the sounds room suggest skipping a track or brightly announcing, 'This is my favourite.' At the end of 'The Great Gig In The Sky' the record would be turned over. Act Two, so to speak, could then begin with the cash register sounds of 'Money', sounds that were still unusual enough to be quite exciting in themselves. People came to regard *Dark Side Of The Moon* less as a piece of music and more as a theatrical experience. The first time Roger Waters played it to his wife she burst into tears at the end. It could be argued this was a good way of avoiding having to say what her favourite song was. *Dark Side Of The Moon* seemed to be above such petty considerations. You submitted yourself to it and at the end you hoped you might have been changed by the experience.

It was popular in a way no record had ever been popular before. It took seven weeks to get to number one in the United States and it only remained there for one week. Of greater significance was the fact that it stayed in the top ten best-selling albums list for over six months. In the UK it entered the chart at number two. It was kept from the number one spot by a TV-advertised hits collection that is now forgotten. Its staying power, however, was astonishing. A whole year later it was still at number thirteen. This was without precedent for a pop record. A year after its release the *NME* sent a reporter out into the West End to interview the person buying the notional millionth copy. Nobody at the time could believe that a record could just keep on selling like that without the obvious fillip of a further hit single or TV exposure. This was something beyond mere word of mouth. Two years later it was still at number eighteen. Three years later it was still at number thirty-nine. Fully ten years after its release the American record company Capitol, while refusing to give the *New York Times* actual sales figures, assured them that *Dark Side Of The Moon* was the biggest-selling long-playing record the company had ever put out. Considering the company had also put out long-playing records by Frank Sinatra, the Beach Boys and the Beatles this indicated just what a quantum leap *Dark Side Of The Moon* represented.

It represented the triumph of long-form rock music. Where it led, others followed. *Dark Side Of The Moon* wasn't the only record released in 1973 that marketed itself as an experience and became arguably more famous than the artist who made it. The year before, Richard Branson had started his own record label. On 25 May 1973, just two months after the release of the Pink Floyd album, Virgin Records' first release, which appeared with the catalogue number V2001, was by a completely unknown guitar player called Mike Oldfield.

At the time of release Oldfield was barely out of his teens. He was the first of what were to be a succession of sensitive boys from middle-class backgrounds who had dealt with family trauma by retreating to his room and teaching himself to play unnecessarily difficult things on the guitar. Experiences with LSD had further loosened his already fragile mental wiring.

His talent aside, Oldfield was not temperamentally cut out for the hurly-burly of the music business. He was living in a flat in Tottenham when he left Kevin Ayers' band with what was then the unimaginably precious loan of a very basic tape recorder. Using this he started to lay down his musical ideas. These had been fired by hearing the 1969 album *A Rainbow In Curved Air* by the American experimental composer Terry Riley.

He played these to a few of the established record companies, none of whom were interested. It was only when he happened to find himself playing sessions at the Manor, a studio which Richard Branson's company was trying to establish in the Oxfordshire countryside, that he managed to get anyone to take an interest. It was eventually agreed that he could use the studio downtime to turn his ideas into a complete LP. Since he had no talent for, nor sympathy for, songs or hook lines and he couldn't, like a classical composer, actually write his ideas down, he was just guided by his desire to make an extended piece of music.

When Mike Oldfield's *Tubular Bells* came out at the end of May 1973 it got respectful attention, mainly because it was different, accomplished, and came from a new company. It had some unlikely disciples. Writing in the *Listener*, John Peel, who played it in its entirety on his radio show, hailed it as covering 'new and uncharted territory' and, since he had small hope that his employers at Radio 1 would have any interest, devoutly hoped that the upcoming performance of the work at the Queen Elizabeth Hall would be broadcast by Radio 3. *Tubular Bells* took a few months to chart but once it did, like *Dark Side Of The Moon*, it stuck around. What put it over the top was its use on the soundtrack of *The Exorcist*, which came out at the end of 1973. The film's director William Friedkin didn't like the score he had originally commissioned so he went to Warner Brothers Records looking for something he could license. They pointed him towards a pile of demonstration records they had no intention of putting out. He listened to a few minutes of the beginning of side one of *Tubular Bells*, decided the glockenspiel had precisely the child-like quality he was looking for, and a deal was done. It went on to sell more than fifteen million copies.

Ever since *Sgt Pepper* it had been taken as an article of faith among certain people that rock would eventually have to grow up.

In growing up it seemed inevitable that it would have to graduate to long-form. In the UK the two most prominent advocates of this line of thinking were the critics Derek Jewell and Tony Palmer, who wrote about 'popular music' in the two major Sunday newspapers, the *Sunday Times* and the *Observer*. Neither belonged to the rock generation and they brought to their job as gate-keepers the instincts and prejudices of jazz people. The qualities they were listening out for – the ability to improvise, a clear demonstration of the mastery of an instrument, and compositions that appeared to be animated by a higher purpose than to get a girl to come across or to celebrate the purchase of a brand-new set of wheels – were the kind of qualities they had applauded during the apparent ascent of jazz from the music that made the masses dance to the music that relatively small numbers of educated folk made a show of appreciating in the concert hall. In Philip Larkin's words, in this process jazz had 'been removed from our pleasures and placed among our duties'.

It was possible to listen to both *Dark Side Of The Moon* and *Tubular Bells* and persuade yourself something similar could be made to happen in rock. The talents Palmer and Jewell lionized were apparently too great to be encompassed in the four-minute single. Bravely naming Yes's six-sided live album *Yessongs* as one of his albums of 1973, Jewell applauded the fact that it was eighty minutes long and pleaded, 'How can it be compared to normal pop? It's in a league of its own.'

As far as these long-form prophets were concerned, expecting skilled musicians to direct their talents to the fashioning of great singles was like taking creatures used to having the freedom of the wide open spaces and confining them in cages. Surely they needed the space to roam free, to follow their muse, to develop their musical ideas, to ascend to the top of the beanstalk and find out what, if anything, was there, and for this they needed the freedom of the long-playing record. Of all the ideas that were not fashionable in

1973 the foremost was that in all vessels for the carriage of music and entertainment limitations are always strengths.

These critics were not the only people feeling this way. Many of the artists felt the same. Not all of them were in favour of the long form purely for the opportunities it offered for self-indulgence. Ever since *Tommy* in 1969 Pete Townshend had been obsessed with doing something that was along the lines of another opera. He had been headed off from doing that with the over-ambitious *Lifehouse* project in 1971, the best songs from which turned up as *Who's Next*, but in 1973 he was girding his loins for the release of *Quadrophenia*, a rock opera based on the mods and rockers of his youth. What drove him was the need to prove that he could do better than he had already done and because, as he said in an interview, 'People don't want to sit and listen to all our past.' Time would eventually prove that this was precisely what they did want to listen to.

At the same time there was the prospect of further technological innovation. In early 1973 quadraphonic sound was being touted as the inevitable successor to stereo. In February of that year RCA released their recording of Elvis Presley's *Aloha from Hawaii* satellite TV special in their new Quadradisc format, which was supposed to be compatible with non-quadraphonic turntables. Since it was only available in this one format, this became the first quadraphonic album to top the *Billboard* chart. It was also the last. By 1976 it was clear that the market for quadraphonic would always be limited to those middle-aged men who considered a living space dominated by speaker leads a greater priority than a partner with whom to share said space. There were isolated cheerleaders. In December 1973 the *New York Times* carried a piece extolling the 'significantly different listening experience' that the new quadraphonic sound offered. 'The additional sound channels,' it said, 'provide a sense of truly "being there" that the usual stereo set-up can't provide.'

In the case of *Dark Side Of The Moon* and *Tubular Bells* it would have been asking a lot for the recording to reproduce the sense of 'being there' because there had never been a place and a time when that music was actually there. This music wasn't played in the usual sense, instead it was assembled over months in the recording studio. There had not been one original performance. The performances came after, when the band went on tour. Both used the new multi-track recording equipment to simulate experiences that had never actually taken place in order to provide the listener at home in front of his precious stereo, which was equally precious whether it had cost a couple of hundred pounds or many thousands, with another experience altogether.

The most important aspect of this experience, which applied as much to Roger Waters' weighty examination of sanity as it did to Mike Oldfield's pretty instrumental, was submitting to a piece of music that required as much patience as a piece of classical music. In 1973 people were aching for substance and were prepared to risk being bored in pursuit of it. Many people have written about the first time they heard *Dark Side Of The Moon*. For some it suddenly threw new light on the whole canon of Western philosophy; for others it was their first experience of how stereo headphones could make sounds seem to travel from one side of their head to another; for yet more it was their first experience of a soaring wordless vocal; for many it was the first intimation of the possibility that anything could be transformed into a rhythm loop; for even more its use of voices and sound effects planted the idea that henceforth music would be 'cinematic' in its scope; and for all of them, as they sat there letting it wash over them and trying to put together the words they would use to describe the experience once it had come to an end, it was ultimately the weightiness that made the biggest impression. What was *Dark Side Of The Moon* like? In the sounds room in Finsbury Park everyone agreed that it was heavy.

And that is how it has gone down in history. If rock music could be said to have a canon, *Dark Side Of The Moon* is one of its corner-stones. Like *Crime and Punishment* or Beethoven's late quartets, it's used as a measure of earnestness. Bands of all shapes and sizes and traditions, from bluegrass to dub reggae, have tried their spin on *Dark Side Of The Moon* in an effort to get some of its reflected glory for themselves. It's one of the handful of rock albums that are better known than the bands who made them. You could mention *Dark Side Of The Moon* on the nightly news and it would need no further qualification. People are familiar with it as an LP not as a bunch of songs; they know it as the ne plus ultra of inner space. When they think of it, they think of that cover with the light entering the prism and, whether they have actually done it or not, of sitting in the dark for forty-two minutes forty-nine seconds. Nearly half a century after its release, 'It's like *Dark Side Of The Moon*' is a commonly heard and widely understood expression.

Only a handful of long-playing records have been responsible for starting their own myths. Only in the case of *Dark Side Of The Moon* does that myth relate directly to the forty-two minutes forty-nine seconds it takes to play the record. In the early days of the internet, more than twenty years after the record had been released, a theory arose that if you played the album while you watched *The Wizard of Oz* things referred to in the lyrics would appear to be happening on the screen at the same time. You would have to be naive to believe a band capable of such a feat of synchronicity given the technology available in 1973. You would have to know very little about human nature to believe that having done so Pink Floyd would be capable of keeping it a secret. Repeated reading of a novel will often yield layers of meaning which are not evident the first time through. The same thing doesn't always apply with classic albums, which is why devoted listeners will go to unaccountable lengths to somehow enhance and make new the experience of listening the first time. In his book *Lost In Music* the writer Giles

Smith recalls walking in on his older brother, who was a big fan of *Dark Side Of The Moon*, to find him playing the vinyl and cassette version simultaneously in the hope of creating a pleasing echo effect.

The more a record becomes part of people's lives the more susceptible people are to believing that every part of it has some kind of purpose. This is particularly the case with *Dark Side Of The Moon* because the members of the group who made it have not cultivated any mystique of their own. Well over forty years after its making its ownership has long passed from the people who made it to the people who, one way or another, have lived with it.

All records seem like a job of work at the time. *Dark Side Of The Moon* was a record that transformed the lives of all the people involved in making it. The principals will probably be arguing about it until their dying day. For them it became a part of their identity. But even the people who were paid a day rate would spend the rest of their lives looking back at what happened and what almost didn't.

In March 1973 Clare Torry only knew the record was out when she saw a cryptic-looking album cover pinned in the window of a record shop on the King's Road. She got the cover out of its plastic, saw her name on it, bought it, took it home and was amazed they had used as much of her vocal as they had. Her original fee had been £30, which was double time since it was a Sunday. In 2004 she finally won a part-composer credit in a legal action. The record's success put Pink Floyd into the super league, turning this wilful bunch of longhairs from Regent Street Polytechnic into a byword for wealth beyond the dreams of avarice. They made hugely successful albums after it. They never, however, outstripped it.

A couple of years ago I was in Studio Two at Abbey Road with the record's engineer Alan Parsons as he went through the original tapes on the original recording desk, lifting faders to audition instrumental parts that had been abandoned during the final mix, locating the little fluffs and amusing asides that were for him reminders of a day at work over forty years earlier. The process was like trying to find chalk marks on the Great Pyramid. Parsons knew there was a time when it was just a bunch of tracks that were being done to make up Pink Floyd's new record. He knew how accidentally LPs like this one came together and how unwilling fans are to believe that anything on a so-called 'Classic Album' could ever have happened by accident. Finally he restored the faders to their original positions. He knew that as soon as it became *Dark Side Of The Moon*, which wasn't definitely the case until that Abbey Road commissionaire just happened to say, 'There is no dark side of the moon – it's all dark,' it was no longer acceptable to change a single detail. Once it had become *Dark Side Of The Moon* it was bigger than everyone, including the people who made it.

1974

'Rock is dead. Long live popular music'

P ink Floyd had made *Dark Side Of The Moon* with barely any involvement from their record company, which was how things worked in those days, at least for bands who were not struggling to attract an audience. In the course of the six years since the success of *Sgt Pepper* the record business had come to hope that every new act that came through its doors knew something about how to excite the great, unknowable mass audience. The majority of those who ran major record companies were sophisticated enough to know there were things they might not know and willing to believe that bands were best left to their own devices when making an album. After 1974 they would never be quite so laissez-faire again.

From 1974, the economy's problems became the record business's problems. All the way from the days of Elvis through the time of the Beatles to the era of Led Zeppelin the record business had been surfing on an uninterrupted post-war boom. This came to an end with the Yom Kippur War of October 1973. Following this, the predominantly Arab states of the organization of Oil and Petroleum Exporting Countries (OPEC) decided to penalize those nations that had supported Israel by imposing an embargo on their product. This raised the price of the commodity on which the developed world in general and the record business in particular depended. When the price of oil went up by a factor of four in a single year it was a sharp reminder to a world grown complacent that peace, progress and prosperity came at a price. The rise in the price of petrol added to the cost of transporting everything. It also forced everyone to look at how much they were spending. Because it was in the business of manufacturing and distributing an oil-based product, the rise in the price of its raw material had a very specific effect on the record trade.

In the winter of 1974 this was exacerbated in Britain by the imposition of a three-day limit on the business use of electricity. During off-days the giant HMV shop on London's Oxford Street erected a table near the door and restored emergency counter service. Customers would ask for the record they wanted at the door. Store assistants would be dispatched with torches into the gloom of the unlit shop to return some time later with recent releases such as T. Rex's *Zinc Alloy And The Hidden Riders Of Tomorrow* and Steely Dan's *Pretzel Logic*. The effect was felt beyond retail. Roy Matthews was running the EMI pressing plant at Hayes at the time and remembers scouring the country for generators to keep the presses going during the times they were denied the use of electricity from the grid. 'Vinyl, which was an oil-based product, became difficult to get and the price went up. We always managed to get enough but some manufacturers responded by making their product thinner and less substantial,' he remembers.

The oil crisis also made the record companies tighten up their commissioning process. The pressure on vinyl gave them the ideal excuse to change their strategy for signing and recording talent. This policy had been going hell for leather in the same direction since 1968. However, it soon became apparent that the ability to go over big with audiences at festivals or benefits did not always translate into the ability to make records that might appeal to an audience of home listeners.

There were a handful of bands that broke through by simply recording their live set, notably the Grateful Dead whose 1969 *Live/Dead* helped pay off the debts they had incurred in trying to make their own *Sgt Pepper*. It took them three years of treating the studio as a convenient place to take drugs and experiment with the latest recording equipment, in the course of which they junked an entire album and recorded it again on sixteen-track, to make the dismaying discovery that they now owed Warner Brothers $180,000 and that this state of affairs simply couldn't go on. It was only then that they finally realized a successful studio recording might call for actual songs, an element which had never previously figured in their calculations. Having made this connection, Jerry Garcia and Robert Hunter promptly went away and wrote the concise, country-ish tunes that made up 1970's *Workingman's Dead*. They rehearsed these for a week and came up with a running order, only then going into the studio and recording them in exactly that order. Henceforth, they concluded, the studio would be no place for experimentation.

1974 was the year Clive Davis, the company lawyer who had guided Columbia from the Mitch Miller years to the years of the Rock Machine, was eased out in a corporate coup, re-emerging as the head of a new company bankrolled by Columbia Pictures called Arista after his old school honour society. It became a vehicle for Davis's tastes, which were nothing like as interesting as Ahmet Ertegun's at Atlantic but were probably better suited to more cautious times. Although no music man, Davis fancied himself as somebody who could select the kind of songs that the American housewife might sing to herself. He wasn't prepared to sanction any LP releases that didn't have any such songs. Davis would have no compunction about refusing to put out an album if, in the time-honoured record company parlance, he didn't hear a single. His reasoning was that to spend further money promoting an album that he didn't believe in was simply sending good money after bad. In this he was possibly right. There are albums that prove to have more commercial appeal than the record company think but they are few and far between. Far more numerous are the albums that never achieve escape velocity despite the heartfelt belief of the people who made them.

The basic record deal of the early seventies was as follows. A record company would advance an act up to $75,000. This sounded a lot. It wasn't quite so much in practice because they had to use part of it to pay off the debts they had inevitably accumulated while waiting for the record deal. They had to house and feed themselves, their crew and their 'old ladies', they had to pay for some rehearsal time, and then, most expensively of all, they had to pay for the recording of the new album in which all their hopes for the future would be invested. In the pre-rock and roll days record companies didn't expect studio time to cost much at all. A Frank Sinatra or an Andy Williams would make an album in four days tops. After *Sgt Pepper*, that changed. It changed again when studios began to offer sixteen- and then thirty-two-track recording facilities. Bands could and did take months in the studio, either because they were keen to discover what each and every button on the console did or because the producer was waiting to hear something the record company could sell.

Dark Side Of The Moon and *Tubular Bells* may have been selling week in and week out without the help of hit singles but they were the exception. In most cases it was still hit singles that stimulated the albums market. Hit singles attracted casual buyers. Hit singles reached beyond your fan base. Hit singles gave you power. Hit singles might even put you in profit.

When an album was released the record company started making money back if it turned out to be one of the 10 per cent of albums released that sold 60,000. The act didn't start making money until it sold over 100,000. If it went gold, which was 500,000 copies in the United States and 100,000 in the UK, the act could then start thinking about buying their apartments. Their percentage royalty might start off at 6 per cent for the first 100,000, rising to 7 per cent for the second 100,000 and up accordingly. If it went platinum, which was 1,000,000 copies in the United States and 300,000 in the United Kingdom, they could look at buying houses in the country. To sell that kind of number they would need to have a hit single, such as might get played on daytime radio and have them invited on to late-night chat shows, and unlock a stream of publishing income that might make at least one member of the band, the person who wrote the songs, quite comfortable.

The majority of acts that made their albums in 1973 and 1974 never hit such heights. For most of them, having a recording contract simply allowed them to claim they were in the game. The small amount of money they could get from the record company in 'tour support' could, with a bit of luck and some skin-of-the-teeth management of unforeseen expenses such as tax demands, keep them in the state of genteel poverty which was the working musician's lot back in the 1970s. Anything below those levels, they went into their next record deal needing even more money to pay off their debts and begin the whole process all over again.

The oil crisis put a stop to all that. *Billboard* reported in 1974 that record companies were now signing acts on the basis that they would try a few singles and see how those worked out before committing to an album. For his book *Starmaking Machinery*, Geoffrey

Stokes spent part of 1974 with Commander Cody and His Lost Planet Airmen, a country-ish outfit from the West Coast who were popular with college kids, as they tried to ensure that their fifth album would be more successful than the previous four. To increase their chances they were forced to do something they had never done before: hire a producer.

For any band taking on the services of a producer amounted to an admission that making records was a lot harder than they had initially believed and that there might be tricks they had missed completely. The role of the producer in making successful records is analogous to the role of the manager in developing successful football teams. Nobody on the outside can actually put their finger on the things these fabled figures do to make a difference but they are prepared to spend a lot of money in the hope that, whatever that is, they will continue to do it. There are other similarities. A good producer, like a good football manager, knows when to withdraw the carrot and when to introduce the stick. Just as in a football team, nobody ever quite knows whether the act would have been successful without him but they're not prepared to take the risk involved in finding out. Furthermore, like the football manager, the producer's job is to get the best out of the talent at his disposal, not to order up superior talent.

Finally, some producers, like some managers, become better known than the artists they produce, which invariably causes resentment. In 1974, the American producer Richard Perry's track record of success with Harry Nilsson, Ringo Starr and Barbra Streisand meant he asked for and got his name on the front cover of the album he produced that year for Martha Reeves. This might have meant it got more attention on radio or in the press than would otherwise have been the case. It didn't stop it from dying a terrible commercial death and abruptly ending Reeves's association with MCA. Perry moved on to other projects.

There were other producers who were seen as being desirable despite not really having a CV heaving with hits. In 1974, Todd Rundgren was sufficiently au courant to be given the job of producing albums for former Rascal Felix Cavaliere, the still-hitless Daryl Hall and John Oates and the over-the-hill Grand Funk Railroad. This was all in the same year he was recording and releasing his own double album *Todd* and the first record by his band Utopia.

None of these acts particularly benefited from the association with the hip producer but it didn't lessen the record companies' belief in the power of the producer to insure against the commercial failure which seemed to be the lot of the overwhelming majority of records. Most acts, like most football teams, fail. Changing the producer is one of the few ways the people who control the money can give themselves the illusion that they're not simply at the mercy of dumb luck.

Bands have long talked wistfully of just being able to plug in and play and have the recording machine eavesdrop on their performance, as though the secret of a successful recording lay in simply capturing them playing in their rawest state. This is rarely the case. The most poignant episode in the Beatles' career came at the beginning of 1969 when Paul McCartney tried to get them to play and record in the way they had done in 1963. In truth they were no more likely to be able to do this than to rekindle the instant of a first kiss. When you're in the presence of a band playing live the clear air turbulence alone will be exciting enough to block out the fact that the beat keeps speeding up, the bass needs retuning or the vocalist is phlegmy in the chorus. When you're listening at home, these shortcomings come into pin-sharp focus. Just as the most effective fight scenes in the movies are the ones that have been carefully choreographed, repeatedly practised and skilfully edited, rather than the ones that have simply broken out on the studio floor, a successful recording is a brilliant contrivance. What Paul McCartney loved about the sound of the band on *With The Beatles* was not simply the way they happened to sound at the time. It was also George Martin's idea of how they sounded best at the time.

Back in 1963 that was largely dictated by what was set down on tape. By 1974 the recording of the actual music had become only half of the process. Once everything had been committed to one of sixteen or even thirty-two tracks, often instrument by instrument and voice by voice, it had to be mixed, which involved a thousand tiny decisions about the relative balance of the instruments, the amount of reverb and the judicious sprinkling of what was widely known as 'fairy dust' in the hope this would please the ear of the band, the people at the record company, the radio programming people, the press and, eventually, even the public.

The experience of Commander Cody with Warner Bros in 1974 is a perfect illustration of how the system worked better for the record companies than for the bands they signed. John Boylan was the man the management and record company decided was the best producer to get something commercial out of them in 1974. He and the band went into the Record Plant in the rich Californian hippy haven of Sausalito and tried to find a way of working together. Boylan had the usual producer's frustrations: a drummer who couldn't quite keep time, musicians who played too loud and sang too quietly, and performances which were insufficiently uniform for him to be able to splice together the best bits of different ones. He also couldn't hear a single.

The best they could come up with was a 1958 Jesse Stone tune called 'Don't Let Go'. The promotion men of their new record company managed to get some early radio play on the single. The radio stations then looked nervously for signs that the record was selling in local stores. As soon as they didn't see any they began to cool on the single, which meant the album came out with nothing going for it but the possibility of good reviews in the press. Neither the

Village Voice nor *Rolling Stone* liked it, both detecting the truth about the record, that in trying to make it a hit they had ended up with something that was likely to please neither their old-time fans nor the country crowd, and thus, effectively, it was all over for the record. The album sold almost 100,000 and then stopped. Stopped utterly. It made some money for the record company but simply put the band deeper in debt. It had cost over $100 an hour to record. That was in 1974 when the average annual salary was under $10,000.

In the fifties and sixties the producer's role had been largely restricted to locating the microphones properly and making sure the right people were in front of those microphones. As the seventies advanced the producer had more and more tools to enable him to fix it in the mix. He also had executives who had an idea of how they wanted a record to turn out. Ideally they wanted a producer who could reverse-engineer the desired result.

In 1972 the great British producer Glyn Johns thought he was finished with his work on the first album by the Eagles, a band managed by David Geffen. Geffen, who also ran their record company, wouldn't leave Johns alone until he had recorded a second Jackson Browne composition with lead vocals by Don Henley to provide what he thought should be a second hit from the record. Johns wound up flying across the Atlantic just to re-record the song ('Nightingale') again, to prove that it wasn't as good a song as 'Take It Easy'. Geffen was the pre-eminent executive of the age of the rock LP. His process-driven approach to making albums until they maximized every last bit of commercial appeal got its crowning reward in 1976 when *Eagles: Their Greatest Hits* became the biggest-selling long-player in the history of the United States.

There are two LPs that came out in the year 1974 that could reasonably claim to be works of art. Neither of them shied away from the demands of the marketplace. They were nonetheless works of art in the sense that they took on adult themes, did full justice to the complexity of those themes and explored them via simple, memorable songs that tempted the listener to play them again and again. This last is the unique challenge of the LP. On finishing a novel that has given satisfaction we generally set it aside. It's in the nature of a successful LP that we should want to play it again and again. The first of these works of art was made by an artist who had been managed by Geffen and was released on Asylum, the label Geffen had designed as a refuge from the moneychangers in the temple. It was also, in some senses, about him.

The habit of describing an LP as being 'about' something dates from this time. Hopes were being entertained that the album was becoming a mature artistic form, capable of describing and reflecting the culture much as a novel might. Nobody was entirely sure what 1974 releases such as Bob Dylan's *Planet Waves*, Neil Young's *On The Beach*, Jackson Browne's *Late For The Sky* and Van Morrison's *Veedon Fleece* were about, other than Watergate or the hangover from the sixties. The mere fact that they were so downbeat made them feel reassuringly adult. Gram Parsons' *Grievous Angel* was even more so because the artist died before it could be released.

Court And Spark, which was released on the first day of 1974, is arguably the best record Joni Mitchell ever made. Insofar as a pop record, which has to be about hit tunes as much as anything, can be said to have a theme, Joni Mitchell's *Court And Spark* is about what a successful young woman might, or might not, be prepared to give up for love. Each of its songs frames the flickering moment during which she faces choices. Does she go with the dreamer at her door with the sleeping roll or stay in the city of the fallen angels? Does she continue to look for warmth and beauty in the singles bar or settle for the first acceptable screw? Does she keep waiting for his car on a hill? We love our loving but not like we love our freedom. This particularly applies to people on the high wire of show business. They sing about true love but the truth is that success and prestige trump everything. Joni Mitchell has never hidden that side of her. She likes success. She likes nice things.

The best of the many great songs on *Court And Spark* was actually inspired by David Geffen. He and Mitchell were sharing a house together at the time and they both had difficulty committing to much beyond their careers. She visited Paris with him and Robbie Robertson, which is where she got the idea for the song. 'Free Man In Paris' is sung from the point of view of a man who can only throw off his self-imposed responsibilities when he's in the City of Light. Because her arrangements and the playing of Tom Scott and his LA Express are so weightless and sublime the best lines ripple into the cerebral cortex on wings of melody, there to be chewed over at leisure by the subconscious. The key detail here is in the verse which goes 'If I had my way I'd just walk through those doors and wander down the Champs Elysees . . .' The words tumble towards the two syllables of 'wander' (a single letter away from 'wonder'), which she then extends into three and a half beats and holds. As she does you rush through the revolving door of that posh hotel lobby and into the Parisian sunshine with her. At that point, halfway through side one, the entire LP opens up. Geffen, who may have thought that song was a bit too close to home, didn't want her to put it on the album.

She was at a party at the time with fellow Asylum artist Bob Dylan. When they put on *Planet Waves* everybody enthused. When they put on *Court And Spark*, Dylan pretended to go to sleep. This was not in itself surprising. Recording artists hate any situation which compels them to listen to and be polite about other artists' recordings. Most musicians take fellow musicians' successes as daggers to the heart.

Court And Spark went on to become more successful than *Planet Waves*. It was eventually Mitchell's most successful album. This was not because it anatomized the thoughts of a generation of women, most of whom were not in Mitchell's privileged position, but because it sounded so pretty. One of the people who grew up knowing its every word was Madonna Ciccone, who was fifteen when the album was released.

The other album of 1974 that might be called, with a straight face, a work of art wasn't quite as pretty but still it had wide commercial appeal. It was also probably the most provocative long-player of the long-player's golden age.

On 9 August 1974, Richard Nixon went before the television cameras in the White House to announce that he was resigning the Presidency. Among the people watching this epochal event on TV were three Californians in their early thirties who had all grown up in privileged circumstances in the bosom of the entertainment business. Randy Newman, Lenny Waronker and Russ Titelman had known each other since their school days and had contributed to each other's careers ever since.

After they had watched this most dramatic episode in the history of America and its politics, the three of them gathered around a microphone and sang a political song. It was not a conventional song of protest. In fact it was a campaign song that had originally been used by Huey Long, the rascally governor of Louisiana. And it wasn't ripped from today's headlines. It dated from the mid-1930s. The song was called 'Every Man A King' and it was planned to come after a Newman original about the disastrous Louisiana flood of 1927 and before 'Kingfish', another Newman composition about Long's appeal to the voters in the wake of that flood.

The Long triptych forms the core of the historical section of the Randy Newman album *Good Old Boys*, which was released in September 1974. The legacy of slavery runs all the way through American history in general and American popular music in particular. Newman's mother was from New Orleans; he had spent a lot of time in the south when he was young and had not been shy of touching upon highly charged topics such as slavery and racial tension in his songs. The great virtue of Newman's work is the same quality that is always destined to get him into trouble. Believing that being on the side of virtue is neither interesting nor instructive, he makes sure the devil gets some of his best tunes.

The opening song of *Good Old Boys* is 'Rednecks'. This was inspired by an incident which took place in December 1970 when the segregationist governor of Georgia Lester Maddox walked off Dick Cavett's TV show after feeling he was being patronized by the host. 'Rednecks' is a song in defence of Maddox written by a notional character whose resentment of the smart eastern elite is stronger, and goes back further, than his resentment of the African Americans that his forefathers kept in chains. The key line explains that the historical role of rednecks was 'keeping the niggers down'. When Newman wrote out the song he missed out the word. Nonetheless he knew its use was vital to achieving the shudder of recognition which makes the song work. Like Mitchell's *Court And Spark*, *Good Old Boys* wasn't just stimulating and didn't just bring with it a new way of looking at the world, it was also simple and catchy in the traditional meaning of those terms. In song after simple song on *Good Old Boys* Newman delves into the residue of America's original sin and in each case he does as much justice to its complexity and intractability as could be expected of even the most advanced pop song.

When they first got into the music business, Joni as a folk purist and Randy as a backroom boy, neither of them could have seen themselves doing what they ended up doing in 1974. In truth they were neither of them rock people. Nevertheless it was rock that allowed them to do what they did in 1974, rock money that paid for the top musicians and studio time, rock's relaxed attitude even when it came to things it didn't pretend to understand which permitted them to stray anywhere they pleased on the musical map as long as they didn't lose sight of the fact that they were there to entertain. This was music that had charm first of all and everything else afterwards. Too often in rock serious intentions are foreshadowed by the sound of grunting and brow-furrowing. *Court And Spark* and *Good Old Boys*, on the other hand, were above all seductive. Their primary weapons of seduction were melodies you could hum and words you were hardly aware you were singing. Popular music is a branch of the art of the possible. If it ever gets too far away from something a person might play on the radio, it's sunk. *Good Old Boys* started life as a concept album, *Johnny Cutler's Birthday*, but it was pared back to a standard album, which proved to be a good thing. Both Newman and Mitchell in the years that followed periodically gave in to the siren call of high culture. On these records they didn't. These records walked the tightrope between art and commerce with supreme grace and in the process, probably by accident, perfected the grown-up rock album.

Michael Watts in the *Melody Maker*, in his review of *Court And Spark*, said 'few other rock musicians have so refined personal experience that it succeeds as genuine art'. It would turn out that what made it her most successful album was the fact that it produced her most successful single. In the same week in June 1974 that Bob Woodward and Carl Bernstein published *All the President's Men*, there was Joni Mitchell at number seven in the *Billboard* chart with 'Help Me'. In the vulgar variety show that is the weekly singles chart there it was, just below Ray Stevens and 'The Streak' and just above the theme from *The Sting*. Singles success is the great leveller. That's where you've got to be if you want to be in people's hearts.

At the same time her album was reviewed in the UK in a little magazine called *Let It Rock*. *Let It Rock* never quite made the grade. It was too early. It was under-financed. The advertising that many years later would permit magazines such as *Mojo* and *Uncut* to prosper doing something very similar simply didn't exist. However, despite its title, *Let It Rock* was reflecting the fact that the music which had been marketed as rock by Clive Davis was now outgrowing the category. Not everybody who wrote for *Let It Rock* agreed. In the issue that began 1974 Nick Kent had looked back on the previous year and said that the worst thing about it was Gram Parsons dying and Neil Young not dying. He also hoped that in the following year 'hordes of deranged mutant youth will spring from the suburbs primed on Iggy Pop', and finished 'viva rock'n'roll fascism', whatever that meant.

The *Let It Rock* review of Joni Mitchell's *Court And Spark* was something very different. In it Stephen Barnard concluded in the light of recent records by Randy Newman and Paul Simon that writers seemed to be breaking out of the old confines of rock and looking to older musical styles to express their musical ideas. He finished: 'Joni may speak for a generation that's been reared on a music casually and very loosely referred to as "rock" but she's actually playing a music that bears more affinity with jazz. So: the message is this. Rock is dead. Long live popular music.'

In 1974, both Mitchell and Newman benefited from the fact that they had small but devoted followings who attended closely to their new records. They had good listeners. One of the reasons these people paid such close attention was because they didn't really have many other options. In the year these exceptional records came out, I was sharing a rented flat in north London with three other young men. The flat didn't have a telephone, TV or radio. The cooking was done on a gas cooker that wouldn't have passed even the lax safety standards of the time. There was no kitchen technology. No toaster. No electric kettle. No vacuum cleaner. The fridge was good only for storing cider. Central heating was a far-off dream. During the winter we would gather around a heater powered by Calor gas. And yet, in the midst of a domestic set-up that was in many senses Third World, we had three record players.

The invention of the long-playing record in 1948 meant all the music on this towering stack of 78s could be contained in the new 33⅓ rpm LPs under the arm of inventor Peter Goldmark. The term 'album' derives from the wallets in which the 78s had been kept.

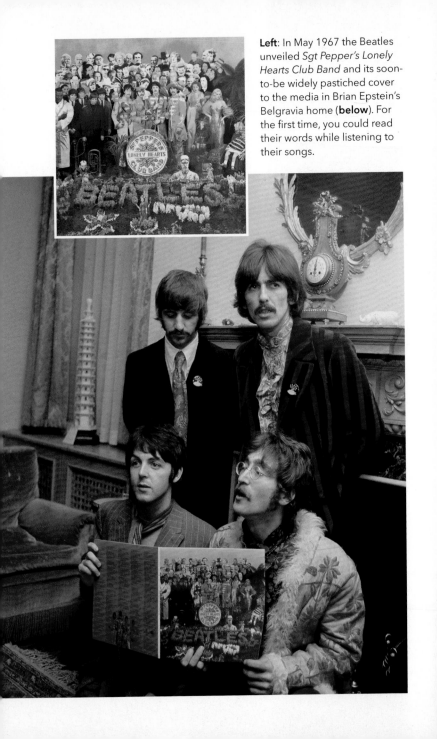

Left: In May 1967 the Beatles unveiled *Sgt Pepper's Lonely Hearts Club Band* and its soon-to-be widely pastiched cover to the media in Brian Epstein's Belgravia home (**below**). For the first time, you could read their words while listening to their songs.

THE ROCK MACHINE TURNS YOU ON.

Bob Dylan
Leonard Cohen
Moby Grape
Spirit
United States Of America
The Zombies
The Peanut Butter Conspiracy
Blood Sweat & Tears
The Byrds
Taj Mahal
Simon & Garfunkel
The Electric Flag
Roy Harper
Tim Rose
Elmer Gantry's Velvet Opera

Above: In 1968, young people couldn't afford to simply splash out on LPs and so budget-price compilations like *The Rock Machine Turns You On* provided an affordable bridge to the songs of people such as Leonard Cohen (**left**), here embraced by Joni Mitchell at the Newport Folk Festival.

Left: Bruce Findlay outside his Edinburgh record shop in 1969, the year he ordered 250 copies of the first King Crimson LP and was forced to replenish his stock by the end of the week.

Above: Barry Godber, a computer programmer and friend of the band, painted the striking cover picture of the first King Crimson LP (**right**) in 1969. He died from a heart attack at the age of twenty-four within months of the album's release.

Above: The Band broke all the rules when making their magical second LP. They faced each other in the swimming pool house of a rented Hollywood home. Levon Helm's drum kit had been bought at a thrift store. Producer John Simon has his boots on the recording desk.

Right and **below**: Record labels responded to the threat of bootlegs by putting out their own officially sanctioned recordings in covers which consciously mimicked the outlaw-chic of the illegal variety.

Stereo for the man who has nothing.

No turntable, no speakers, no amplifier, no tuner—nothing.

The Sony HP-188 stereo gives you everything you haven't got in one compact package.

A 4-speed BSR automatic turntable with cue-ing control for safe, easy record handling. And a featherweight cartridge we designed ourselves.

An FM stereo FM/AM tuner with FET circuitry in the FM for more sensitivity and less distortion.

An amplifier with all-silicon transistors.

And a pair of two-way high-compliance speakers for true high fidelity sound.

Everything is just $239.95.* (The HP-156, everything minus tuner, $179.95*) So you'll have something left to spend on other lovely things.

The Sony HP-188. A complete stereo music system.

Left: In the seventies, when hip people didn't have TVs and it was still possible to invite somebody up to listen to your new Van Morrison record without risking mockery, an impressive hi-fi system was the dream of every bachelor.

Below: Jack Nicholson gives Crosby, Stills & Nash his undivided attention on his new headphones in 1969. The Buffalo Springfield are poised on the auto changer of his record deck, ready to follow.

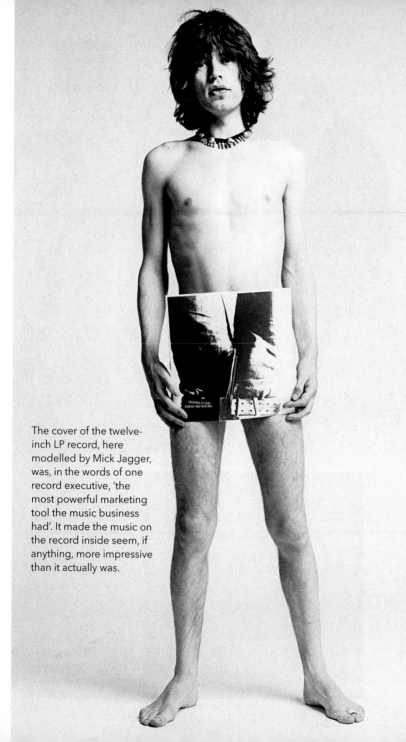

The cover of the twelve-inch LP record, here modelled by Mick Jagger, was, in the words of one record executive, 'the most powerful marketing tool the music business had'. It made the music on the record inside seem, if anything, more impressive than it actually was.

Above: With the encouragement of Atlantic boss Ahmet Ertegun (*on the left*), Cream made sure their breakthrough LP *Disraeli Gears* was packed with radio-friendly rockers. The one LP by Clapton's next project, the super-group Blind Faith, came in a cover (**left**) which proved too much for America but could be bought on any UK high street.

At the same time, the artist soon to be known as Elvis Costello was sharing a flat in London with other music-obsessed young men. He remembers them living on toast and jam and spending all their spare money on long-playing records. Every evening they would gather and play one another their records, each one taking turns to be the DJ and amuse his housemates, with 'The Gift' by the Velvet Underground running into Monty Python's Cheese Shop sketch. As for the television, he doesn't remember there being one. His whole world revolved around records just as those records revolved in his world. It was the availability of this huge audience waiting to be delivered from its miserable circumstances that helped provide the conditions for this brief flowering of long-form popular music.

1975

'Take Donna home and make love to her'

In the spring of 1975 a customer from overseas came into the large record shop where I worked in the West End of London. The man was based in Beirut where he ran a club of some kind. He would come into the shop once a year to buy the latest hot records. He would generally carry a shopping list of what he wanted but he would also ask for suggestions. At that time he was taking away with him new releases like David Bowie's *Young Americans*, Led Zeppelin's *Physical Graffiti*, *Chocolate City* by Parliament, Cockney Rebel's *The Best Years Of Our Lives* and *Blue Jays* by Justin Hayward and John Lodge, as well as new albums by Abba, Manhattan Transfer and the Pointer Sisters. He always bought a lot of different records. He always paid cash. He always took them back to his hotel in a cab. On this particular occasion, when he'd got to the bottom of his shopping list, he fixed me with a 'Can I trust you?' look before furtively enquiring, 'Do you have any sex music?'

This was the first time I had been asked for sex music. I said I wasn't clear what he was talking about. It turned out he was referring to a particular record he'd recently heard in a Dutch discotheque, a record so instantly appealing that he had just naturally assumed that it had to be the leading title in a wave that was bound to have resulted in an entire new category in the record shop. He felt sure that what he'd heard meant that there must be a section labelled 'sex music'.

There never was such a category but in every other respect the man from Beirut was on to something. The record he had heard in that Dutch disco was 'Love To Love You Baby' by Donna Summer. That record and the many that came after it would change the way people bought LPs.

The story had begun with Giorgio Moroder, an Italian record man working in Germany, who was talking to Donna Summer, an American who had come to Europe with a touring production of *Hair*. I would like a sexy song, he said, with the somewhat clinical air of a Swiss banker asking directions to the corner of Sin and Iniquity. If you ever have an idea for a sexy song, Donna, he added, I would like to hear it. Donna had been raised in the Church but she knew a lead when she was faced with one.

A week later she came back and sang him her idea for a sexy song. It was no more than a wisp, little more than a fragment. It was just the line 'love to love you baby' sung again and again. Moroder was sufficiently taken with her fragment to record her singing it and to make it up into a demo. Any shortcomings of the lyrics were more than compensated for with moans and sighs which seemed to arise from the depths of the kind of sexual delirium described in some detail in the correspondence pages of *Forum* magazine. The only precedent for her idea was 'Je T'aime . . . Moi Non Plus', Jane Birkin and Serge Gainsbourg's heavy-breathing hit from 1969, which was certainly not played on the radio.

By 1975 the sexual climate had changed. The best-selling book of the year in the United States was *The Total Woman*, which had been written by an impeccably respectable middle-aged lawyer's wife from Miami called Marabel Morgan. Mrs Morgan sold twenty million copies of her book which advised wives that if the price of keeping their marriages alive was to unleash their inner slut then they should have no compunction about greeting their husbands at the door dressed as a showgirl. The same year, the hero of Malcolm Bradbury's novel *The History Man* was a sociology lecturer who believed in what he liked to call an open marriage. Judith Rossner's *Looking for Mr Goodbar* was about a New York City schoolteacher who cruised the singles bars at night. Even the teenage fiction area was shaken up at the time by Judy Blume's publication of *Forever...*, a novel where the young heroine has sex with her boyfriend and her life doesn't come apart.

Moroder's partner took Summer's demo to a music business fair in Cannes in an attempt to scare up some interest. This found its way to Neil Bogart of Casablanca Records, who demanded that they record more of it. He didn't want something different. He didn't want something similar. He wanted more of what was already there. Bogart wasn't expecting the song to go anywhere, to add a second voice or to relieve the monotony with an interesting middle eight. Bogart, who was never handicapped by modesty, simply sensed that he needed more. How much more? Well, long enough to make up one side of an album, he said. Or, to put it another way, he wanted something long enough to soundtrack an orgy.

Sixteen minutes. That was the length of 'Love To Love You Baby' when it was first released in the USA in November 1975 as a twelve-inch single. Practically speaking, sixteen minutes was asking a lot of the stamina of musicians, let alone sexual athletes. Because the drummer on 'Love To Love You Baby' was playing live, the rhythm section could only sustain the tempo by effectively starting the song again a few times in the course of that sixteen minutes. This was a problem that would in the fullness of time be addressed by the replacement of human drummers with rhythm machines. But already, the traditionally made album *Love To Love You Baby*, which had come out in August 1975 with the title track taking up the whole of the first side, exemplified three key changes brought about by the disco boom.

The first was that it exchanged the dynamics of the standard rhythm and blues-derived dance hit, Motown's so-called 'heart-beat' rhythm, for a four-on-the-floor rhythm such as might appeal to dancers who were neither black nor Latin, and also to people who couldn't dance at all but remained happily unaware of the fact.

Here was the most profound shift in popular music in the whole of the seventies, far more profound than the progressive rock that had already happened or the punk rock that was to come. It changed dance music from something that coaxed you on to the floor into something that simply demanded submission to its big mama heartbeat. The boom-boom-boom-boom of four on the floor was not there to seduce; it demanded surrender, and usually achieved it. Two years later the same production team would set the controls for the future with 'I Feel Love', but by that time musicians had been largely supplanted by machines. Brian Eno, who was in Berlin recording with David Bowie at the time, interrupted a session to announce, 'This single is going to change the sound of club music for the next fifteen years.' He wasn't wrong.

The second thing the disco boom proved was that people liked to be provided with the same rhythm relentlessly for long periods of time, and the long-playing record was ideally placed to do this. Whereas it had previously been thought ideal that a long-playing record should showcase the range of what an artist was capable of while at the same time ministering to the different demands of a diverse audience – the few records that weren't titled *The Many*

Moods Of . . . seemed to be called *Two Sides Of . . .* – now it seemed that there was a demand for LPs that offered the fresh reassurance of no variety whatsoever. If people liked four minutes of Donna Summer's 'Love To Love You Baby' then it followed they would love sixteen minutes even more. This was the beginning of the boom in twelve-inch singles with their promise of more of the same. And it wasn't just the hard-bitten unromantic record men who were beginning to think this way. The whole of the first side of Kraftwerk's *Autobahn*, which had been released in 1974 but began its British chart run in 1975, was taken up by the title track which mimicked and celebrated the monotony of travelling the network of the new motorways that now spanned Europe. The fact that its twenty-two minutes went past without any change in its tempo led some people to think of it as a novelty record. They were surprised when Kraftwerk came back with further musical ideas.

The third big change brought about by disco was that henceforth it was taken as read that nobody was singing about love. What they were singing about was sex. Hyping the success of 'Love To Love You Baby', Neil Bogart of Casablanca would say that it had succeeded because out there in the marketplace were a lot of people like him who felt there hadn't been a long-playing record that provided proper accompaniment to sexual intercourse since Iron Butterfly's 'In-A-Gadda-Da-Vida'. Using the opportunity to advertise his personal stamina, Bogart added that he had initially asked for a twenty-minute version and was slightly disappointed when they only sent him sixteen.

Bogart was delighted when radio stations proved reluctant to play the record. All the more reason, he said, 'to take Donna home and make love to her – the album that is'. Bogart was on to something here. The people who bought Summer's record and also at the same time the overheated love operas of Barry White were not kids or students or the same people who bought Bob Dylan's *Blood On The*

Tracks, which was released the same year. They were people who regarded music as something that was primarily there to enhance their lifestyle. The many people who couldn't keep pace with Bogart on his sexual marathons nevertheless liked to feel that they ought to be able to. Thanks to Donna Summer, society seemed to take on board the idea that sex was something you should be able to hear from a nearby building. *Time* magazine labelled her the queen of something they called 'sex rock' and, with their American commitment to exactitude, reckoned they counted no fewer then twenty-two simulated orgasms in the long version of her record. Sex music it was. My friend from Beirut was ahead of everyone.

Nobody knew quite how to react to the sound of a woman, a married one with a child no less, bringing herself to a climax over what seemed like an amiable piece of travelogue music kept on track by a more excited heartbeat than the one that had begun *Dark Side Of The Moon*.

There was little chance of such sounds finding their way into your home entertainment diet any other way. At the time the record was released, one episode of *Fawlty Towers* was still hinging on the chances of an unmarried couple being able to share a bed in a hotel without the owner discovering them. The same episode was made memorable by a scene in which Connie Booth took off her T-shirt to reveal her bra. Desperate to arrest the slide in cinema attendances, the film industry was beginning to flirt with porn, both softcore and hard. *Emmanuelle* had appeared in the UK at the end of 1974, and in America there was a run of porn films, such as Marilyn Chambers in *Behind the Green Door*, that briefly opened up the possibility that there might be a respectable audience prepared to go and see such things in movie theatres. Even Bob Hope and Johnny Carson were cracking light-hearted jokes about *Deep Throat*.

Sex and the long-playing record had seemed to belong together ever since the medium was invented. In 1956, *Playboy* magazine had published a pictorial dedicated to its dream apartment. This idealized environment for modern living was beyond the means of 99 per cent of the magazine's readers but contained a feature that probably appealed to them even more than the well-equipped kitchen and state-of-the-art bathroom. This was 'an entertainment wall' containing all the audio equipment the discriminating man about town might desire. The key feature was that all could be controlled by a number of magical switches which could be easily reached from the most important item of furniture in the apartment, the bed. The link between playing records and getting a woman into bed didn't have to be spelled out any further.

This was clear to the people who marketed hi-fis and the records to play on them to young men. Album after album seemed to promote the idea that single women were just waiting for the right tune to be played on the right turntable in order to surrender their virtue. *Have Mood Will Call* by the Will Davis Trio, which came out in 1959, is a perfect example. On the cover of this an Anita Ekberg lookalike reclines on a perfectly made bed alongside, for some reason, a bowl of fruit. She is holding a phone. From this we deduce that she has just put a call through to her eager swain. He is now racing round with all speed, a copy of Davis's newly purchased release on the Sue label under his hot little arm. In those days putting on a long-playing record for a woman was as close as most men came to an emotional gesture.

In the same year Omega Records put out a compilation called *Bedside Companion For Playboys*. This cover features a Vargas-like woman naked but for a pair of shoes. She is regarding the camera from an upside down position, presumably urging her beau to put on the other side so that she might hear the Frank Comstock Orchestra doing 'Island Of Desire', or 'Limehouse Blues' as rendered by the Brussels World's Fair Orchestra. In the majority of cases the music didn't quite live up to its aphrodisiac billing but that didn't stop it pouring forth. Never in the history of recorded music have the puffings and scrapings of so many over-mortgaged middle-aged men been packaged inside so many covers emblazoned with pictures of pretty women trying to look relaxed while draped on a tiger-skin rug or sexually primed while giving his sidecar that all-important shake. The shot of a beauty relaxing at home with a gramophone, the floor of her apartment covered with the sleeves of her limitless collection of long-playing records, was a standard weapon in the armoury of the Hollywood studios. LPs meant sophistication, the good life and the possibility of sex.

The gramophone was a home-bound item of furniture and therefore it was expected to be able to solve the kind of problems that arose in the home. Men who were otherwise impervious to the most basic ideas of how to please a woman had nonetheless taken on board the idea that soft lights and sweet music would always help. The first of these prerequisites could be hard enough to arrange. At college, I remember a brisk trade in coloured cellophane to wrap around the single central light bulbs that illuminated the average rented room. This was clearly a fire risk but probably not much more of a fire risk than everything else in the room. A lot of men had a lot of recorded music but it was possible that not a great deal of it was sweet. When comedian Jackie Gleason fronted a series of albums of romantic mood music in the fifties he had said his aim was to provide practical help for gentlemen who weren't used to entertaining women in their quarters and were unlikely to have cooked a meal. 'Every time I ever watched Clark Gable do a love scene in the movies,' he said, 'I'd hear this really pretty music, real romantic, come up behind him and help set the mood. So I'm figuring that if Clark Gable needs that kinda help, then a guy in Canarsie has gotta be dyin' for somethin' like this!'

In the 1950s and 1960s few men were sufficiently established in the single life to be able to organize their domestic environment to maximize the chances of a successful seduction. By the 1970s this had been changed by increasing prosperity and wider access to higher education. A *New York Times* survey of universities in March 1974 had found that for this new generation of baby boomers records were simply 'one of life's necessities'. In a survey of student halls of residence all over the country they found that everyone bought records and that listening to them had replaced dances and rallies as a way of passing the time. And it wasn't just men. Susan Kahn of Smith College in Massachusetts reported that whereas two years before there had only been two women in their seventy-five-berth dormitory who had a component stereo system, there were now more than thirty. 'When I first came to Smith three years ago, an interest in good quality stereo equipment was equated in many students' minds with the use of marijuana,' she said, obviously relieved that such ill-repute was now a thing of the past. Reporting from the ivy-clad walls of Harvard, Arthur Lubov added, 'Stereos are now as common as armchairs.'

This dependence on record players continued as this generation moved on from halls of residence to rented apartments. The hi-fi was the first thing that had to be installed and working as soon as they moved into a new place. It was a comfort. In the absence of a living fire, a favourite photo or the purring of a much-loved family cat, the record player alone provided a sense of home. It was the sole possession of any consequence. It was the only conceivable reason why one's home would be of any interest to burglars. The ownership of as few as forty albums to play on it would also increase your standing among your circle of friends. The quality of the set-up and the music you had available to play on it could transform you from a person of no social consequence to someone it was worth visiting. Some of these visitors would be of the opposite sex. In the 1970s you could ask a girl back to your place 'to listen to my albums' without being openly laughed at. Why was that? Primarily because the only way you were going to hear Marvin Gaye's *Let's Get It On* at the time it came out was to go to the home of somebody who owned a copy. The experience of listening to records like these simply wasn't available any other way. Simply saying, 'I have a record' became a legitimate opening gambit. Jonathan Morrish, who was starting to work in the record business at the time, almost blushes as he remembers that 'There was a certain power in owning a record, in being able to say, "I've got the new Neil Young album". There was a feeling that if you invited a woman back Neil Young might charm her on your behalf.' It wasn't just the civilians who recognized this power. Back in 1965, Jackie DeShannon had tempted guitarist Jimmy Page back to her hotel room with the promise that he could listen to her copy of the new Bob Dylan album.

As well as the small bump of delight that came from being able to introduce somebody to something they hadn't heard before, there was also the fact that certain long-playing records imbued their owners with prestige. In the early seventies I was aware there were other males who spent their disposable cash on cars rather than records but reasoned correctly there was no future for me in a girl who was more impressed by an old MG Midget than the new album by Todd Rundgren. Also, there was something intimate about the two of you just *listening to a record* in your room, a place which had no other facilities or distractions. It wasn't like watching a video was to become in the following decade. It wasn't a distraction from what was going on between the two of you. It increased the chances that something might happen between the two of you. Responding to a record was something both personal and public. There was nothing to look at apart from each other and the album cover. In this way, playing a record *to* a girl became a form of wooing. With a little bit of luck the record – its sound, its appearance, its fresh, unscratched surface, its manifold associations, the conversation it might spark – would melt the space between you and render possible things that in its absence would have been difficult to imagine.

Much of the time the choices were clunky and the moves gauche. In his autobiography *Some Fantastic Place*, Squeeze's Chris Difford describes how his efforts to get to know a Swedish au pair while listening to Todd Rundgren's *Something/Anything?* (a record whose fourth side runs almost twenty-six minutes, thus comfortably accommodating the average orgy) came to grief when he rolled off the single bed directly on to the record player. Small wonder so many people were attracted by the idea of records that promised to do the job for you.

Barry White prospered mightily in 1975 on the basis that the ownership of any of his LPs promised to turn even the least beguiling suburban front room into some kind of boudoir. A former gangster from South Central, White had kicked around the music business for years as a producer and writer until he stumbled on a new career as a narrator/singer/preacher figure whose every text involved love, which was pronounced 'lurve'. White made the discovery that the primary erogenous zone for the woman is the ear. Women bought his records to listen to and men bought them in the hope of getting women round to listen to them. His success during this period, on his own, with his female trio Love Unlimited and with his Love Unlimited Orchestra, was immense. He was so successful that simply referring to 'putting on a Barry White album' came to stand for an entire repertoire of foreplay. It was the male equivalent of slipping into something more comfortable. Barry White was supposed to put her 'in the mood', as if this could be simply achieved by locating the right switch. It was taken for granted that while women needed a reason to have sex, men simply needed a place (and a record player). If you put on a Barry White album and didn't get your way then it seemed reasonable to conclude that you might as well shoot yourself. Part of the appeal of

White's records was they set a mood and then maintained it. The band got in the pocket and remained there while Barry made encouraging noises over the top. White was so dedicated to ensuring his listeners were getting as much lurve as he was, you were surprised when he didn't make himself available to turn the record over at the end of side one.

Disco was the tide that raised all boats. Even David Bowie's first real hit in the United States turned out to be 'Fame', a disco number from his breakthrough album *Young Americans*. Disco gave a new lease of life to acts from the fifties and sixties like the Isley Brothers and the Staples Singers. Patti LaBelle and the Bluebells came back as Labelle, issuing direct sexual invitations while arrayed as Bacofoil Amazons. Old songs like the Jackson Five's 'Never Can Say Goodbye' were given disco paint jobs and did great business for singers such as Gloria Gaynor. There was no idea too lame to be given a disco twist. Carl Douglas had enjoyed a huge hit in 1974 with 'Kung Fu Fighting', which proposed that even a martial art could develop its own dance.

Anyone who wanted to sell a record had to have a tune on it that people could allegedly dance to. Elton John had them dancing to 'Philadelphia Freedom', ELO did the same with 'Evil Woman' and, most unlikely of all, disco proved to be the way back for the Bee Gees with 'Jive Talkin''. Nobody suspected they might be on the verge of their big moment. In 1976, while making their new single 'Stayin' Alive', they solved the problem Giorgio Moroder had faced with his Donna Summer record. Rather than over-taxing the drummer they took one bar of Dennis Bryon's drum track, the one that they felt was the most infectious, and then jerry-rigged a tape player so that it played that bar again and again and the rest of the band could just play along to it. According to Albhy Galuten, the man who was at the desk that day, 'That first loop was a watershed event in our life and times.'

Disco was not just music. It was also, of course, an activity. The word itself summoned up for people not just the driving, insistent sound of music that was made for dancing and not just the lyrics which were predominantly exhortations to start dancing or keep on dancing; it also evoked a world of achievable make-believe, of peacock men wearing white suits with wide lapels, of vampish women in sheer fabrics over ballet tights, of heterosexual men behaving in a way that had previously only been permissible among gay men, and of attractive spaces in the dark that could only be accessed if you knew the doorman. This move upmarket was preferable to the rough manoeuvres in the dancing barns of the past. It was also a competitive sport. It seemed to extend permission to every cost accountant or shop assistant to transform themselves into a disco vamp, magnetizing the men of their dreams with their mastery of the Spanish Hustle. Disco was not about stars. It was about the audience. It was about the opportunities it provided for them to be the star in their own movie, walking down the road with a pot of paint like John Travolta at the beginning of *Saturday Night Fever*, supposedly doing a job of work but in fact living for the weekend.

By the time that film came out two years later the word about disco had spread to every suburban living room in the country, where it was widely believed that the right record could transform that room in Penge into a scene from a Jackie Collins novel. One of the themes of Mike Leigh's play *Abigail's Party*, first produced in 1977, is that just the same friskiness was lurking beneath the skin of every suburban home. The play starts with the terrifying hostess Beverly coming on to the stage and putting on a record. It is, of course, 'Love To Love You Baby' by Donna Summer.

In 1975, Donna Summer, Barry White, Millie Jackson – whose *Caught Up* had successfully introduced the concept album to soul music – Roy C, Labelle and a few others did well out of the fact that they were prepared to be more sexually overt than the competition.

The people who bought their albums weren't teenagers. When they talked about love they meant sex, and the sex was far from teen-aged. The Grammy for best sleeve design that year was won by *Honey* by the Ohio Players for a cover which featured Ester Cordet, a *Playboy* playmate, spooning honey from a jar on to her naked body. There was speculation that the screams that could be heard on one track on the record came from the model's reaction to the pain of the honey, which had been heated to make it run, contacting her naked skin. There was no truth whatsoever in this story but it managed to reach the UK without any help from the press or radio. It was the video craze of the next decade that properly cemented the connection between music and sex. For the moment it was all in the ear of the listener.

At the same time a new puritanism was abroad. By 1975 even a wave as powerful and all-enveloping as disco couldn't monopolize the music market. The album's market was maturing. The big names of the sixties and early seventies were being joined by new contenders who were in their mid to late twenties and had yet to break through. As well as *Blood On The Tracks* and *Physical Graffiti*, 1975 was the year of Bruce Springsteen's *Born To Run* and Bob Marley's breakthrough to popular acclaim with his live album. There was also *The Myths And Legends Of King Arthur And The Knights Of The Round Table* by Rick Wakeman, if that was to your taste. But if there was one dominant strain of music, it was disco.

There was also the first sign that the widening age range of the people listening might be making it untenable to sustain a consensus over what was good. People no longer felt they were on the same side. In some quarters there was a yearning for a new poison. Generational fissures were beginning to open up. At the end of 1975 art student Viv Albertine saw the picture of a new album sleeve in the reviews pages of the *NME* and immediately determined that she had to have it. 'I saw this picture and I almost had a little jump in my throat,' she wrote many years later in her autobiography. 'I thought: "My God, I think I might have seen, for the first time, a female whose music is going to resonate with me." I was scared.' This record was only available on import and so she went into the West End to find a shop that stocked it. Outside the shop she bumped into Mick Jones, another art student who was there on the same mission. Neither had yet heard a note of the music of Patti Smith's *Horses*. However, they felt they knew all they needed to know just by looking at the cover.

1976

'What's the worst job you ever had?'

The weekend of 11 September 1976 was wet. The heatwave which had set records for the United Kingdom that summer had broken at the end of August to be replaced abruptly by thunderstorms. James Callaghan's Labour government had spent most of the year attempting to stave off the prospect of going cap in hand to the International Monetary Fund to be bailed out by the countries who had been on the losing side in the Second World War. Those seeking further signs and portents of the decline and fall of Great Britain since Churchill's Finest Hour needed to look no further than Big Ben, the clock atop the Houses of Parliament, which had recently broken down for the first time in 117 years. It remained stuck at a quarter to four for the next nine months.

The newspapers that week were dominated by obituaries of Chairman Mao Tse-tung, who had died in Peking at the age of eighty-two. A TWA flight from New York to Chicago had been hijacked by Croatian separatists, eventually ending up in France. At Wembley, an England team captained by Kevin Keegan had drawn with an Ireland team led by Johnny Giles. The Sex Pistols, as yet unsigned and unrecorded, were on their way to Whitby in Yorkshire to play the Royal Ballroom. Among the new releases being played that week by John Peel, the edgiest DJ on the BBC, were 'More Than A Feeling' by Boston, 'Rose Of Cimarron' by Poco and *Modern Music* by Be-Bop Deluxe.

In the United States ABC Television was getting a lot of advance publicity for its new show *Charlie's Angels*. This would break all records on its debut, ushering in an age of what came to be called 'jiggle TV', because each episode built to a climax in which the three beautiful young operatives working for the private detective agency would give chase to some villain in a manner that would encourage the audience to speculate about their underwear. In this, TV was belatedly following the example of the big screen. Among the big movies of 1976 was *King Kong*, which set a lot of store on tethering the delectable Jessica Lange between two trees and offering her up to the appetites of a giant gorilla. There was also the film adaptation of Stephen King's *Carrie*, which memorably began with a changing room full of high-school girls undressing and showering in steamy slow motion.

British TV was a good deal primmer. On the BBC the suburban comedy *The Good Life* and American cop show *Kojak* had both returned with popular new series. In the same week Leonard Rossiter debuted in *The Fall and Rise of Reginald Perrin*. This was a comedy about an executive in the confectionery business who went to work in a morning coat and bowler hat but was beginning to feel that everything in his life was hopeless. Each day when he left for work his wife would say, 'Have a nice day, darling' and every day he would answer, 'I won't.' Each day when he arrived at the office he would apologize for being eleven minutes late and offer the rail company's explanation. 'Somebody stole the line at Surbiton.' These were just the first of many of the show's catchphrases which would be taken up by the public. They seemed to chime with a mood of exhaustion and resignation that was gathering around the country.

There was a feeling that nothing worked. This feeling was not without foundation. If you undertook a car journey in an English-made vehicle that was anything less than brand new there was a reasonable chance that you would end up by the side of the road waiting some hours for a recovery truck. If you wanted a drink in a hotel after the bar closed you would have to wait for the night porter to bring you a bottle of warm light ale. The Chancellor of the Exchequer, Denis Healey, who had spent much of the year trying to fend off the economic crisis that seemed imminent, had decided to escape the heatwave by spending much of August in the Highlands of Scotland. His holiday did not run smoothly. While out on a walk he strayed into a bog and had to be rescued by a local teenager. He tried to buy a bottle of whisky from a local shop without his wallet and was refused credit. And finally, one night he was woken up in his hotel in Ullapool by frantic calls from the Treasury in London to tell him that the pound was collapsing on the New York exchanges and he had to intervene. The reason for including this anecdote in a book about entertainment is to highlight the fact that in the year 1976 the second most senior member of Her Majesty's Government had to step in to rescue the country from the prospect of waking up to ruin while standing in a corridor in his pyjamas because the hotel in question had only one phone. The widespread feeling was not simply that the country was going to the dogs. There was widespread agreement that it had already got there.

Where some nations might have responded to this crisis with an urgent call for national regeneration, Britain clearly felt it was time to call upon its long tradition of calculated disrespect and reflexive bawdiness and act as if all its problems could be solved by sticking two fingers up to all that was decent. The time was ripe for a piece of entertainment that celebrated the spirit of can't-do in which the British prefer to wallow at times of crisis. This was the perfect moment for a piece of entertainment that TV would not have dared broadcast, print could not properly deliver, and not even the cinemas showing *Emmanuelle 2* at the time would have dared exhibit. Of course nobody saw it coming.

On the weekend of 11 September 1976, fourteen-year-old Nick Moore was doing his usual Saturday job, working in a record shop in a small town in suburban Essex. One of his tasks was to log all the new releases when they came into the shop. In this particular week, alongside the Electric Light Orchestra's *A New World Record*, the soundtrack from *Car Wash* and the live album *Hard Rain* from Bob Dylan, he booked in the store's single copy of a mysterious-looking record called *Derek And Clive (Live)*. He knew nothing about it and took little notice of the fact that the cover, which had been designed to look like a bootleg, announced it as the work of Peter Cook and Dudley Moore.

Later that same day Nick sold this one copy to a teenage girl who had come into the shop and asked for it. Two hours later the girl returned. This time she was accompanied by her mother, who was not amused. The mother had somehow heard enough of the record to ascertain that it involved a great deal of obscenity, notably multiple uses of the word 'cunt' (thirty-one in the space of a minute to be precise), and she wished to know why the shop had sold it to her daughter, particularly since a stamp in the corner of the cover clearly said 'Warning! This record contains language of an explicit nature that may be offensive and should not be played in the presence of minors.' The record shop manager was called for and the aggrieved mother was given a refund and sent home with her daughter. The daughter was presumably mischievous enough to have thought the record worth buying but not quick-thinking enough to keep her mother from finding out about it.

Variations on this scene were played out in record shops up and down the country. In the next couple of weeks an amazing 100,000 copies of the album would be sold in the UK. *Derek And Clive (Live)* eventually went as high as number twelve in the album charts where it nestled between the Eagles' *Greatest Hits* and *The Roaring Silence* by Manfred Mann's Earth Band.

In later years Peter Cook would boast that it was the biggest-selling comedy album of all time. This is the kind of claim artists can usually get away with making because newspapers don't wish to spoil a headline by checking to find out whether such a claim is true. It was by no means the biggest-selling comedy album of all time. It wasn't even the most outrageous comedy album of all time. But it was the first time a really outrageous long-player had become a mainstream best-seller, and the fact that it was allowed to happen at the moment it did indicated that something was shifting in the world of entertainment.

Of all the many varieties of long-player, the one that seems most moribund these days is the comedy album. Humour is now so inescapable, via the tiny fragments of internet memes or the intimidating abundance of Netflix, there seems small reason why anyone would pay to own an actual record of something funny. There was once a time when comedy seemed to be one of the forms of entertainment the long-playing record might have been designed for.

Record companies rarely went round looking for funny people and giving them the opportunity to make funny records. Hence the long-playing comedy record was a product which had grown by trial and error. In 1960 the record label attached to the Warner Brothers film studio in the USA was looking for a way to justify its continued existence. Having begun ingloriously with contract player Tab Hunter, who it was said 'couldn't carry a tune in an armoured car' and having later commissioned their own military band in the hope that the market might go for *Sousa In Stereo*, by the end of the fifties Warner Brothers Records were so desperate they were prepared to try anything. The anything came in the shape of Robert Newhart. Newhart was an accountant by profession but fancied himself as a humorist. His speciality was to record himself supplying just one side of a telephone conversation, allowing the listening audience to assume the unconscious hilarity of the other.

Jim Conkling, the head of the label, heard Newhart's tapes, liked what he heard and was prepared to underwrite the cost of recording him in front of an audience. The problem was, Newhart didn't perform live and had no dates lined up. Warner Brothers arranged a fortnight of support slots for him at a club in Houston called the Tidelands. By the time they were ready to record, Bob Newhart had developed half a dozen routines. Two of them – the 'Cruise Of The U.S.S. Codfish', which took the form of an address from a submarine commander to the sub's company at the end of a disastrous tour of duty, and 'Driving Instructor', a nervous instructor's attempt to teach an even more nervous pupil to drive – became, thanks to radio play, particularly on request programmes, absolute smash hits. There is no other word for it.

The LP, *The Button-Down Mind Of Bob Newhart*, was released in the spring of 1960. It eventually went to number one on the pop LP chart and stayed there for fourteen weeks, holding off Frank Sinatra, Elvis Presley and the Kingston Trio. When Newhart was eventually introduced to Jack Warner, the mogul hailed him as the man who had saved Warner Brothers Records. He wasn't joking.

Following Newhart's success there was no arguing with the idea that comedy and the LP were made for each other. After the Kennedys moved into the White House in January 1961 Cadence Records prepared an album called *The First Family* which gently spoofed the Kennedys' star quality and Bostonian mode of speech. It sold a million copies a week on its release in 1962 and won the Grammy for Album of the Year in 1963. When Kennedy was assassinated in November of the same year the company promptly withdrew the album and its follow-up from sale. It would not see the light of day again until the end of the century.

This vogue for comedy albums wasn't just happening in the United States. In London the young George Martin had been put in charge of the Parlophone label in 1955. Parlophone was the least successful and least prestigious of EMI's labels. It seemed only a matter of time before the parent company would close it. In 1957, Martin went to see a show called *At the Drop of a Hat* at a small theatre in Notting Hill Gate. The stars of this revue were Michael Flanders and Donald Swann, two evidently well-brought-up men down from the varsity. Swann sat down because he played the piano. Flanders sat down because polio had confined him to a wheelchair.

Their stock-in-trade was the comic song. Their compositions took aim at standard features of English life such as the bus conductor, the social-climbing neighbour and the proper pronunciation of the names of less celebrated animals. In their 'Song Of Reproduction' they even had a swing at the absurdity of the new high-fidelity set-ups which promised to make it sound as if there was a symphony orchestra in your living room. Flanders and Swann said they couldn't think of anything worse than having a symphony orchestra in your living room. Martin was not just impressed with the show, he also believed it would be possible to record it for an LP without sacrificing any of its charm. The resulting album came out in 1957 and was a great success. Excerpts were regularly requested on the radio and played so often that most Britons over the age of fifteen could recite the lyrics of such favourites as 'The Gas Man Cometh' and 'I'm A Gnu'.

Martin didn't stop there. He believed there could also be a

market for extended programmes of humour, programmes devised specifically for the long-playing record. He was a fan of Peter Sellers and recognized that the actor was capable of a daydreaming form of humour which could be amusing and seductive without requiring the trigger of a live audience. He faced opposition from colleagues at EMI who couldn't believe that anyone would want to listen to one person's comic musings and insisted he restrict himself to a ten-inch record. The record was such a success, going to number three on the British LP chart in 1959, that its tongue-in-cheek title *The Best Of Sellers* was no longer a joke and he immediately set about making a twelve-inch version. Then, in emulation of Sinatra's recently released *Songs For Swingin' Lovers!*, he produced the album *Songs For Swingin' Sellers*. This wasn't merely an LP full of jokes. It was also a joke about an LP. The cover showed the booted and spurred feet of a man, presumably the artist, hanging from a tree above one of those record players that the adventurous might take on a picnic. On the back cover there was a tongue-in-cheek injunction to play the record using only needles of Burmese plywood.

Sellers and his fellow actors populated the record with memorable characters. There was the grass widow flirting with her French admirer in the park and the rapacious major who kept a stable of would-be rock and roll stars sequestered in his Mayfair house. They were all characters who were not quite obvious enough to be snapped up by the people who did radio comedy. Between them George Martin and arranger Ron Goodwin placed Sellers' inventions in a soundscape which meant that you kept playing the record long after any belly laughs had exhausted themselves. There's a strong argument for saying that one of the artistic forerunners of Martin's later production *Sgt Pepper's Lonely Hearts Club Band* was *Songs For Swingin' Sellers*.

Throughout the sixties and seventies all shops would have a rack of comedy records. Some people were more inclined to collect comedy records than musical records. With a comedy LP you could do something that you couldn't do with the TV or the radio. By providing fans of particular humorists or performers with a unique opportunity to bask in the work of their favourite and, crucially, by carefully lifting the stylus and moving it back to the beginning of a particular track, actually to repeat a favourite joke on demand, comedy seemed a more sensible way to use up the forty minutes of playing time than, for instance, pop music. It was the first form of home entertainment that could be replayed on demand.

For an increasing number of people, comedy LPs justified having a record player. Most collections of LPs in most homes contained a treasured sub-set of much-loved and oft-loaned comedy records: these might range from souvenirs of favourite radio programmes such as Tony Hancock's *The Radio Ham* to material which could never have got on the radio such as Lenny Bruce's *The Berkeley Concert* and, when the counter culture eventually decided it needed to invent its own form of humour, as far as National Lampoon's tribute to the Woodstock generation, *Lemmings*, and the stoner humour of Cheech and Chong.

Comedy records were often at the centre of new social rites among the kind of sophisticated young marrieds who regarded the record player as the key piece of equipment in their home. As Bob Newhart pointed out, 'Nightclubs had kind of priced themselves out as far as a young family was concerned; they became quite expensive. So my understanding was that a lot of the college kids and the young marrieds would get together at somebody's house and they'd have pizza and beer and they'd play a comedy album.'

Certainly there seemed something almost perverse about listening to a comedy album alone. Bob Merlis, who did PR for Warner Brothers Records at the time, observed, 'There is a natural tendency to proselytize about a comedy album.' When you bought a comedy album it was rarely just for yourself. There was an implicit under-standing that you would share it with others. You would play it for a friend – or even somebody you wished to be a friend. It would not be enough to loan it to them. The key pay-off of owning a comedy album came when you played it to somebody else and they evidently liked it as much as you did. The more you played it the more you internalized every phrase, every accent, every nuance of the record and the more deeply embedded it became within your social group.

Some people found a deep relationship with comedy LPs that other people only found with music. Comedy albums were among their most precious possessions, and since they sold slowly they were apt to disappear from the catalogue. The American writer and comedian Stephen Colbert was ten when he suffered a family loss. Following that, every single night he would listen to Bill Cosby albums like *Wonderfulness* and *Why Is There Air?* with the speakers underneath his pillows so his mother wouldn't hear. 'You could drop a needle anywhere on those albums and I would know what came next. I think Bill Cosby's albums saved my life,' he recalled.

There had always been dirty records just as there had been dirty films and dirty books. The trail-blazing female comic Rusty Moore sold large quantities of such albums as *Knockers Up* and *Sin-Sational* after her gigs in the sixties without ever once using a word that would have been unacceptable to the moral guardians of prime-time TV. What placed her beyond the pale was the combination of her chosen subject, sex and her gender. The idea of a woman comedian talking about sex seemed a prima facie threat to the established order. Nobody predicted at the time that at some point in the future all the comedians talking about sex would be female and that men would no longer dare go near the subject. In 1963, *Time* magazine sent a reporter to find out how Rusty had sold three million albums without the help of radio or TV and came back sniffing, 'She is just another dirty comedian who deprives sex of all its grace and sophistication.'

Things changed in the late seventies, and as usual it was technology that was in the forefront of the change. In 1976 the cable TV company Home Box Office, which was owned by Time Warner, identified dirty comedy as a way to drive subscriptions to its service, reasoning it was one of the few obvious advantages they enjoyed over network TV. The following year they hired George Carlin to perform his act on one of their shows, thereby ensuring that you would no longer have to buy his album *Class Clown* in order to find out what were the words you couldn't use on network television. Then they gave their subscribers the opportunity to see Redd Foxx doing the same adults-only act that he had been doing on the Chitlin Circuit for thirty years. 'People say I'm a dirty old man,' he began. 'Well, let me tell you, that's a load of shit.' The laugh that arose in response to this suggests the audience had never heard that word in an entertainment context before. On the same weekend that *Derek And Clive (Live)* came out in the UK, Warner Brothers released *Bicentennial Nigger* by Richard Pryor, the comic who as a young man had paid Bob Newhart the compliment of entering a record store in Peoria and walking out with *The Button-Down Mind Of Bob Newhart* under his jacket. Suddenly many comics were concluding there was a future in the material they had previously had to hold back for their friends.

Although Peter Cook and Dudley Moore had made their names through the stage show *Beyond the Fringe* and then on BBC television in shows like *Not Only . . . But Also*, both of which were broadly suitable for family audiences, they were known within the business for their sideline in after-hours routines which didn't so much skirt the border of acceptability as burst right through it. This particularly applied to Cook, who was tall, upper class and never met a line he didn't want to cross. As early as 1962 he was entertaining the other public schoolboys in the office of the satirical magazine *Private Eye* with his portrayal of a gormless mechanical who blankly related how the worst job he had ever had was removing lobsters from the sphincter of the fifties starlet Jayne Mansfield.

In the autumn of 1973, when Cook first suggested to Moore that they should go into a New York recording studio and just see what happened, both of their careers were at a low point. Cook was bored and drinking too much. Moore had not yet found his niche in Hollywood. Cook was always the instigator of whatever mischief was about to start. As soon as the tape was rolling in the studio at that first session, Cook took the lead.

Cook: I'll tell you the worst job I ever had.

Moore: What was that?

Cook: The worst job I ever had was with Jayne Mansfield. She's a fantastic bird – big tits, huge bum, and everything like that – but I had the terrible job of retrieving lobsters from her bum.

And thus it continued, with Moore doing his best to keep up with Cook's remorseless flow. The joke went nowhere, which was the point. The adjectives used were the kind no radio station at the time would have broadcast, no newspaper would have printed and no record shop would have sold to the public. Simply committing such words to tape seemed danger enough. There seemed no question of it going any further. Cook and Moore called these characters Derek and Clive but had no idea what to do next.

One group with an insatiable appetite for anything considered too strong for the general public was rock musicians. It was rock bands who entertained themselves on their tour buses and planes with pornographic films and anything that was not and seemingly never would be available to their fans. That was the excitement. Copies of the Derek and Clive tapes were soon circulating among people who worked in recording studios. These people enjoyed access to a store of unpublished material which others could only dream of. Hence the Derek and Clive tapes eventually became popular with bands like the Rolling Stones and Led Zeppelin. In 1976, Cook gave the tapes to Chris Blackwell, the owner of Island Records. Blackwell, having nobody else to answer to but himself, decided he would put the tapes on a long-playing record and release them.

At the time there were only a handful of independent record labels. It would have been out of the question for any of the majors, all of which were public companies with people on their boards with thoughts of knighthoods and similar, to have released it. Blackwell could get away with doing things that others couldn't. He knew that EMI, who manufactured Island's records, wouldn't touch it. This was not least because their Hayes factory was heavily unionized and the shop stewards would have the factory out on strike if the middle-aged women in the quality control department were compelled to listen to this filth in the course of their work.

Therefore he contracted out the manufacture and distribution of the record and relied on the fact that no radio station would play it and none of the major retail chains would stock it to create interest and drive sales. It came out on 10 September 1976 and was an immediate success on notoriety alone. In the absence of HMV, WHSmith and Boots, the small independent record dealers made hay. Island were more than happy to be stoking the controversy. The company's sales manager was arrested for spraying 'What's the worst job you ever had?' on a wall in London. Some people seemingly couldn't wait to be offended by it. One Dennis Jude of Kegworth was alerted to it by reading about it in the *NME* and complained to his MP, who passed the details to the Home Secretary. Meanwhile, in Wolverhampton Sgt David Wilson went to Sundown Records accompanied by WPC Veronica Reynolds, bought the record and took it back to the station where they dutifully listened to both sides to see if they could justify a prosecution under the Obscene Publications Act. The DPP listened to it and the case officer said it was 'fourth form lavatory humour'.

It was such a success that it restarted the careers of Cook and Moore and led to three follow-ups, each with less impact than the one before. Even the first could never follow up on the promise of track one side one. For Cook and Moore, the whole point of the Derek and Clive project was simply to put the album out and to have it on display in the average high street. In November 1976 the pair did a signing at Virgin's shop at Marble Arch. While fans queued for autographs the record echoed around the shop and out into the street. Although pleased with its success they were worried about it being heard closer to home. Neither of them wanted their parents to hear it and Cook's wife was embarrassed about having to answer questions about it from other parents at their daughter's school. Most people didn't mind that they only played it a couple of times. For the people who bought it and took it home the process of lowering a stylus on to a £2.99 record, listening to the pregnant rumble of the run-in groove and then hearing unrestrained obscenity ring round their own living room seemed justification enough.

Alan Fisher, who bought *Derek And Clive (Live)* in a shop called the Long Player in Canterbury, remembers its arrival: 'Our group of mates played it to death, endlessly quoted lines from it – and no doubt appeared utterly tedious to everyone else. The copy passed furtively between us. Sometimes one of us would take care of it over the university holidays. Even now at the age of sixty-two I still use phrases from it.'

It proved to be the thin end of a very significant wedge. *Derek And Clive (Live)* was still in the top forty albums on 1 December 1976. On that day Queen were booked to appear on a regional TV magazine show in London. They cried off because of illness and the record company offered a substitute, their brand-new signing the Sex Pistols. Johnny Rotten and co's live exchange with host Bill

Grundy, in which they swore in order to live up to what they saw as his expectations of them and he goaded them into swearing even more in order to prove that he didn't find it shocking, was a watershed moment in British pop culture. It began their career, finished Grundy's, and remains their most noteworthy achievement. Once they had sworn on live TV there was nowhere else to go. Even the records seemed beside the point after that.

In an article about the record's release in the *Guardian*, Robin Denselow began, 'It's been such a long time since a record actually shocked anyone, or caused even the slightest ripple of controversy, that I suspect many people won't know how to react to a new comedy album with the innocuous title Derek and Clive Live.' It wouldn't be long before there would be a small industry devoted to making records whose highest aspiration was to find someone to shock, and also newspapers rising to the challenge of making sure that anything even slightly shocking came to the attention of the people who were only too happy to cooperate by pretending to be shocked. It would only be a matter of months before the greatest compliment you could pay a record would be to call it provocative, subversive, iconoclastic, abrasive or shocking, and record companies would find themselves wishing to publish material that might even land them in court. In years to come, Peter Cook would ruefully claim that Johnny Rotten had pinched his act. He wasn't entirely wrong.

1977

'With their fretboards pointed directly at the music of the spheres'

I n February 1977 the *NME*, originally known as the *New Musical Express*, which was at the time the leading music paper in what was already the most competitive market for music publications in the world, could afford to flex its muscles. At the time it was selling over 200,000 copies every week. Under the stewardship of the shrewd Nick Logan it had manoeuvred itself into a position where it was by far the most influential voice in all matters pertaining to music and, every bit as importantly, the poses with which that music was associated. With the latter in mind it felt entitled not simply to reflect where music actually went but also to publish increasingly weighty 'directional' think pieces about where the music ought to go. This was the kind of thing more commonly found in literary magazines or scientific journals.

Only the previous year Mick Farren, one of the *NME* writers who had cut his teeth on the underground press of the late sixties, had all but written a prescription for punk rock in an editorial for the paper which had called for rock to be taken 'back to street level and start all over again'. The *NME* had an obsession with the street, possibly not unconnected with the fact that it seemed so far away from the paper's office high up in King's Reach Tower, the head-quarters of their owner, the International Publishing Corporation, which was also home to titles as varied as *Woman's Weekly* and *Horse & Hound*. In the months following that piece each of its star writers, from the established ones like Charles Shaar Murray and Max Bell to the new ones like Tony Parsons and Julie Burchill, appeared to be vying with each other to be the ones to identify who might be best placed to lead this seemingly inevitable revolution.

Being the first one to identify, celebrate in print and form a personal relationship with the next emerging talent was a game that rock journalists liked to play. If you were right it could lead to all-expenses-paid trips to the United States and Japan, lucrative freelance work writing official biographies, a rise in one's status within the paper and, for a few, jobs as A&R men, a role which they soon discovered wasn't anything like as congenial as sitting at a typewriter. If you were wrong and your pick to click didn't happen, then you weren't the only one who had made that mistake and readers were likely to quickly forget. Dozens of bands who came out of the London pub-rock movement of a couple of years earlier had been tipped for success but only Dr Feelgood had achieved it.

Dr Feelgood were right up the alley of the people at the music papers in that they seemed to be getting back to something valuable that had been lost. At the time it seemed that all the squares on rock's rich tapestry had been marked out. Similarly, all the *NME* writers seemed to take it for granted that the new new thing would look and behave enough like the old thing for them to be able to employ the same terms of reference to write about it. The new new thing would probably be a group, it would probably be a group of young white men, and they would probably play guitars. *NME* were more comfortable with guitars than anything else. A couple of weeks earlier they had divided the appraisal of David Bowie's new album *Low*, a record which embodied the sound of the future if anything did, between two reviewers as if no mere individual could be expected to decide what to make of it.

On 5 February 1977 they published a piece which the people who were readers of the *NME* at the time still remember over forty years later. It came from Nick Kent, the writer who had probably the greatest authority of anyone on the paper. This owed something to the fact that he looked like a version of Keith Richards who had been put to the rack. It didn't hurt that he also squirrelled away hipster jargon which he then slung together in sentences so serpentine they seemed to be every bit as liable to topple over as their languid author, who would then miraculously rescue them via some unsuspected flourish near the end, a flourish which was the pen-and-ink equivalent (Kent never mastered typing) of the chord at the end of one of Pete Townshend's windmilling arms. He would follow the long sentence with something pithy and colloquial. Kent wrote the kind of reviews that people would read two or three times. This was not merely to work out what he had said but also for the sheer joy of the way he said things.

The *NME* didn't sell over 200,000 copies every week because it was simply one of the few places you would find out that a band was going to go on tour and where exactly you should send your stamped addressed envelope and postal order for tickets. It didn't galvanize large numbers of readers purely because you were unlikely to read a review of the new albums by Gregg Allman, Abba or the Amazing Rhythm Aces anywhere else. It didn't do such good business because in those days a Niagara of information about the wider world of popular music would have to travel down its frail filaments or not travel anywhere at all. It did all those things and more because, like all the truly successful music magazines of the pre-digital era, it was an entertainment in itself. If hardcore readers could have had a choice between being able to access the *NME* or being able to access the music it wrote about they would have had difficulty deciding which they got the most value from. For people up and down the country, but particularly the people in those faraway towns where the main form of interaction with youth culture came from sitting around the base of the war memorial and watching the traffic go past in the direction of somewhere more exciting, the *NME* was a lifeline. It benefited greatly from the fact that if it hadn't been there an entire internet's worth of information, amusement, provocation, pseudery and accidental education would never have found a mark on which to land. In those days it had the greatest blessing any publication can ever have: it had readers who read the very print off it every week. On those many occasions during the mid-seventies when industrial action of one kind or another stopped it from being printed and distributed it left at least a hundred thousand people feeling bereft of entertainment, lost for guidance and suffering from a mild form of depression.

At the same time the *NME* as well as the other papers, *Melody Maker*, *Sounds* and *Record Mirror*, performed an absolutely invaluable function on behalf of the record business. They made its products seem more important than they were. *NME* might have been the first to dismiss records that it felt were not up to its lofty standards. The record business may have tutted over its cynicism. On the other hand, anything that it took a liking to it would tend to elevate to the status of an unarguable classic. It made the bad albums seem not to be worth anything at all but it made the good albums seem as though they had been handed down from heaven. It established, celebrated and sustained the culture of the long-playing record. It may have savaged individual examples of the form but it never once argued that the form itself wasn't a good idea and that the readers weren't perfectly justified in expecting new masterpieces to turn up on a regular basis.

And when Nick Kent spoke, as he spoke in that issue in February 1977, those readers took notice. It helped in this case that the editor took the step, no doubt in the absence of a more bankable alternative, of putting Kent's review on the cover of the paper. (The last few issues of the *NME* leading up to it had featured Ry Cooder, the Rolling Stones and Joan Armatrading.) Hence the cover of the 5 February issue announced 'Patti Smith trips and busts her neck, Peter Green flips and gets put away, Stranglers in obscene tee shirt row', and then, beneath a picture of four undernourished New Yorkers posed against a cellar wall, 'Nick Kent finds genius on page 29'.

Occupying the whole of page twenty-nine and half of the following page was Nick Kent's review of *Marquee Moon*, the first album by the New York group Television. In those days it was difficult enough to get to hear an emerging group from Stockton-on-Tees. There was no chance of hearing somebody who was playing the clubs in New York. Consequently people grew used to reading about music for months or even years before they actually got to hear it. This meant their perception of the music was coloured by criticism, and their relationship with the people who played it deepened by the enchantment inevitably lent by distance. All the bands that emerged in the late seventies, just before the expansion of TV made everything visible before it was audible, were beneficiaries of the mystique that comes from spending hours reading about someone before spending mere minutes actually listening to them.

The Kent review of Television, whose mystique had been building steadily in the music paper hothouse, was less a review than a testimonial. Here he hailed a group which for him had clearly been long overdue, that is a group who seemed to possess the musical ability to match their ambitions. This was during punk's phoney war. We were already getting intimations that the claims being made for new acts had more to do with whether they were seen as being pure in heart than whether they sounded any good. Charles Shaar Murray's embracing of Patti Smith's *Horses* two years earlier had established the ground rules of this reformation. Anyone who was not convinced of the message of the cover of *Horses*, as Viv Albertine and Mick Jones had been, was unlikely to be persuaded by anything in its grooves. Punk was about style or it was about nothing at all.

Nick Kent's personal idea of a glorious future seemed to contain something of his idea of a glorious past. He likened Television not to the Velvet Underground or the Stooges, the standard canonical bands to which every other release was compared in 1977, but instead to the likes of Country Joe & the Fish, Fairport Convention and the Doors. Profoundly aware of the noises-off coming from the *NME*'s so-called Kinder Bunker wherein Julie Burchill was promoting the view that only the young would be able to truly appreciate the next big thing when it arrived, Kent was saying that here was a group all sorts of people could appreciate because – and here he didn't use this expression, but if this review had a sub-text it might well have been a headline – Television could play.

He finished his review by saying that if Charlie Murray hadn't already spent the line about fine first albums like this being hard to come across on Patti Smith's *Horses* two whole years earlier he would be using it himself. Some of us took this to mean, if you were one of the suckers who took Charlie's advice back then and were bitterly disappointed, don't worry because this record is worth every bit of praise I've lavished on it.

At the time this review was published the record still hadn't come out in the UK and was only available on import at certain shops. However, as soon as Kent's review appeared all those copies vanished from the racks. Instantly. Good reviews sold albums in

1977, but I don't recall any record enjoying such instant acclaim purely on the basis of a review. In terms of the claims he made for Television, who were a group with a certain kind of sound but an altogether different kind of haircut, Kent was pushing against an open door. People poured into the shops and bought it without needing to hear it first. Art-rock snobs bought it, jam band enthusiasts bought it; it was loved by everyone from those who had been missing Quicksilver Messenger Service to those who couldn't wait for the first album by the Clash. And miraculously, unlike in the case of Patti Smith's spindly *Horses*, Bruce Springsteen's muddy *Born To Run* and all the other albums which were proclaimed as marking rock and roll's long-sought moment of reset, Television's *Marquee Moon* was that rare thing, a record which sounded as good as the review had promised it would.

All forms of criticism obey the rules of their particular sector. Record reviewing has its own. There are so few new plays that they're all reviewed by the same handful of theatre critics who have little trouble keeping their enthusiasm in check. All novels are reviewed by other novelists who are acutely aware that what goes around comes around and will therefore lay off in case they cop a packet when it's their turn. Film reviewers spend all their time in the company of other film reviewers and therefore tend to arrive at a consensus without much need to talk about it.

With records it's different. Record companies apply very little science to what they release and what they don't. Experience has taught them that experience is no guide to what will capture the public's imagination and what won't. Consequently they put out an awful lot of records that are literally only of interest to the people who made them plus a few people who hate them and wish to see them fail. (Morrissey once wrote a song called 'We Hate It When Our Friends Become Successful', a sentiment which in the music business is so familiar most people couldn't believe he had bothered.)

Only three people can quote a bad review verbatim: the artist it was written about, the person who wrote it and the artist's deadliest enemy.

Those who have been the victim of an unfavourable review tend to think they have been the victim of a great conspiracy. This is not the case. Because there are so many records to review the editor charged with doling them out has to rely on a small army of free-lance contributors. All these supplicants at the reviews cupboard, which was the holy of holies of all music magazines, would like to be entrusted with reviewing one of the more anticipated new records but most often are sent off to do their worst on some record which the editor has promised some PR he would make sure was reviewed. The freelancers, in order to shore up their self-esteem and get noticed within the publication's near-medieval pecking order, will tend to big up or do down the qualities of the record. That is why most records are either underrated or overrated. Once you have reviewed, say, a dozen of the records that make up the bulk of most of the companies' release schedules you start to glimpse the inescapable truth about rock albums. Most of them are not terrible and they're not brilliant either. They are OK if you like that kind of thing. Sadly, 'OK if you like that kind of thing' does not make for hot copy and therefore there is a tendency to pretend this OK record is brilliant and that OK record is such an abomination that it should be placed in a lead-lined box at the bottom of the deepest ocean and its precise whereabouts excised from all charts. Too many acts carry the scars of their early reviews. They pretend to forget but they never do.

Performers are convinced that everyone is ganging up on them. They don't understand that records are like life in that you wouldn't worry so much about what people think about you if you knew how little they did. Bands can't accept this. They have lived with the record for so long, have taught themselves to love its every last wrinkle, know how much of a struggle it was to get this effect on that track, remember how much time and argument went into the running order and the cover. Given all this they find it impossible to believe that anyone who is less than impressed by it has actually listened to it at all. What they fail to give sufficient weight to is that what most reviewers want most of all is a record that is easy to write about. This favours a record with a story, a record with incidents within it worth relating, a record worth devoting a few hundred words to. This is why the likes of Patti Smith got so many column inches. She dealt in words. Writers also deal in words therefore it's not a stretch for them. Music, on the other hand, is very difficult to write about and therefore critics get round the problem by writing about everything in the artist's world apart from the music.

What artists can't bring themselves to believe is that in most cases bad reviews are just collateral damage in a battle being waged each week to fill the magazine with readable copy. The reviewer didn't think you were that good and they didn't think you were that bad either. They were just trying to keep the bright red ball of human interest in the air. And most rock writers of this time were very good at it. While many of them could be – whisper it – quite surprisingly boring in company, most made up for it by appearing incapable of being boring once they were behind a typewriter. Entertainment was their higher calling. That and, in some cases, the fact that they felt they ought to be acting as talent spotters for the music business. It was this that led to their eventual obsession with finding the next big thing. Following Mick Farren's call for a new breed, the British music papers became seized with the need to convince themselves that the new thing was always just around the corner – a need which grotesquely resulted, ten years after Nick Kent's review, in Sigue Sigue Sputnik.

Nick Kent wound up his review of Television with one of those predictions which are irresistible bear-traps for rock reviewers. As so often is the case with the rock press it began with a sideswipe against what he saw as the prevailing orthodoxy. 'In a year's time, when all the current three-chord golden boys have fallen from grace Tom Verlaine and Television will be out there hanging fire, cruising meteor-like with their fretboards pointed directly at the music of the spheres.'

This was a good line, but Kent was mistaken in believing this would just be the beginning. Television never managed to either match or outshine their opening offer. Their first album was the most famous thing about them. In that sense *Marquee Moon* was like *Catcher in the Rye* or *To Kill a Mockingbird*: the promising start which also proved to be the end. On the other hand many of the three-chord golden boys – 1977 also saw the first albums of the Damned, the Jam, the Clash and the Sex Pistols – did far better than anyone would have predicted. They did better because they offered something Television didn't – the promise of a gang you could join. They had lots of things besides music. Television just had the music. When they first appeared in London in May 1977 their thunder was stolen by the support group, Blondie. They were never special again.

But why should they be? The Ronettes never improved on 'Be My Baby'. A great LP like *Marquee Moon* is a perfect snapshot. By the time it's in the shops the band who made it have changed, grown up, moved on, maybe even lost interest. The air in which they made the music is no longer quite there in the same way. Television instantly became a cult that stood for something, in their case a blinding incandescent moment of inspiration and realization never to be repeated.

Danny Kelly was a student in north London when *Marquee Moon* came out. Like many others he responded to the siren call of Nick Kent's review, bought the record and placed it at the top of any list of greatest albums he was called upon to make. Years later he became the editor of the *NME*, in which capacity he got the opportunity to compile many such lists. This, he would assure his colleagues, is the greatest guitar record ever made. In time CD came along and vinyl copies of *Marquee Moon* began appearing in bargain bins like so many unloved children. Danny was so moved by their plight he started picking them up whenever he saw them. 'I would buy them and give them a home next to all the other copies of *Marquee Moon*. I eventually had about thirty of them.' He took to giving these copies away to people. 'Finally one drunken night me and a friend listened to it and decided it was a little bit cold in places. Next day we announced to an astonished *NME* office that the greatest guitar LP was the even less fashionable *Layla*. I'm very happy with that – except when I'm listening to *Electric Ladyland*.'

Once albums begin to be regarded as 'classics' people can stop actually listening to them. They can carry on putting them on lists but they don't play them. This can particularly apply to those which have a reputation for being austere or difficult. If you listen to *Marquee Moon* now it sounds impressive in places and uncomfortably shrill in others. If you listen to it now you realize that it's very difficult to write eight songs. If you listen to it now you realize that the world is divided into people who took it as their *Revolver* – who regard *Marquee Moon* as the starting point of the whole wonderful world of indie, the inspiration for generations of pallid young white men playing spidery guitar lines and singing songs the wider audience found it difficult to connect with – and the rest of us.

The people who were there at the time of punk have a far less reverent attitude to it than the people who came afterwards, to whom it was handed down as some kind of Year Zero. The people who were there at the time tend to remember things taking place at 45 rpm. Punk was about capturing moments rather than starting careers. Many of the most celebrated punk acts made one half-decent album. Hardly any of them made more than one. This didn't stop them continuing to make albums. Sham 69 released more albums than the Beatles. The punk bands have wound up sticking around every bit as long as the old hippies they once scorned.

Just as Television were playing Hammersmith, the Clash's first album was greeted in certain quarters as though it was a masterpiece, largely by people who were so busy enjoying liking it that they weren't actually listening to it. A year later the band took the disastrous step of making an album of the kind the American record company wanted them to make with an American producer. Literally nobody has listened to that album since the day it came out. Then, a year after that, they produced *London Calling*, a record whose coherence and swagger everybody attributes to producer Guy Stevens. Who knows? On every record they made they sound like a completely different band.

Punk rock undoubtedly changed the tastes of those who were the right age when it came along, but all the English punk bands foundered as soon as they got to the United States. They were accustomed to audiences you accumulated on the basis of what people had read about you in the music papers, not audiences such as the ones in Moose Droppings, Ohio, who couldn't read your social and cultural references, didn't read the *NME* and just expected to be won over. Many of these bands came home from American tours, retired to their tents and sulked. Some of them, such as the Jam, made very good careers by staying at home.

In the USA, 698,000,000 units of recorded music were shipped in the year 1977. This was an increase of more than a hundred million units over the previous year. It was the largest percentage increase in the history of the music business. This was the highwater mark of the record industry. The biggest global albums of 1977 had nothing to do with punk rock. An appreciable number of those many millions sold had to have been copies of one of three major albums, all of which were released in 1977, each of which in their own way reached far beyond the tight circles of those who read the *NME*, and each of which sold to people far beyond the traditional heartland of record buyers.

There was *Rumours* by Fleetwood Mac, which came out in February and eventually sold forty million copies. It's a record that people still, over forty years later, regularly reach for and play for their own pleasure rather than their moral improvement. It's also a record whose critical standing is a great deal higher now than it ever was in its pomp. There's *Bat Out Of Hell*, a sub-operatic pastiche of Bruce Springsteen by the previously unknown Meat Loaf, which had been shopped around all the record companies in the world before a division of Columbia wearily agreed to give it a go. This too eventually sold forty million copies. Four decades later musicals based on *Bat Out Of Hell* are playing around the world. The third was the soundtrack to a low-budget feature film which was loosely based on a story about night life in Brooklyn written by the Irish writer Nik Cohn. *Saturday Night Fever* went on to sell over forty million copies, making it the biggest-selling soundtrack album of all time. If you put on the soundtrack from *Saturday Night Fever* today it would sound as fresh and as contemporary now as it did then. While so many of the cool customers of 1977 have been forgotten the world is still catching up with the Bee Gees and Fleetwood Mac.

Of additional significance is the fact that an increasing number of the copies of those three albums weren't sold on vinyl. They were sold on a format whose popularity was beginning to climb dramatically just as sales of LPs were beginning to flatten. In some people's eyes it was making vinyl LPs look dated. That format was the compact cassette. For the immediate future this was where the growth would be. The LP wouldn't be the only game in town for much longer.

1978

'The kids need new shoes'

t was usually near the door, where the customers would see it first on entering the shop, or near the counter, where the people working there could easily reach it. Wherever it was, the 'Just Released' rack was the most exciting place in any record shop. It was like the changing front page of a magazine that in most other respects would remain the same. It was the first place you would look. You would be searching first of all for the records you were expecting but also, more excitingly, it was the place you would look to be surprised or delighted.

In the early days of the albums market, even as late as 1972, we were still intrigued by novelty. Thus new albums were innocent until proven guilty. I hadn't yet arrived at a point where I was familiar with my own prejudices. In September of that year I bought not just the ultra-progressive *Close To The Edge* by Yes but also *Full House*, the ultra-regressive live album by the J. Geils Band. I ended up with *Bandstand* by Family and also *My Time* by Boz Scaggs. Furthermore, if somebody had offered me the chance to hear Steeleye Span's *Below The Salt* and even *Phoenix* by Grand Funk Railroad I would have leapt at the chance. All these records were in the same 'Just Released' rack. It was either there or 'Groups A-Z' and 'Solo Artists A-Z'. Music wasn't yet being hived off into taste ghettos. This openness to different musical styles was not a unique virtue of my generation. It was more a reflection of the fact that most of what was going on in the albums market was happening for the first time.

Six years later, in 1978, many of the same acts were doing many of the same things but with inevitably diminishing returns. Often the album was heralded by a claim that something was fresh and exciting this time. *Street Hassle*, Lou Reed's eighth solo record, was the first rock album recorded using the binaural method. *Here, My Dear*, Marvin Gaye's eighteenth, was so-called because he agreed to give half its earnings to his ex-wife. In both cases the market remained unmoved. Big acts were still making a living because the market was bigger and was beginning to splinter into tribes, but the spirit of adventure had gone. By 1978 it seemed unlikely that any of the same people would be buying both Yes's *Tormato* and the J. Geils Band's *Sanctuary*. Most listeners had decided who they were and what they were interested in. They were no longer so apt to be dared into trying something lying outside their comfort zone.

Therefore a good half of the records in the 'Just Released' category would be things you weren't interested in. You recognized there was a market for them but you recognized that market didn't include you. By 1978 there was no room for doubt that what was once the music business was now the music industry. As with other industries, the product does not wait upon the arrival of magic. The product must be there no matter how uninspired its producers might happen to be. Industries do not wait for inspiration. The mills of any industry must grind regardless of how uninspired the elves on the shop floor may be feeling. Release schedules must be compiled, sales forces sent forth with their message of eternal hope and record-breaking returns tomorrow, raw material has to be ordered, covers must be designed, and promotion men have to continue to take radio programmers to lunch and let slip that they've heard a couple of tracks from the big act's new one and they were blown away but meanwhile they would really like your view on this new act who are a bit of a priority for us this year. That is what an industry does. It creates the impression of doing something important even when there is nothing important to do.

By 1978 the LP industry was settling down to a new reality built on the management of reduced expectations. None of the acts thrown up by the recent punk rock/new wave convulsion had gone major league, as the publicity might have led them to expect. Most of them had found their level and it wasn't approaching the level of the Eagles or the Bee Gees. They might never rise to those giddy heights but it was still possible to make money out of them if you could keep the product flow going. At the same time there was an echelon of older acts, the kind who in time would come to be known as 'classic', whose golden years may already have been behind them but who still had fan bases prepared to buy pretty much anything they put out, often regardless of quality. These were the catalogue sellers, the names that would keep on turning over in unspectacular fashion.

The most popular tool to manage all this surplus was a crude form of ageism, although this, like most other isms, was in its infancy at the time. For many people the world was divided into those who were new to the public and those who had made the mistake of being around prior to 1977. At the age of thirty-three in 1978 Debbie Harry was only a year younger than Ray Davies of the

Kinks but there was never any question which side of the acceptability divide she was on. At the age of thirty-seven in 1978 Bob Dylan was only eight years older than Hugh Cornwell of the Stranglers but the former was an old fart whereas the latter was permitted to be a young Turk.

The age profile of the people buying pop records was also changing. Whereas at the end of the previous decade the overwhelming majority of people buying LP records were between the ages of twelve and thirty, by the end of the seventies they were between the ages of ten and forty. A new template began to emerge. Just as bands no longer gave up and took a more respectable line of work once the first flush of fame was over, fans similarly retained their youthful enthusiasms into middle age. Indeed some of them kept on buying records by their favourites even when those records weren't as good as the records that had made them their favourites in the first place.

This was always more than the dispassionate exercise of a consumer choice. There were already a certain number of people for whom not buying the new album by Wishbone Ash or Jethro Tull felt like reneging on vows of fidelity, vows that they had made when they were young. There are an appreciable number of people who remain more faithful to the pop group that excited them when they were fifteen than to the person with whom they exchanged the considerably more solemn vows of marriage. Pop music fans are a byword for fickleness and music is seen as more ephemeral than the rest of the arts. This reputation is completely undeserved. In fact people keep buying second-rate albums by their favourite musicians long after they've ceased going to see the movies of people who were once their favourite actors or reading the books of people whose works they once found hard to put down. There is a sort of dogged faithfulness underpinning people's relationship with popular music and the people who make it. Often they find it hard to let go of their old favourites because letting go would mean having to admit to themselves that the relationship was rather foolishly entered into in the first place.

Rock stars are brands. The key feature of a brand is you think it's valuable, in many cases more valuable than it actually is. Another key feature is that a brand engenders loyalty and keeps you coming back for the same thing, even when there might be other, more attractive options vying for your attention. Most brands are not stars. Most brands are not market leaders. Most brands never quite dominate their category. Most soft drinks are not Coca-Cola. This doesn't mean that they have no reason to exist. A key characteristic of an industry is that a few stars make most of the noise and the bulk of the profit. However, those few stars sit on top of a seething factory full of honest toilers. That's what happens with an industry. In 1978 the 'Just Released' section was similarly full of honest toil.

People form bands because they seek fame and glory. They remain in those bands because they grow accustomed to the life and after a time they simply don't know what else they could do. What they do every day is not work as most of us would recognize it. They have no employer. They have no routine. Their routine is measured out in recording contracts and tour plans. By 1978, particularly for those bands that had made their names in the sixties, begun making albums in the seventies and had recently suffered the unfamiliar indignity of being cheeked in the public square by a new generation of chippy upstarts, it started to feel like work.

The albums revolution of the late sixties had been an immensely exciting idea at the time. You could be paid for doing what appeared to be fresh creative work. The record company advanced you a certain amount of money and promised to make a fuss about you on those occasions when a new album came out. By the time they had been doing this for five years or more the bands began to realize the truth of their situation, which was that their LPs had not been successful enough to propel them into the super league, where you could make up your own rules, and the only option that remained at the end of their contract was to sign on again at slightly less advantageous terms and just do the same things everybody else was doing to feed the market.

The number one albums of 1978 may have been Fleetwood Mac's *Rumours*, Gerry Rafferty's *City To City*, Billy Joel's *52nd Street* and above all the soundtracks of *Saturday Night Fever* and *Grease*; the most celebrated albums of the year were clearly *This Year's Model* by Elvis Costello, *Darkness On The Edge Of Town* by Bruce Springsteen and *More Songs About Buildings And Food* by Talking Heads; but the majority of the albums released that year were made by well-known names who were clearly no longer going to be contenders but were equally clearly not planning to go away either. This is the one respect in which the work of rock stars is different from the world the rest of us inhabit. In the world of rock nobody ever gives up. Here retirement is not an option.

Around this time I happened to interview members of the original Merseybeat band the Searchers, whose hit-making days had ended in 1965. But now the advent of punk and then power pop seemed to be providing them with another spin of the wheel. After years without a record deal they were suddenly picked up by Sire, the label behind the Ramones and Talking Heads. Suddenly they were no longer old hat. Suddenly they were classic. Suddenly they were being asked to record songs which were in their idiom but which had been written by performers from a later generation. They were quite happy to do this but were equally at pains to make it clear that in the years since 'Needles And Pins' and Beatlemania they had never stopped. The Searchers had carried on playing even when nobody had apparently been thinking about them. I asked them the same question everybody asked of a band that had been around more than two years. Why did they still do it? They gave me the same answer they gave everyone else who asked the question. The kids need new shoes.

What I couldn't have known at the time was that in the future the majority of bands would be like the Searchers, making a modest living from eking out a brief moment in the spotlight, playing when they were paid, recording when somebody asked them, no longer dreaming that they would ever be toppermost of the poppermost, simply going out to work like window cleaners or van drivers, because the kids needed new shoes. The immediate consequence of this for anyone entering a record shop in 1978 was an oversupply of new product from people who were names but were not stars.

For example, all the New Dylans were still around. Regularly through the seventies some new folkie would come along who wrote stream-of-consciousness songs and played the guitar, often with a harmonica in a holder slung round his neck. Some even wore Levi jackets. Inevitably they would be hailed somewhere as 'the New Dylan'. There were some quite well-known New Dylans, such as Bruce Springsteen, John Prine and Loudon Wainwright III. 1972 was a big year for New Dylans. Then there were others who were less well known, people like Elliott Murphy and Willie Nile. None of the New Dylans broke through to mass acceptance in the seventies. Most of them never broke through to mass acceptance at all. But whereas in the fifties and sixties that would have meant that most of them would have dropped out of contention, by 1978 all the New Dylans were still going. In 1978 they were all still there, putting out albums. Indeed in that same year, as if to prove that in the record business hope springs eternal, they were joined by Steve Forbert, a New Dylan from a new generation. There was clearly a living to be made in the niches.

The big acts kept trundling along although they didn't know quite how to respond to the heckling they had recently got from punk rock. The Rolling Stones' *Some Girls*, their fourteenth album but only the first of scores which were to be hailed as 'their best since *Exile*', didn't seem to worry overmuch about the challenge, though the last track 'Shattered' contains Jagger's last autobiographical line, 'Love and hope and sex and dreams are still surviving on the street and look at me, I'm shattered'. He was thirty-five. Inevitably Pete Townshend, who was all of thirty-three, agonized a good deal more about his age. The Who's eighth album *Who Are You?* was a veritable midlife crisis set to music. Its recording was a catalogue of disasters, most of them instigated by the increasingly chaotic personal lives of the members of the band, Keith Moon in particular. They changed studios twice, losing backing tracks in the process, and when they finally lined up to have their pictures taken for the cover by Terry O'Neill, the photographer suggested Moon should hide behind a chair to conceal his alcohol-related paunch. Moon died three weeks after the record came out. He was thirty-two.

Bob Dylan's eighteenth album *Street Legal* was recorded in just four days in 1978 during a brief pause from a world tour that lasted almost a year and anticipated the 'never ending tour' he has been on ever since. Dylan's record company needed a new album in order to justify helping him out with the expenses of touring with a ten-piece band. He had to keep touring because he had spent two years trying to put together the film *Renaldo and Clara* and needed the money. Even the man who wrote 'Mr Tambourine Man' has to buy the kids new shoes. His need was even more pressing because he was facing the cost of getting divorced in California, his marriage to Sara Lownds having finally come to an end in 1977 when she came down to breakfast to find herself sitting opposite his latest girlfriend.

There were many big-name records that really shouldn't have come out at all. Some, like the Beach Boys' *M.I.U.*, were desperate attempts to distract attention from the fact that the band had to all intents and purposes fallen apart but still had its side of a record contract to fulfil. Their twenty-second studio album, this was chaotic even by the standards of the Wilson family. Most of the Beach Boys weren't even there when it was recorded. Because the record company had rejected their attempt at making a Christmas album they hastily excised all the original festive songs and put new ones over the same backing tracks. Via this process a song called 'Bells Of Christmas' was transformed into 'Belles Of Paris'. This process of piecing together a new album from fragments that had not been considered good enough to be on a previous album was to become increasingly common as bands tried to avoid recognizing the dirty secret of the music business, which is that most groups have only got enough good ideas for two or three albums but enter into financial arrangements obliging them to provide many more.

Once you have an industry you have a variety of product lines. One of these is the solo project. 'Project' implies something in the nature of a short-term experiment, which is rarely how its author sees it. Solo projects exist because every member of every band feels he has an idea, a song, an arrangement, a title, even the flimsiest nano-wisp of an idea; furthermore he feels that idea is his and his alone. This is either something his fellow band members do not properly appreciate or, more likely, something he simply doesn't wish to hear their views on. Consequently he will do it himself. And since putting the idea out on a single would seem insufficiently grand, he must have his own attendant marketing campaign, his own fuss, his own opportunity to go off on his own and do his own interviews and set the world to rights in his own particular way. That means he must have an album.

In the year 1975, for instance, all five members of Yes 'took some time off' to do their own solo albums. Once that kind of hiatus is in a band's diary even the members of the band who aren't particularly fussed about solo records – and here we're thinking primarily of drummers – feel they may as well do their own. Since these solo efforts are sometimes written into the contract between the band and the record company they worry they would be missing out on a payday if they didn't.

The reductio ad absurdum of this approach came on 18 September 1978 when Casablanca Records released four solo albums from each of the four members of Kiss in the same livery on the same day. This would have been foolish had the four individual members been known for their contrasting musical styles and their ability to come up with arresting original material. Since Paul Stanley, Gene Simmons, Ace Frehley and Peter Criss were largely notable for having approximately the same rugged individuality as the occupants of a pantomime horse this seemed to verge on the insane.

Like the overwhelming majority of solo albums these records only came into existence thanks to the surprising cynicism of the individual members, who were perfectly ready to short-change their young fans if they thought there was something in it for them, and the unsurprising cynicism of the record company, which dreamed it might be possible to sell four times as many units by putting out four albums on the same day. They were wrong. While all four records went into the *Billboard* chart, all four swiftly dropped out again. Casablanca had shipped a million copies of each, enabling them to briefly claim platinum status. It seemed that even more unsolds came hurtling back than had gone out and the band, who had only the year before been voted the most popular in the USA, would never be the same again.

Another product line is the live album. These provide the record companies with new product for each new season without anyone having to come up with any original songs. The first time an act does a live album there's genuine anticipation among the fan base. They can take it home, draw their curtains, turn up the volume and luxuriate in the fantasy which underpins all rock stardom and accounts for nine out of ten sales of live albums, to wit the dream of glorious transfiguration in which they become the star and all the people they know in the world and most wish to impress are just voices out there in the dark expressing their full-throated approbation and their willingness to provide sexual favours. In most cases live albums are more sex aid than musical experience.

Very few acts should ever do a live album more than once. In 1978 Bob Dylan, David Bowie, Blue Oyster Cult, Todd Rundgren, the Band, Bob Marley and many others provided the market with something that nobody was particularly asking for – a second live album. All these records had significant post-production help to excise the gremlins that invariably attend live performance. Thin Lizzy's album *Live And Dangerous*, which came out in the middle of 1978, was particularly notable in this respect. The original plan had been that to save them the trouble of doing a new album they would quickly mix some live recordings that had been done over the previous two years. In the event it took five weeks with Phil Lynott going into the studio every day to do a great deal more than tidy up the odd bum note. Producer Tony Visconti has since said that the only parts that survive from the original recordings done at the venue are the drums and bass. It's impossible to put a figure on how much of a live album is actually how it originally went down on the night. Bands never speak the truth about this. It is only human nature to want to give the best possible impression of oneself and the fact remains that anything that can be changed in post-production will be changed until you get the album as the artist likes to think it sounded, rather than the way it did sound. The most successful live album of 1978, which actually went to number one in the USA, Donna Summer's *Live And More*, doesn't sound remotely live. The audience noise seems as though it's been flown in from another dimension altogether.

Then there are the records that have absolutely no artistic impetus behind them. These come into being the same way most films come into being: because somebody powerful has got hold of the rights to some valuable property and thinks if he can package that up with some bankable names a multiplier effect will come into play and fortunes will be made. As if to drive home the point that no matter how much insurance you take out there are no sure things in the music industry, the emblematic stinker of 1978 hinged on bringing together the most gold-plated name of the past, the Beatles, with what were supposed to be the most bankable names of the mid-seventies, Peter Frampton and the Bee Gees, in a wholly uncalled-for soundtrack for the film version of *Sgt Pepper's Lonely Hearts Club Band*. This farrago somehow got into the American Top Five for three weeks in July 1978 until America shook itself awake, threw cold water over its face and vowed it would never speak of the matter again. Peter Frampton's career never recovered.

The vast majority of records from name acts came out and simply disappeared. Even from the vantage point of today, when it sometimes seems that we have rediscovered and reassessed more unsuccessful albums of the past than could ever have actually existed in the first place, the fact that 1978 saw the release of Leon Russell's *Americana*, something called *Hobo With A Grin* by Steve Harley, a fourth album from Brass Construction and a long-playing record from the Three Degrees – named, with enough wistfulness to break your heart, *New Dimensions* – still somehow boggles the mind.

Even punk rock succumbed to the dictates of industry in the year 1978. Blondie, one of the many bands that had come out of New York's arty downtown scene on the same wave that had lifted Television and the Ramones, had made their first two albums with minimal interference from the industry. By the time of the third one their contract had been bought out by Chris Wright and Terry

Ellis of Chrysalis Records, who were determined that they should follow a more obvious commercial path. It was they who insisted on Mike Chapman as producer for the third album.

Chapman came from the school of pop hits. He and his partner Nicky Chinn had been behind scores of corny but catchy chartbusters in the glam rock era. Blondie were the kind of group that talked a good pop record but could be erratic when it came to making one. Chapman, on the other hand, had the know-how to get from a sliver of an idea to the kind of fully-fledged hit that the radio simply can't resist. (I spent some time as a radio promotion man around this time and saw with my own eyes how radio producers decided whether there was anything on an album they wanted to programme. They put the stylus down on track one, listened for forty-five seconds, then skipped to track two, did the same thing, then gave track three the benefit of thirty seconds of their attention and then took it off, leaving you with the strong impression that they would never return. I don't blame them. Hits leap out at you. The rest don't.)

Chapman described his role as producer with Blondie as 'song manipulator and song construction consultant/technician'. He found the band far more difficult to work with than the people he was used to. 'People like Suzi Quatro were easy because they were nice people to work with. Blondie, on the other hand, was all about suffering. None of them liked each other, except Chris and Debbie, and there was so much animosity. They were musically the worst band I ever worked with. I basically went in there like Hitler and said, "You are going to make a great record, and that means you're going to start playing better."'

Chapman was performing the most valuable service any producer can provide, which is setting the bar and doing everything in his power to make sure the record comes up to it. If anybody has any doubts about what a producer does they should go and listen to a recording of a song called 'Once I Had A Love' that Blondie did in 1975. The song is familiar. The performance, one of those halting, everybody's-looking-at-their-fingers stumble-throughs which you can get away with on a radio live session but which sound laughable on a record player, is not. Listening to it now you can't believe that anyone ever spotted the potential of the song in question.

Chapman asked them to stop doing it the way they were doing it. He asked Debbie Harry what sort of music she was listening to at the time. 'Donna Summer,' she replied. Chapman said, well let's try it in that style. Some members of the band objected to doing something in a style – disco – which they had thought they were there to banish from the earth. They eventually went along with it. Then Chapman suggested that they should call it not 'Once I Had A Love' but 'Heart Of Glass'. He also suggested they should use a Roland drum machine, and then when they had set up the track they should record live drums over the top of it. Eventually they pieced it together, agonizingly, until it sounded not like Blondie but like Debbie Harry singing a disco song.

It also sounded like a hit. It was surprising that they put it in the middle of side two where radio programmers wouldn't hear it first time through. It could have been a victim of the traditional syndrome whereby the band hear it as one thing and the world hears it as another. As far as the band were concerned this was their avant-garde Kraftwerk tribute. As far as Chapman was concerned it was a hit. At every stage in the life of *Parallel Lines* the obvious course had to contend with the snobberies of some members of the band. They even refused to smile on the cover of the album until their manager suggested that Debbie should scowl and they should smile, thereby presumably in their minds subverting the entire music business. 'Heart Of Glass' was the third single from the album. It went to number one. The album sold a million copies. For about a year they were the biggest thing in the world.

Once you are the biggest thing in the world, even for quite a brief time, there will always be a living to be made, either reminding your original fans of the time when they were young and full of hope or, more likely, representing a vanished era for the benefit of the children and grandchildren of your original fans. Interest in any new music you are thinking of recording may be limited, but thanks to the steady generation-by-generation growth of the market for pop your old music will be familiar to far more people now than it ever was back then. I'm finishing this chapter exactly forty years after the release of *Parallel Lines*. Last night Blondie, who still feature three members of the band who recorded it, played the Hard Rock Hotel at Catoosa, Oklahoma. There they played three songs from *Parallel Lines*. They finished with 'Heart Of Glass'. Clearly somewhere out there somebody's kids still need new shoes.

1979

'Oh I just don't know where to begin'

The first album of 1979, Elvis Costello's *Armed Forces*, which was released in the first week of the New Year, had one of the best opening lines any album can have. 'Oh I just don't know where to begin,' Elvis sang at the beginning of the first song, 'Accidents Will Happen'. This is an opening salvo fit to stand alongside Mick Jagger's 'What a drag it is getting old' at the beginning of *Aftermath*, or the line that begins Roxy Music's 'Do The Strand' and gives this book its name. That line notwithstanding, it sounded as though *Armed Forces* knew its business. Costello's album came front-loaded with possible hit singles, as was increasingly the custom with new albums in 1979. Such decisions were still made by the artist and the producer rather than the record company, which sometimes resulted in notable songs being lost. The Derek and the Dominos album *Layla* might have done better if the title track hadn't been placed next to last on the fourth side of a double album.

In the previous decade priorities had been different. In most cases British LPs by the Beatles and Rolling Stones wouldn't have any singles on them. In fact potential buyers would be disappointed if they found that a single they already possessed was on an album. Why should they spend money on something they already owned? Consequently LPs were sequenced primarily for the impact they would have on the person listening at home rather than the shopper who was just browsing. George Martin's priorities when he sequenced Beatles albums in the early sixties was to make sure that each side started with something up-tempo, you closed the first side with something strong enough to make the listener want to turn the record over, and you kept the louder tracks away from the middle of the record where their dynamic range placed too much pressure on the narrower width of the last tracks. This began to change in the seventies as bands took more of a hand and preferred to treat the end of a side like the ending of Act One of a play, placing something ballad-like or seemingly thought-provoking there. Christine McVie's 'Songbird', which closes the first side of Fleetwood Mac's *Rumours*, 'Wasted Time' in the same position on the Eagles' *Hotel California* and 'You're Gonna Make Me Lonesome When You Go' on Bob Dylan's *Blood On The Tracks* all play the same trick.

In the case of *Armed Forces* the first single, 'Oliver's Army', was the third track. Elvis later told me that he actually considered track four the key to an album because it lay just outside the hit single zone. He reasoned that this was where people try something unusual, something that will never be a single but nonetheless deserves to be heard. In some quarters it was believed that this was where you put the track that you hoped might intrigue the critics. 'Big Boys' was *Armed Forces'* track four.

From its running order to its absorbing packaging, which was designed by Barney Bubbles, *Armed Forces* exuded confidence.

Bubbles, the reclusive genius who provided the design signature of many of the most memorable LPs of the era, including Ian Dury's *Do It Yourself* and the first Damned album, was, like many of the prime movers in the independent record scene of the time, a graduate of the Notting Hill alternative scene of the late sixties. His *Armed Forces* cover, which involved complex fold-outs and postcards to be used for subversive purposes, was a direct descendant of the first cover he did, *In Blissful Company* by Quintessence, which had come out ten years earlier. Jake Riviera, one of the bosses of the Stiff label and Elvis's manager, also liked to have fun at the expense of the dignity of the LP format. On the run-out groove of the previous Elvis album, *This Year's Model*, had been a phone number of the company that distributed the album plus the name of somebody to ask for if you wished to claim a prize. A number of early copies of the first Damned album had a picture of Eddie and the Hot Rods on the back, supposedly printed in error.

Contrast the playfulness of Elvis and the people in his corner with the elephantine gestation of Fleetwood Mac's double album *Tusk*, which after more than a year in the studio finally came out in October of the same year. Whereas Elvis, who was in his twenty-fifth year at the time, was young enough to feel he still had everything to win and nothing to lose, Lindsey Buckingham, the musical leader within Fleetwood Mac, had approached the task of following the massively successful *Rumours* as if he believed it was bound to misfire and he was going to get the blame. Buckingham was only thirty when the record came out but at that time, when there was no battalion of forty-something elder statesmen of rock, that seemed to be on the wrong side of the generational divide that had opened up during punk. Even somebody like Declan Mac-Manus, who had taught himself to play all the songs from the second Band album and worshipped the Beatles, realized that in order to get himself on the right side of history he had to deny most of his previous allegiances, narrow his trousers, conduct himself like somebody who had a grudge against all convention, speed through his catalogue like a man pursued by a forest fire and change his name to Elvis Costello. Even the writers of *Rolling Stone*, which in the year 1977 was treating its readers to a succession of blow-dried cover stars from Peter Frampton through Rod Stewart to Boz Scaggs, had decided at the end of the year that the most important album of the year was the Sex Pistols' *Never Mind The Bollocks, Here's The Sex Pistols*, a record still more notable for its packaging than its content.

Any artists who had made the basic error of being around before this new wave – and they could usually be identified by the length of their hair and the nervous manner in which they rolled the sleeves of their jackets up – were expected to be able to account for themselves, like members of the bourgeoisie being quizzed on what they had done during the storming of the Winter Palace.

For people like Lindsey Buckingham, who five years earlier had been kept by his girlfriend's waitressing, who had had his nose pressed against the window of the music business for years and could reasonably claim to know more and care more about popular music than anyone, it was agony to be seemingly marooned on the wrong side of history. Pop music had always been about what you don't like as well as what you do like, but the era of punk rock was the first time that people self-identified on the basis of the music they were against. One of the first stories about the Sex Pistols that gained traction was the one about Johnny Rotten wearing an old Pink Floyd T-shirt on which he had scrawled 'I hate'. Anybody who was an established success was targeted on the basis that they were somehow scheming to keep the next generation from their place in the sun and their position in the charts. In 1979 the most conspicu-ously established success was *Rumours*, which was clearly the work of the devil. Trying to follow it was impossible.

On 8 August 1979, just as the follow-up was being mixed, the *New York Times* reported that the unthinkable appeared to be happening: the market for recorded pop music, which had been growing exponentially since the Beatles, was no longer expanding. Companies were merging, staff were getting laid off, people within these companies were beginning to question practices that had previously gone through without demur. The writer John Rockwell pointed out that whereas in the past the cost of making a record had been possible to contain, certainly compared to the spendthrift movie industry, it now seemed arguable that the companies' traditional habit of just letting artists work in their own way at their own pace might be resulting in 'neurotic self-indulgence, absurdly inflated recording studio costs and a loss of control by record companies over when they can release records by their key money makers'. He didn't mention *Tusk* by name but it would have been the perfect illustration. If any artist was made to feel that he had the fate of the record business on his shoulders it was Lindsey Buckingham in 1979.

Lindsey was the person who was charged with making it all happen. He was the lead songwriter and the producer. Mick Fleetwood was the leader of the band in management terms but Lindsey was the Brian Wilson of the group. The more the previous album sold the harder his task seemed. By the time the new album was ready, its predecessor *Rumours* had sold eight million copies in the United States alone. This was nothing compared to what it would go on to sell but it had already changed the narrative around Fleetwood Mac from the chaotic progress of a former blues band from England making a happy marriage with a pair of Hollywood go-getters and finding a new future as chart regulars to one that was primarily about revenue and wealth beyond the dreams of avarice. Buckingham's first defence against the inevitable pressure that success brought was to tell everyone who would listen that the next album would not be another *Rumours*. He kept the details of how it might be different to himself, possibly because he wasn't entirely sure. He was starting to record demos on his very basic set-up at home. This was the rock superstar's equivalent of shielding your paper behind your arm during an exam. He wanted to be able to work his songs up without having to listen to any of the comments of the rest of the band. Most of those songs were initially recorded in his basement at home. He recorded the vocals in his bathroom, getting down on his knees to sing to a microphone placed on the floor.

Knowing that this album would take even longer to make than its predecessors, Mick Fleetwood tried to persuade the rest of the band that they should defray the cost by coming in as co-owners of a recording studio. Only ten years earlier bands had been content to record on premises owned and managed by their record companies. Then they had moved to independent studios with freelance producers. From there it was but a small step to tailoring their own studio environment to cater to their unique requirements and better reflect their utter fabulousness. There was also the argument that owning your own studio made sound economic sense.

Fleetwood couldn't get the rest of the band to agree to owning the studio so they would just have to pay the bills like any standard client. By then, Geordie Hormel, the owner of the Village Recorder, had, with Fleetwood's encouragement, designed and built a new studio, Studio D, purely so that the group would have somewhere to record *Tusk*. He didn't merely bring in a few domestic touches to make the band feel more at home as they made music. He took studios that were already the most luxurious, best appointed and fully serviced in Hollywood and transformed them into an opulent atelier which might be worthy of this new record, whatever it should turn out to be. He gutted an existing studio and rebuilt it from scratch, even to the extent of refloating the studio floor so that not the slightest noise or vibration should penetrate from the outside world. It's characteristic of any freshly made millionaire not to wish to use the existing facilities, which is why millionaires always knock down houses and build them again. In Fleetwood Mac's case there were five millionaires and nobody wanted to be the one who could be accused of pinching pennies.

The fact that Fleetwood and Buckingham then had to search out a corner of this temple to high-end audio where they could record a rhythm track direct on to a cheap boom box is one of those characteristics of the recording business which beggars irony. Technological progress is rarely in a straight line. In fact it's rarely progress. It's simply a process of change where you exchange a little magic there for a lot of convenience over here. The tracks on *Tusk* were finally digitally mixed via Soundstream, a technology at the time so new that it could only be operated by the company's own engineer, and then had to be taken to the company's headquarters in Salt Lake City to be edited. All this painstaking effort was aimed at satisfying Buckingham's desire for a 'harder, rawer feeling'.

That authentic raw sound is not something that can be left to chance. Like everything else in the recording process it has to be faked. At the time the finishing touches were being put to *Tusk*, Neil Young released *Rust Never Sleeps*, a record that tried to summon up the magic quality of roughness by beginning with tracks that were recorded live and then overdubbed in the studio. In the summer of 1979 Ry Cooder released *Bop Till You Drop*, which claimed to be the first pop release from a major label to have been recorded and mixed digitally. A note on the cover claimed that this meant it wouldn't have the 'noise and harmonic distortion produced by analog recordings'. Although you couldn't argue with the music or the performances on the record, its lack of heft suggested that it might have been the noise and harmonic distortion that were the things we liked. Cooder's selection of songs might have set out to summon the rank odour of Hollywood Boulevard in the small hours of the morning and love on the wrong side of town, but *Bop Till You Drop* ending up sounding like the kind of record you borrowed from the library. Much of this alleged progress would later come to be seen as a dead end. In years to come Young would say that his fondest wish was to bring consumer-level listening to the point it last reached in 1979.

It wasn't digital sound that was about to change the music industry. That was actually the sound being created at the time in studios like New York's Power Station, where Nile Rodgers of Chic, a man who had 'don't bore us, get to the chorus' in his DNA, was masterminding their new album *Risqué* with the help of a young engineer called Bob Clearmountain. Clearmountain eschewed the dry style of recording that had been favoured in the waning decade, where instruments were captured by microphones placed at close quarters in order to be able to manage those sounds separately in the mix and to foster the apparent intimacy that made sense when played in your bedroom. What he created instead was a big splashy room sound that was the embodiment of the audio quality known as Presence. Within five years Clearmountain would be the most in-demand engineer/mixing specialist in the business, his fingerprint on Bruce Springsteen's *Born In The USA*, David Bowie's *Let's Dance* and hundreds of other records that seemed to have a sense of drama and self-importance baked in. Many of these records were made at the Power Station in New York. In his book *Perfecting Sound Forever*, Greg Milner explained what happened at the Power Station. 'They sacrificed the intimacy [of seventies records] for something more communal – both in terms of the sound of the records and the interactions that went into making them.' Clearmountain would provide the sound of the video age.

Even before Fleetwood Mac went into the studio Mick Fleetwood was telling people that the band's next album would be a double. This should have been a red flag. There can be good reasons for doing a double but more often it is what happens when bands would rather include everybody's songs than tell somebody their contributions aren't good enough. Stevie Nicks's 'Silver Springs' had been left off the previous album by this line-up of Fleetwood Mac and relegated to the indignity of the B-side of a single. Many millions of sales later that wasn't going to be allowed to happen again. Record companies didn't like doubles because they were harder to sell. With certain exceptions such as Stevie Wonder's 1976 release *Songs In The Key Of Life*, double albums were regarded as an indulgence. Hardcore fans liked them because they got more of what they knew they wanted but they rarely added to the fan base. Faced with a double album, which cost more money and took longer to get to know, the casual buyer tended to pass on to something else.

Nevertheless, 1979 seemed to be a good year for double albums. Donna Summer's double *Bad Girls* went to number one. Just three weeks after the release of *Tusk*, when it was already going down the *Billboard* chart, Pink Floyd released *The Wall*, a double that was to be their most successful album apart from *Dark Side Of The Moon*. The Clash's most popular album, *London Calling*, appeared in the UK at the end of the same year and the following year Bruce Springsteen broke through to mainstream acceptance with his first double, *The River*.

Warner Brothers might not have liked the idea of a double but there was little that they were able to do about it. They had no control over Fleetwood Mac. They didn't get to hear anything. Nobody from the company was allowed beyond the studio's outer rooms when the album was being recorded and they weren't played demos or given any idea what it was going to sound like. The previous two albums had been made without any reference to them and this wasn't going to be any different.

The project developed a life of its own. Buckingham was the senior creative officer, along with the two engineers who were his confederates, and therefore nothing could move unless he said so. There was still tension between him and erstwhile girlfriend Nicks. She would appear in the studio trailed by a posse of assistants and a poodle whose job it was to assist her in the all-consuming business of being Stevie Nicks. During this time Nicks had a brief affair with Don Henley of the Eagles, which must have preyed on Buckingham's mind. Christine McVie, meanwhile, was consoling herself with Dennis Wilson of the Beach Boys, a man who was beautiful but startlingly self-destructive even by rock star standards. John McVie couldn't wait to do his bass parts so that he could set sail on his yacht to Maui. Mick Fleetwood, whose marriage had broken up and who also had an affair with Nicks, was at a loose end and was in the studio as much as anyone. It was a mess everywhere you looked.

Fleetwood later recalled, 'By the time we got into the studio the whole thing was like a Fellini flick. Studio D was our place of worship. It was really a trip, everything we'd ever dreamed of, including a replica of Lindsey's bathroom at home, which had a particular ambience he cherished.' Stevie Nicks remembers it less fondly as an 'intense heavy' experience, 'locked up in Studio D for a year – with shrunken heads and leis and Polaroids and velvet pillows and saris and sitars and all kinds of wild and crazy instruments and the tusk on the console, like living in an African burial ground'. At one stage she wanted a vocal booth which had a mural of a sunset in Tahiti so that she could get into the right frame of mind when she recorded her contributions. Comfort and convenience were more important than productivity. Couches lined the room. The coffee tables were glass, ideal for the chopping of lines of cocaine. The ceiling of the outside listening room was a notional sky covered with tiny stars.

Fleetwood Mac had commenced recording on 26 June 1978.

They finished recording on 22 June 1979. On both days they were working on the same song, which was called 'I Know I'm Not Wrong'. The fact that they were working on the same song on the day they finished as on the day they'd begun suggests that recording, like rehearsal, is an activity that expands to fill the time available for it. For most of the fourteen months that they were recording and mixing the album they were not all present.

All through the time they were making *Tusk*, *Rumours* was still selling 200,000 copies a week in the United States alone. In a piece in *Rolling Stone* in January 1978 Dave Marsh noted that there was a new super class of hit album and that while gold status had once been something to celebrate, now real success was measured in how many times platinum you went. When you're selling 200,000 copies a week and you know that in an office somewhere somebody is preparing another cheque for your part of that success there's a tendency to behave as though it would be wrong to deny your body all the sensual pleasures that could be available.

During this period the members of Fleetwood Mac were rarely seen without a drink. Even when working they would sashay from room to room holding their drink of choice as though the real business of their lives was an expensively catered party. In this there was no real difference between the American members of the group and the original Brits, whose bloodstream was already 100 per cent proof. Everywhere they went they made sure there was a fully stocked bar – in the studio, at rehearsal, even on photo sessions. The studio redesign even called for a bar with English beer on tap in the outer room. During the open-air recording of the rhythm track for 'Tusk' Christine McVie wandered around with a glass of white wine in the middle of the day. When Daisann McLane dropped in on rehearsals for the *Tusk* tour she found people taking long hits from a bottle of Harvey's Bristol Cream. To counteract the depressive effects of the alcohol there was cocaine. This was maintained in the same steady supply that later bands would require of mineral water. Based on Mick Fleetwood's later calculation that he had snorted an eighth of an ounce of cocaine every day for twenty years and Stevie Nicks ending up with a hole in her nose through over-ingestion, it seems reasonable to assume that not one single day in the period when the album was being composed and written could be described as sober.

But even *Tusk* needed a single. Because they were more bothered about telling the faithful they had a new album out than converting the casual buyers with one of the album's many tuneful selections they chose to lead with a song that wasn't representative of the record but had the advantage of having the same name. 'Tusk' was a name they had eventually given to a rhythm part they used to play at sound checks. It satisfied Buckingham because it didn't sound like Fleetwood Mac and appealed to Fleetwood because he had wanted to make a percussion album in the first place. They began entertaining grandiose visions. They felt the riff would only sound right if it was accompanied by the horns of a hundred-strong marching band. They furthermore felt these marchers should be recorded in the open air. Thus the University of Southern California Trojan Marching Band was assembled in full uniform at Dodger Stadium in LA and recorded with Fleetwood attempting to conduct them. His plan was they would be able to replicate this sound by inviting the marching band to accompany them in every city they played on their next tour.

The record company didn't get to hear any of *Tusk* until it was finished. When they did, the word they used about it was 'challenging'. They didn't understand why it was called *Tusk*. In this they were joined by Stevie Nicks, who never liked the name. When she discovered, as she subsequently did, that it was a reference to the male member that went back to the days when Jeremy Spencer was the group's front man, she liked it even less. The cover execution was a combination of punk obduracy and superstar lavishness such as only the record business would allow. The only picture on the outside was a shot of engineer Ken Caillat's dog Scooter tugging at the leg of his jeans. The expensive visuals, the photographs taken by three different name photographers on different occasions, in different places – some involving rented houses, stylists and make-up artists, each one involving diplomacy, ego-fluffing and lip-biting on a scale that would have been familiar to a courtier at Versailles – were relegated to the inside of the packaging where each record was unaccountably housed in two separate art paper covers. No expense had been spared to ensure that those who bought the LP would feel satisfied by what they had bought. Hardly any thought was given to how you might interest other people in buying it in the first place.

Even before it had come out it was known in the press as 'the million dollar record'. Because they didn't own the studio they were presented with a bill for the best part of a million dollars in recording costs. That million dollars became part of the narrative of the record. And also its millstone. This meant that when *Tusk* came to market it had a list price of almost sixteen dollars, making it the first album to cost more than a ten-dollar bill. It came out on 12 October and it was soon plain that it had engaged their hardcore fans but hadn't penetrated much further. Michael Jackson was at number one in the US singles chart that week with 'Don't Stop 'Til You Get Enough'. At the top of the album chart was Led Zeppelin's *In Through The Out Door.* Also released in the USA that week was *Reggatta De Blanc* by the Police, hailed by *Rolling Stone* as their 'band of the year' in the same issue that *Tusk* was reviewed. *Apocalypse Now* had just opened and Bo Derek was starring in *10*. The big TV shows were *The Rockford Files* with guest star Lauren Bacall and *M*A*S*H*. *Tusk* confused the market. In the end it sold four million copies. This would have been more than respectable for most acts but Fleetwood Mac had set their own standards and had to live with them.

'Tusk' the single stalled at number eight in the USA. The album got no higher than number four. Its reviews weren't bad but nor were they laudatory, which is standard for a double album. Doubles take a long time to get to know, which doesn't help with reviews. The songs were sequenced in a way that did them no favours. The record begins with 'Over And Over', a stately Christine McVie tune which in the normal run of things would have turned up halfway through side four. This is followed by 'The Ledge', which sounds as though it should be thrown away on a B-side. Here Buckingham has left in his mistakes and fluffed takes as though in an early display of his determination that there was no way this was going to be seen as *Rumours* part two. The first stand-out and the record's biggest hit song, Stevie Nicks's 'Sara', is the final track on the first side.

Every decision about *Tusk* seemed to have been taken to please the artists who made it and the devotees who were certain to buy it and nothing had been done to reach out any further. It may well have been the last major label record you could say that about. In the seventies, records were made exclusively by the people in the studio. Beginning with the next decade they would increasingly be influenced and shaped by the people outside who were paying the bills. Records were beginning to be made, like many other consumer goods, from the outside in.

1980

'Suddenly we were floating'

I n the spring of 1980 I interviewed all three members of the Police in their homes. At the time there was no more happening act in the world than the Police. The money hadn't yet begun pouring in and even if it had they would have been too busy to spend it; consequently they still lived the same kind of lives they had lived before their success. Sting was with his first wife, the actress Frances Tomelty, and their small child in a basement flat in Bayswater. Andy Summers, as befitted a more established musician, was in a mansion block in Putney. Drummer Stewart Copeland was in a modest house in Shepherd's Bush which he shared with his girlfriend Sonja Kristina, who was formerly the singer with his old band Curved Air.

The band had just returned from Japan. Before I left, Stewart was keen to show me the gift he had recently been given by Sony Japan. In the latter part of the seventies Sony's tape hardware division had been threatened with consolidation and therefore it was banking on this new product to guarantee its future. Up to this point hand-held cassette players had been exclusively aimed at the business market, where they were used to record letters for typing up by secretaries. The new product he had been given was an adaptation of an earlier cassette recorder called the Pressman, which had been developed for journalists to record interviews on. In an effort to come up with something that might appeal to a broader market the engineers had removed the record function to improve the sound quality and paired it with lightweight headphones with foam pads that went over the ear.

They didn't look impressive. They looked as though they might be adequate for secretarial use but wouldn't be equal to the immersive experience a home listener expected of headphones. When Copeland handed them over and invited me to put them on I wasn't expecting much. But when he depressed the play button with his thumb and the sound of the Police's latest album flooded into my ears the experience was more of a revelation than any audio baptism I'd undergone before or since. We stood there in his hall, me smiling with amazement and him smiling at my amazement. This was clearly why he had wanted to demonstrate them to me. He'd obviously done it before. Introducing somebody to their first Walkman was the party trick of 1980. Throughout the year hundreds of thousands of people all over the world were to experience versions of the same epiphany. Almost all of those epiphanies resulted in a sale. The Sony Walkman, as it eventually came to be known, went on to sell in the hundreds of millions, securing not just the future of Sony's tape division but the parent company as well.

The Walkman epiphany wasn't simply about sound. The sound wasn't any better than you would hear through headphones attached to your home stereo. The epiphany was how freeing it was. The amazement was that all that sound could come from anything so small and, more importantly, portable. The realization that you could take the immersive experience of listening on headphones and walk into another room was revolutionary. Its impact on anyone who heard it was so immediate it seemed amazing that it had taken the audio industry this long to understand that the personal stereo could be a game changer.

Originally it wasn't Sony's idea. The concept of a light portable player had actually been thought of some years earlier by a German-Brazilian called Andreas Pavel. Back in 1972 Pavel had jerry-rigged a cassette player with headphones to allow him to listen to his favourite music in the great outdoors. Pavel was in the mountains near St Moritz when he had his epiphany. The tape he was listening to at the time was the singularly unpromising *Push Push* by the jazz flautist Herbie Mann. On this occasion the snow was beginning to fall. This significantly increased the seemingly magical nature of the experience. 'I pressed the button, and suddenly we were floating,' he remembered. 'It was an incredible feeling, to realize that now I had the means to multiply the aesthetic potential of any situation.'

Pavel intuited early on what the audio trade took years to realize – that the innovation the public would appreciate most was not the one that improved the sound; instead it was the one that untethered music from the immovable object in the corner of the living room and allowed it to wander into every corner of our lives. The greybeards in the audio business couldn't see it at first. It was only when Sony managed to come up with headphones that were a tenth of the usual weight that it began to look promising. Even then they still saw music listening as something essentially social. Their experience of the LP and the home stereo system had taught them that people played music primarily to share it with others, which is why their early Walkman (also named the Soundaround and the Stowaway in early incarnations) had two headphone sockets in it. It was assumed that people would think it anti-social to be enjoying something that nobody else could hear. In fact that was what people liked about it. The advent of the Sony Walkman in 1980 would mark the beginning of our long march back into solitude.

By 1980 cassettes were clearly the fastest-growing sector of the market for recorded music. In the UK in that year almost half the albums sold were sold on cassette. In the United States, 1980 was the first year cassette sales overtook sales of eight-track cartridges. By 1985 the market for pre-recorded cassettes had overtaken the market for long-playing vinyl. This also indicated a change of emphasis as recorded music grew more popular. In the record business it was widely accepted that the market for tapes was different from the market for LP records. Fans and enthusiasts bought LPs; cassettes were bought by people who liked the tunes. The cassette department in the shop where I worked in the middle of the 1970s was patronized by more older women than you would have found among the LPs. There were some artists, like the Carpenters, Elton John and Abba, who always did better on cassette than on vinyl.

From the retailers' point of view cassettes were a lot easier to stock, sell and handle than twelve-inch records. They were also far easier to steal, which was a problem for the increasing number of shops that had gone self-service. The rise and rise of the cassette demystified the music business. Because cassettes didn't seem to demand any special handling you could sell them at petrol stations or via mail order. For many people they became the only sensible music carrier. Many new customers entered the music market without ever dealing with the long-playing record. My own mother was one of the legions who acquired a radio/cassette player around this time to keep in the kitchen. Henceforth she would quite unself-consciously refer to all music carriers, from seven-inch singles to (in the fullness of time) compact discs, as 'tapes'. It was easy to see why she preferred them. They took up less space, she didn't have to live in fear of damaging them, and she could take them out with her to play in the car. She had no problem adapting to tape because she had no emotional attachment to any format. Unlike her son, she didn't think a record represented a special category above and beyond any other consumer good.

The rise of the cassette marked a fork in the road for music lovers. It wasn't the only one that happened that year. Whereas a cassette was just a music carrier that did its job efficiently, a record seemed more than that. One of the main driving forces behind punk rock had been the desire on the part of lots of people to celebrate that very specialness by actually making their own records. For thousands of them up and down the country punk fame or notoriety would lead to a brief ride on the giddy carousel of show business and all sorts of adventures. They forgot lots of it but the one part of their adventure they never entirely got over was that time when they enlisted the aid of a friend who had the use of an unsafe motor car and drove to the local pressing plant, there to collect a small cardboard box containing their very own record, the solitary mark they might hope to leave upon a heedless world. For some it was just a one-time thing. For others it was a precious opportunity to call themselves a record label.

Punk rock had been responsible for a huge growth in the number of small independents. Some were started just to get a local group off the ground and would disappear just as quickly as the group. Others had the ambition to become mini Motowns. At first their ambitions didn't stretch far beyond putting out singles. What all of them craved, more than fame and money, was some sort of recognition of their efforts. Although many of the records from these labels sold respectable quantities, they were rarely likely to trouble the compilers of the official charts on which radio play and TV programmes like *Top of the Pops* were based.

The likelihood is they would have slipped back into the

obscurity from which they had sprung had it not been for Iain McNay of the independent label Cherry Red, who came up with the idea of a chart that exclusively featured independent records. The first independent singles chart appeared in January 1980 with 'Where's Captain Kirk?' by Spizzenergi at its top. Since everyone is a devout believer in the authority and accuracy of any chart in which they're included, the independent chart was not short of supporters. It provided a kind of safe space for those who feared they would never sell as many records as Pink Floyd or Blondie but nonetheless wanted to be able to prove that they mattered. The indie chart instantly provided a place that could reflect the import-ance you had, even if it was in a slightly smaller version of the real world. As Geoff Travis of Rough Trade, which was subsequently to become the EMI of the independent chart, recalled many years later, 'We were happy in our own little world – there was a logic and beauty to it. And the real world's taste is so terrible.'

The arrival of the indie chart was the thin end of the wedge lead-ing to the eventual Balkanization of pop music. Pop was already starting to become too big and too various to be covered by one lens. 1980 was the last year when it was possible for a person to say with any conviction that they knew everything that was going on in music. In time, other taste groups – dance, folk, reggae, heavy metal, even Americana – would also make their unilateral declar-ation of independence from the mainstream of the music business, and their first stake in the ground would be a chart of their own.

Initially the independent chart was only open to those whose records were independently distributed and didn't benefit from the marketing muscle of the major labels. Over time, the more success-ful independent labels would be bought up by the same majors and the word 'indie' would come to mean music by bands with a cer-tain way of arranging their hair and a taste for jangly guitars and opaque lyrics. These acts did some things differently but the one thing they did in the old-fashioned way, and did the moment they got the chance, was to prove their seriousness by making their own long-playing record.

At the same time as the first indie charts were being published the Manchester group Joy Division were in Britannia Row, Pink Floyd's studio in Islington, making their second album. Everything about Joy Division was lightly undertaken but doggedly morose, from their name – a reference to a concentration camp brothel lifted following somebody's skim of a schlock paperback – to their big single 'Love Will Tear Us Apart', so called because it was recorded at the same studio where Neil Sedaka had done the chirpy 'Love Will Keep Us Together'. Joy Division made a sound as rainy as Manchester's weather. In doing so, like Black Sabbath ten years earlier, they dropped a coin in the deep well of the English subconscious.

Their singer Ian Curtis was, like so many men of his generation, obsessed with LP records. LPs were the main thing that mattered to him as he was growing up. When he was a teenager he didn't have enough money to feed his album habit so he would go to the indoor market in Macclesfield wearing a greatcoat big enough to secrete new records beneath. If he didn't like the records he stole he'd sell them back to the shop the following week. He and his young girlfriend Debbie used to sit in the front parlour of his parents' house listening to Lou Reed and Iggy Pop for hours at a time. She wasn't even eighteen when they got engaged. By that point he was already exerting such control over her that she was only allowed to have one school friend as a guest. He wasn't as loyal to her as he expected her to be to him. Only later did she find out that he had given their copy of *The Man Who Sold The World* to the local beauty. Records were eventually their only friends.

In March 1980 Curtis's marriage was unravelling at the same time as Joy Division started recording their second album. The opportunity to work away in London provided a welcome relief

Left and **below**: Neil Young's first big long player, 1970's *After The Gold Rush*, wasn't just about the music. It also promoted a lifestyle which seemed tantalizingly achievable to anyone who could grow their hair and look deep while reclining on a couch.

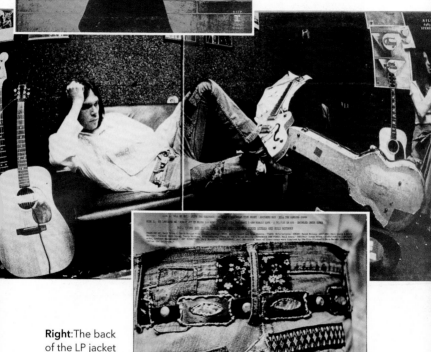

Right: The back of the LP jacket features a close-up of the artist's backside with the credit 'patches: Susan Young'. Young's look was widely emulated.

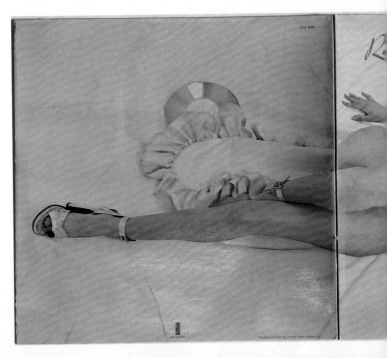

ILPS 9200

Phil Manzanera

Eno

Side One
Re-make/Re-model
Ladytron
If There Is Something
2 H.B

Cover concept · Bryan Ferry
Art · Nicholas deVille
Photography · Karl Stoecker
Artwork by C.C.S.
Clothes, make-up & hair · Anthony Price
Kari-Ann's hair by Smile
Equipment by McInnes Laboratories & Torner
Transport by Wragg
Dedicated to Susie and all the
others, who made this album possible

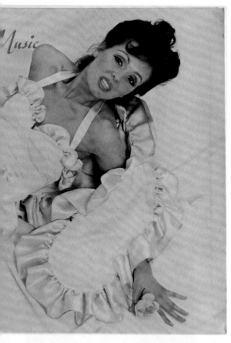

Left and **below**: Released in 1972, the first Roxy Music LP marked the arrival of a new aesthetic which self-consciously quoted from the past in both music and pictures and had more credits for people involved in the cover than the record. Like the King Crimson record a few years earlier, it sold right out of the shop window (**bottom left**).

Andrew Mackay

Bryan Ferry

Graham Simpson

Paul Thompson

Side Two

The Bob (Medley)	(5.48)
Chance Meeting	(3.00)
Would You Believe?	(3.47)
Sea Breezes	(7.00)
Bitters End	(2.02)
	21.37

...ccadilly, 1972: taking a turn off main-...eet, away from cacophony and real-life ...lics, & into the outer spaces myriad ...es & sweet deafening sounds of ...ck'n'roll. And inner space... the mind ...set its bearings. what's the date agxin/ ...'s so dark in here) 1962? or twenty ...ars on?

...this a recording session or a cocktail ...rty?!...on the rocks, please ...where's ...e icebox? — oh! now! that is...so ...ol...(there'd been rumours, of course, ...oching, certain, but the suggestion of ...orb)...

...usicians lie rigid-&-fluid in a mannerist ...nvas of hard-edged black-leather ...ntings, red-satin slashes, smokey ...rrounding gloom...

...listening to the music re-sounding, ...cting the sixlike it was glass, rock'n'roll ...ggernauted into demonic electronic ...personic mo-mo-momentum — by a ...nplit machine-pile, hifi or scifi who ...n' tell? Wailing old-time sax, velvet/

...viscous, vibrato/vicious or ensemble ...jamming (& more)...synthesised to whirls & whorls of hardrock sound... mixed/fixed/sifted/lifted to driving, high-flying chunks & vortices of pure electronic wow — gyrating, parabolic, tantalising (oh ...nces could not spell out the score). ...fantasising: phantomising: echoes of magic-golden moments become real presences... dreamworld & realworld loaded with images (of a style & time & world of celluloid artefacts? heart-rending hardfacts?). Monaural & screate fragments sea-changed & refined to pon ...span the limits of sensation... leaves of gold, crossing thresholds & hearts. Saturday nite at the Roxy the Mecca trio Ritz — your fantasies realized...& are they still? & is this the end, the bitter end? (or the beginning) &, so help me, so many questions? & are the answers naked to the eye — or ear? or are they undercover?

SIMON PUXLEY

Bryan Ferry - Voice & Piano
Graham Simpson - Bass Guitar
Andrew Mackay - Oboe & Saxophone
Eno - Synthesiser & Tapes
Paul Thompson - Drums
Phil Manzanera - Guitar

Recorded at Command Studios,
London, March, 1972
Engineer - Andy Hendrikson
All songs by Bryan Ferry,
arranged by Roxy Music

Produced by Peter Sinfield for E. G. Records
All songs published by Buggane Music Ltd © 1972
an associate of the E. G. Group
℗ 1972 by Island Records Ltd

Left: Neil Bogart of Casablanca Records (*on the left*) demanded that Donna Summer's 'Love To Love You Baby' be long enough to accompany an orgy. When her album came out in 1975, he had its image baked on a cake and booked two airplane seats to fly it to New York.

Below: Joni Mitchell's 1974 masterpiece *Court And Spark* was released on Asylum, the label invented by her manager and friend David Geffen, the harassed millionaire hero of her song 'Free Man In Paris'.

Above: Patti Smith's 1975 release *Horses* was a repudiation of the Roman excesses of the era and was promoted via indie shops like Rather Ripped Records in Berkeley.

Below: Elton John, a man so in love with record shops that he volunteered to work behind the counter, signs copies of his 1973 smash *Don't Shoot Me I'm Only The Piano Player* at DJ Noel Edmonds' (*on the left*) record shop in Kings Road, Chelsea.

Left: *The Dark Side Of The Moon* was made by Pink Floyd (**below**) without any involvement from the record company. The sticker on the cover had to be added later to help buyers find it. It did not get to number one on its release in 1973, but a whole year later it was still in the top twenty. It seemed to represent the inevitable triumph of long-form rock music.

Above: Recording LPs as pristine as Fleetwood Mac's *Rumours* was a job which expanded to fill the time available and placed particular stress on singers like Stevie Nicks (**left**) who might have to wait weeks to spend a few minutes adding a harmony.

Below: Blondie were reluctant pop stars. In 1978, producer Mike Chapman told them, 'You're going to start playing better'. The boys in the band only agreed to smile on the cover (**left**) on condition Debbie Harry did a contrasting scowl.

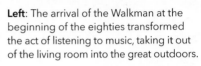

It's Sony! Walkman by Sony. The world's first stereo cassette player for work, play or sport. It's the low-priced portable so stylish and light you can listen to it anywhere.

It's incredible! Only Sony could give you fidelity this high in a package so small. The sound that flows through Walkman's featherlight headphones is phenomenal. There's even an extra headphone jack for a friend.

It's Walkman! That's the name of the fashion and sound sensation that's sweeping the world. From New York and L.A. to Paris, London and Tokyo. Try one on and hear why Walkman's all the rage.

WALKMAN

Left: The arrival of the Walkman at the beginning of the eighties transformed the act of listening to music, taking it out of the living room into the great outdoors.

Below: Michael Jackson's epochal *Thriller* was nominated in twelve categories at the 1984 Grammy Awards and recalibrated the expectations of the music industry. Soon LPs were being outsold by cassettes and then, by the end of the decade, CDs.

and allowed him to conduct his affair with a Belgian woman with whom he had bonded over a shared love for David Bowie's *Low*. During one of Curtis's arguments with Deborah, by then his wife and the mother of his young child, she is said to have broken his copy of the same album.

Joy Division's first album, *Unknown Pleasures*, on the Manchester-based label-cum-art project Factory Records, had been very well received but they still didn't feel either successful or famous. When they went into Britannia Row they were acutely aware that it was costing them £40 an hour and they were only earning £15 a week. The album was recorded in two weeks at the beginning of March. As they finished it, *Kramer vs. Kramer* was released in British cinemas, a new production of *Othello* was running at the National Theatre with Paul Scofield playing the Moor in blackface, ITV was screening *Gay Life*, the first ever programme for a homosexual audience, and President Jimmy Carter had announced that the United States would be boycotting the Moscow Olympics as a protest against the Soviets' invasion of Afghanistan.

Two outsiders shaped Joy Division's album as much as anyone in the band. Producer Martin Hannett may have been unconventional in many ways but he knew that the stage of record making that really mattered was the mixing. That was why he preferred to do this at a time of day or night when the band couldn't attend. Joy Division's Peter Hook remembers that Hannett liked Britannia Row because it was cold and clinical and had all the latest toys. 'He started working at night to take advantage of it at its most silent and dead. You can hear all of that in the album.' Hannett knew how he wanted the band to sound, which was a long way from the Stooges-type sound they would have had if allowed their way. He wanted something that was as appealing to the body as the brains, something that was elemental but not clichéd, something that hinted at great sadness without actually overwhelming the listener, something above all that sounded good in your living room. As the band were to concede in years to come, Hannett was right and they were wrong. Joy Division may have sprung from punk but *Closer* turned out like a more austere version of what Pink Floyd had been dealing in on *Dark Side Of The Moon*.

The other outsider who shaped the record was designer Peter Saville. Saville's choice of an image and typography more redolent of an order of service for a Victorian funeral than a recording by a young pop group from Manchester vastly increased the mystique of the object by removing it from the world it had emerged from and placing it somewhere else entirely. For the cover of the album he chose a picture of the tomb of an Italian noble family taken by a fine art photographer. Where Martin Hannett's mix gave the music grandeur, Saville's cover lent it classical austerity. *Closer* was the original and also the ultimate indie album, partly because of the music, partly because of the package, and partly because of what happened next.

Between the completion of the album and its release, Ian Curtis hanged himself. It was on the eve of what was supposed to be their first tour of the United States. Factory's staff pointed out to the boss Tony Wilson that there might be a problem with the cover.

They said, 'Tony, we've got a tomb on the cover of the album.'

He said, 'Oh fuck.'

They didn't make any changes. They didn't add Curtis's picture to the cover, as a standard record company would have done. They didn't add his dates. It was not Joy Division's way to either apologize or explain. There are not even any track names on the label and only an engraving on the vinyl to distinguish one side from the other, but there is the date of release, which is 9/5/80. The catalogue number FACT 25 suggests the confidence of a long-established brand. In fact Factory gave all its projects numbers, whether they were records or the company's notepaper. Like many small independent labels, the people behind Factory were excited and amused by the idea that theirs was a company and liked to feel that it made things rather than merely published them. The surface of the paper sleeve of *Closer* was matt, the corners of the inner sleeve rounded – the sure signs of something going against the grain of standard record company design and costing slightly more than usual. On the run-out groove of the first side the person who cut the master, presumably acting on the instructions of Tony Wilson, inscribed the words 'Old Blue?' This was a reference to Frank Sinatra, whose singing style Wilson had commended to Ian Curtis as the album was being made.

Like the music itself there was no trace of ingratiation anywhere in the package. It had the same kind of well-placed confidence that made Led Zeppelin refuse to put even their name on the cover of their breakthrough album. They seemed to know when something was right. When it came out in July 1980 it went to number six in the real charts where it sat alongside *The Game* by Queen and *Give Me The Night* by George Benson. Its predecessor *Unknown Pleasures* had never entered a chart of any kind. There was no arguing with the fact that now they had arrived. Following Curtis's death, the other three decided that was the end of Joy Division and henceforth they would be New Order. This was a decision taken on the basis of a vow they had made to each other but it could as easily have been made on a more calculated basis.

Closer is a perfect record of a moment that was never likely to be repeated. It has just as much variation as it needs and no more. It sounds like the future that never arrived and a past that never took place. The musicianship is sufficient to its purpose and not enough to put on airs. It has no stand-out tracks, no particular variations of tone or pace. You put it on, leave it on, surrender to its groove, listen to it as closely or as distantly as you want, and then turn it over. When you tune into the words it's plain that the singer is describing the symptoms of his profound depression. This came as as much of a surprise to the band as to the listeners because, as they recalled later, they never talked about it. And yet, it works. It is oddly playable for something surrounded by so much tragedy. Along with Ian Dury's *New Boots And Panties!!* and Talking Heads' *Fear Of Music* it's arguably the best long-playing record to come out of the long tail of punk rock.

Closer manages to embody all the seriousness about life that most of the band were just too callow to be able to demonstrate at the time. As Peter Hook remembered many years later, Ian Curtis presented a different version of himself to everybody in his life. It's likely even he wasn't sure which was the true one. It was only after his death that they realized that he meant every word of what he was singing about. It was only after his funeral that they realized they were the beneficiaries of one of the most curious aspects of our relationship with death. It makes people buy albums.

The most dramatic case of that syndrome came at the very end of 1980 when John Lennon was murdered outside the Dakota Building in New York. He had been cajoled back to make a record after years of inactivity. *Double Fantasy* wasn't very strong and hadn't been very well received. On the day of his death he had had a meeting with David Geffen, the boss of his record label, at which Geffen made the customary noises about releasing another single and trying again.

By the time the next issue of the trade paper *Billboard* was on the stands the front-page splash was headlined 'Lennon's Death Galvanizes Trade'. The story detailed Geffen's attempts to keep up with the increased demand for *Double Fantasy*, which had suddenly stopped its slide down the charts. Dealers across the United States were reporting unprecedented demand. Some had customers coming in wanting to buy up to a dozen copies. Since they weren't seeing the same effect with the cassette they attributed this to 'the collectors market'. By the following week Lennon and Ono were on top of both the singles and albums charts. For the next few weeks radios all over the world and speakers in every public place poured out the most optimistic songs Lennon had ever written, the ones that celebrated what he thought was a new beginning. Dealers, who don't look for ironies when the tills are turning as quickly as this, were congratulating themselves on this unsought fillip to the end-of-year sales – although many of them couldn't restrain themselves from observing that it was not quite such a jamboree as they had had following the death of Elvis Presley in 1977.

Over the next few days thousands of people gravitated towards the Dakota Building. They brought flowers. They brought home-made banners, some bearing puzzling messages such as 'Goodbye, Nowhere Man'. They wore Beatles T-shirts if they had such things. They lit candles. They behaved for all the world like followers of one of the religions Lennon had disavowed. Many of them brought albums, which seemed the nearest objects of veneration at hand. Obviously there was nothing to play them on but they could hold them up like so many cardboard icons or over-sized party cards. What they had come to represent was far greater than what they were. This is who we are, people seemed to be saying as they held aloft old copies of *Imagine* or *Revolver*. Most of these people were baby boomers. Nothing else in their lives held the same symbolic power as an album cover.

For the same foggy reason thousands of people all over the world in the days ahead wandered as if in a trance into their local record mart and handed over money for a record that a few days earlier they'd not had much interest in. Why exactly? Because it seemed respectful. Because all the publicity around the death had suddenly brought John Lennon and his part in their lives back into focus. Because, truth to tell, they were rather enjoying mourning over the loss of somebody they didn't know and they were keen to let their contemporaries know that they were just as cut up as they were.

Because a death engendered one of those rare moments of unity within a musical landscape that felt increasingly fractured. Because while you wouldn't feel that you ought to read a book following the death of its author, listening to a record is not something that calls for a great deal of commitment. Because when a musician dies, everything they have ever recorded, from 'Twist And Shout' to '(Just Like) Starting Over', is newly suffused with an attractive air of poignancy.

Mark Chapman was one of those people who spent a lot of time, probably too much time, watching LPs go round. He had approached John Lennon earlier in the day and asked him to autograph his copy of *Double Fantasy*. That was what you did in the days of LPs. Had it been the age of the selfie it is possible he would have been delighted at the prospect of having his picture taken next to his idol. According to an onlooker, John asked, 'Is that all you want?'

1981

'Home Taping Is Killing Music'

In the early seventies, one of the young men I was sharing a flat with in north London worked as a lowly clerk in the head office of a government body. This meant he had to adhere to a dress code and everything that went with it. His routine could not be lightened in any way. He got through the day by focusing remorselessly on what he intended to do once the day was over. As soon as it was over he would push his way on to the London Underground where he would be surrounded by fellow members of this army of drones, many reading the *Evening Standard* and most of them smoking. His journey home would be one of unrelieved tedium and discomfort.

On arriving back at our flat he would always do the same thing. I could hear him do it from the room next door. There would be a click followed by a hum, indicating that the record player in his room had just been turned on. Then there would be the speckled rumble that indicated a record was about to be played too loud. This was followed by the fervid, libidinous growl of the Texas blues band ZZ Top playing the song 'La Grange' from their album *Tres Hombres*. 'La Grange' was the sound he used at the end of every day. It was the sound he clearly required to wash away everything the day had done to him, to transition from the person his job expected him to pretend to be to the person that rock and roll allowed him to pretend to be in his spare time. After one side of this LP he would emerge transfigured from his room, as though from a shower or the confessional, his mood visibly lightened, the cares of the day lifted from his brow by this longed-for daily reunion with loud music and everything it did for him. In those days loud music was a sound you could only get at home.

Because LPs lived at home and were played on gramophones requiring a stable floor, wired connection to speakers and access to mains electricity, they were necessarily a home-based form of entertainment. By 1981 the Sony Walkman had changed that for ever. Now you could take your home with you. Out into the street and down into the Underground. It was a revolution.

The idea of no longer being dependent on your home, the idea of being able to take your listening environment with you, was the clinching novelty that made the Walkman such an instant, dramatic success. It was a success with the very people who would not have dreamed of hauling a beatbox around on their shoulders. The Walkman was not for show-offs. As early as April 1981 the *New York Times* began noticing the adopters of the Walkman on the streets of Manhattan. At first their behaviour struck them as odd. For a story headlined 'Private Music and Public Silence' they went out on the streets and talked to these 'waves of people walking about with little foam rubber circles on their ears and expressions of transport on their faces in a scene that was almost Orwellian'. What they found was these people were all giddy with excitement at being able to listen to music in spaces where it had previously been inaccessible or verboten – places such as, whisper it, the office. 'I've even worn them to work,' gushed one Phyllis Stein, 'and I'm a research librarian.' Somebody else enthused about finally being able to take music to the beach: 'Radios are banned at my beach club, but there's no way they can object to this.'

The *Times*, which clearly hadn't made the leap itself, also noted that cheap competitors to the Walkman were available and were making the wearing of headphones a more common sight every day. They confessed they might have to revise their previous view that the original $200 price tag had made the Sony Walkman likely to be 'a middle class indulgence'. As it turned out, the Sony Walkman would be the first in a succession of products that changed our world by turning all our indulgences into necessities. People who would never have spent the same amount of money on a home stereo rushed to embrace the Walkman. The Walkman marked the beginning of a convenience-driven revolution in entertainment, a revolution that led to the world of today.

The success of the Walkman was so dramatic that hardware prices almost halved within a year. As competitors crowded into the market, what had been initially seen as an executive plaything was increasingly sought by everyone, whether they were on the shop floor or the school bus. If it was a middle-class indulgence, we all wanted to indulge, much as we all wanted to be middle class and we all wanted to be young and beautiful. The Walkman fitted right into a lifestyle revolution. In the summer of 1977 the cover of *People* magazine had recommended an exciting new form of exercise known as 'jogging'. They commended it to their readers on the grounds that this was the way Farrah Fawcett Majors and her husband remained beautiful. The arrival of the Walkman just a few years later addressed the central drawback of jogging, its inherent tedium, while also allowing the user (or wearer) to advertise the fact that their pursuit of physical fitness was not at the expense of their interest in fun. 1981 was the year of Olivia Newton-John's video for her song 'Physical' in which she wore a leotard and sweatband and trailed a finger down the glistening abs of a naked man, thus clearly spelling out what all her interest in physical culture was leading to.

Between 1980 and 1985 the number of pre-recorded cassettes sold in the UK doubled but still nobody managed to make pre-recorded tapes seem special. Cassettes were still seen as the poor relation of the long-playing record. At the end of 1980 Malcolm McLaren had made much of the fact that the first collection of songs by his post-Sex Pistols act, Bow Wow Wow, would not only come out on cassette-only but would also start with a song in praise of the petty larceny that was vexing the record companies, a song called 'C30, C60, C90 Go!' The fact that McLaren didn't choose to repeat the trick suggests it wasn't popular. Martyn Ware of the Human League was struck by the fact that this new toy would make it possible for people to design their own soundtrack to accompany them at every stage of their diurnal round and so his group, the British Electric Foundation, released a cassette-only collection of filmic-sounding material and called it *Music For Stowaways* (the early Walkmans were called the Sony Stowaway). This too failed to capture the imagination.

Chris Blackwell of Island Records attracted the opprobrium of his fellow labels when he launched the One Plus One series of cassettes in February 1981. The idea with this series was that you got the artist's new album on one side with the other left blank for you to record your own favourites on. This never entirely took off, partly because technological reasons meant you couldn't have the same quality of tape on both sides and also because people simply preferred to make decisions for themselves. This was one of the early cases of record companies being disturbed by the fact that what their customers did with their exciting new products was often not what they wished them to do, and they were powerless to either predict it or stop it happening.

In the early eighties the record business may have been becoming more scientific than it had been in the past and it was certainly starting to employ more marketing staff, but still its relationship with its customers was characterized by close familiarity in certain respects and total ignorance in others. Most attempts by hardware and software manufacturers to influence how the public use recorded music have failed. If people see a cheaper alternative and it's one that suits the way they prefer to consume music, they will take it.

Pre-recorded cassettes never had the cachet it took to appeal to fashion-conscious youngsters. Unlike the LP, the cassette could never aspire to perfection, to finality. Instead it was a tool for magpies. It was provisional. It was a recording medium. It was all about what happened when you put some sellotape over the safety device that prevented recording. It was all about what happened when you drew your own 'cover' on the inlay card. People made tapes that were like musical Valentines. They were cheap enough for people to be able to swap them with each other. They were also deliberately, proudly lo-fi.

Within two years of the launch of the Walkman it and its scores of competitors had become the one item of audio kit that all teenagers had to have. They used the cassette as a tool, either to copy a friend's copy of an album, to record from the radio or, most likely of all, to cherry-pick the two quality tracks on most albums and completely ignore the rest. Sales of blank tapes soared in the first half of the eighties as people took their LPs and recorded their favourite tracks on their home entertainment system with a view to playing them on the Walkman. In America in 1981 it was estimated that over thirty million were sold, and record executives began to grumble that since they clearly weren't all being used to record baby's first cry the record industry should be compensated by the government. In Britain, from 1981 onwards, the inner bags of many albums came with a graphic of a skull and crossbones over the outline of a tape and the stern warning 'Home Taping Is Killing Music – and it's illegal!'

Cassette wasn't a medium that had any interest in perfection. Bruce Springsteen recorded the original demos for his album *Nebraska* on cassette on a rudimentary four-track Tascam machine. Having tried and failed to record superior versions of these songs with his band he ended up taking the original cassette out from his back pocket and suggesting they simply remaster it from there. They even briefly flirted with the idea of putting it out on cassette-only.

1981 was also the year *NME* started doing its own series of cassettes, which the magazine used as a promotional item. These were not merely good promotion but also successfully brought together edgy post-punk one-offs, nascent club music and abstruse oldies into what started to sound like a new form of entertainment. It pointed towards a new aesthetic which was more about the art of the mix than the work of specific artists.

Sonic Youth's Thurston Moore remembered: 'I was living in downtown New York as a musician when the Walkman came along. Suddenly there was a machine you could afford to buy and put music on. It was a real revolution for us. I would get these cheap cassettes on Canal Street, three for a dollar, and I would go and record the guy upstairs' records. It was an incredible learning experience for me. All the punk rock and hard punk records were so short that you could fit so many on a cassette and to me that felt like you were curating a gig in a way. They were cheaper and the sound was different. Then they were cheap enough to mail to other people. All through the eighties people were making mixtapes for people they had crushes on. They were part of the courting ritual.'

As David Byrne wrote years later: 'The mixtapes we made for ourselves were musical mirrors. The sadness, anger or frustration you might be feeling at a given time could be encapsulated in the song selection. You made mixtapes that corresponded to emotional states, and they'd be available to pop into the deck when each feeling needed reinforcing or shooting. The mixtape was your friend, your psychiatrist and your solace.'

In the winter of 1981 I interviewed Byrne in New York. In those days even a moderately successful recording star could afford to rent an enormous loft space downtown. He was talking about an album he had made with Brian Eno called *My Life In The Bush Of Ghosts*. This record had come about as a result of the cassettes the two men had been making for each other, cassettes that featured snatches of people talking on radio phone-ins, devotional music from overseas, radio evangelists and even an unidentified exorcist at work. These arresting snippets could then be looped over recordings of backing musicians playing an insistent groove. This was strange music. It didn't yield to the standard forms of interpretation but it sounded exciting and current. Byrne wasn't the only one attracted by this new direction. A few months earlier Dave Stewart of Eurythmics had played me a recording of Can's Holger Czukay doing something similar with so-called 'found vocals'.

It was the kind of record Byrne and Eno made up as they went along. There were no predecessors but there would be many followers. Twenty years earlier Cliff Richard and the Shadows had been making their records at Abbey Road without feeling the need to go upstairs to the control room. Fifteen years earlier the Beatles had crossed that divide and everyone else had come in their train, asking what this or that lever did and eroding the division between artist and producer. Now, in 1981, people were starting to play with the idea of making records at home, using the very basic tools that were beginning to become available.

Byrne told me the record would have been impossible if it hadn't been for the Walkman. Before that, he said, you had to tote albums around to play them to friends or potential collaborators. Now you simply had to put a cassette in the mail. At the same time the technology allowed him and Eno to work more like film directors presiding over an edit than musicians looking nervously through the window and asking 'How was that?' With *My Life In The Bush Of Ghosts*, he later recalled, 'we were turning the mixing board into a giant instrument'.

My Life In The Bush Of Ghosts was a bellwether record. Four years later Kate Bush was pointing out the influence it had had on lots of records released that year, presumably including her own *Hounds Of Love*, a much-layered offering which had put snippets of dialogue from old movies and recordings of old folk songs on top of her original home demos. Like *My Life In The Bush Of Ghosts* and almost every record since, the music was built from the rhythm track. As Byrne wrote years later, 'making music is like constructing a machine whose function is to dredge up emotions in performer and listener alike'. It was a world away from *Astral Weeks*.

This was coming at the same time as Blondie's 'Rapture' became the first record featuring a rap to go to number one. 'Rapture' celebrated the advent of hip hop and name-checked various denizens of the downtown scene. Henceforth, particularly with hip hop – and in time everybody would take their cue from hip hop – all records were seen as provisional. In many ways this was a good thing. The second side of my original copy of *My Life In The Bush Of Ghosts* starts with a song that features Algerian Muslims chanting from the Koran. It was taken off the album in 1982 at the behest of the Muslim Council of Great Britain. The legal department never did manage to clear that.

Elsewhere in entertainment bigger changes were starting to happen. In 1981 there were still just three television channels in the

UK. The majority of the output of those channels was still firmly aimed at a traditional idea of the family audience. At Christmas that year there was the customary excitement around the showing of famous feature films on the small screen. These annual showings were huge events because they provided the only opportunity people had to see major films without going to the cinema. Since most UK cinemas had not been given a facelift since the 1950s they were not attractive places. They were even less attractive if you weren't a smoker because there was still no restriction on smoking in public places. If you missed a film the first time around there were few chances to catch it later. In the UK there was still a five-year window between cinema release and the first TV showing. *Star Wars*, which had galvanized a mass audience of young people in a way that no film had ever done before on its release in 1977, was not shown on UK television until October 1982. Consequently there was a huge pent-up appetite for any kind of film. This particularly applied to Hollywood films with their big budgets, better-known stars, racier themes and all-pervading gloss. There was an equal determination on the part of the studios to restrict people's access to these products and to ensure that they only watched them on their terms.

This had begun to change in 1979 when the first home video players became available. Uncertainty over warring formats meant it took a couple of years for these machines to become first rentable, then affordable, and finally indispensable. Because the studios didn't wish to sell their films on video directly to the customers they priced them as high as £80, safe in the knowledge that dealers would pay this premium and then make their money back by renting them out at a couple of pounds a night.

Video rental stores began appearing on the high street from the end of 1981, offering access to a product that had previously been unimaginably distant. It excited the mass audience who suddenly had the option of renting a video rather than settling for whatever the BBC or ITV were providing for them. Living rooms were redesigned. Record players were banished from the main living space to make room for space-consuming Trinitron TVs, heavy VCRs that would only go into record mode when placed under maximum pressure by two hands, and shelves that were soon groaning under the weight of roughly labelled cassettes ('Jane's wedding' or 'Butch Cassidy – do not erase!').

The video industry had a product people really wanted and it made them pay for it. When I first joined 'a library', which was how they styled themselves at this time, I had to pay a joining fee, then pay the same again as a deposit, and then a rental per night. Like everybody else I paid up because I was genuinely excited by the prospect of being able to take home *All the President's Men* for the evening and play it much as I might have played *Pretzel Logic*. And this was the point. The VHS suddenly introduced a new way you could spend the evening. Like the Walkman, it provided a dizzying sense of liberation. It started when you wanted, paused when you wanted, and finished when you wanted. People no longer had to be beholden to the TV scheduler. There was no more 'Quick, it's on!' Suddenly there was time shifting, much as there always had been with LPs. But now people began talking about Home Entertainment. There were now options, and these options didn't require quite so much concentration and imagination as listening to an album had once demanded.

With the advent of the Walkman, listening to recorded music went from being something that took place behind closed doors between consenting adults to something that took place on the street. At first this was something to show off about. In the 1984 movie *Footloose* Kevin Bacon uses his much-prized new toy to teach the teenagers of his sleepy old town in the puritan heartland how to dance to the rock music which the town's elders forbid. The poster for the film gave the equipment more prominence than the star. He is half turned away from the camera, thrusting the miraculous machine fastened to his belt loop towards the viewer. In the 1985 movie *Back to the Future* the hero's father, time travelling from the 1950s, is shocked rigid by the experience of having the headphones clamped to his head and being exposed to the guitar sounds of Eddie Van Halen. The video for 'Wired For Sound', Cliff Richard's 1981 song of praise for the wonders of this new technology, features the then forty-one-year-old pop veteran roller-skating around the streets, enjoying this revelatory experience of listening to pop while on his own personal wheels. The message of the TV commercials for the Walkman in 1981 was 'put on a Sony Walkman and see the whole world in a new light', accompanied by images of mere pedestrians instantly turning into joyful dancers upon donning these magic headphones. The aerobic execution of the ad all but promised that you would shed some more stubborn inches while listening to the superior classical music sound of the Walkman. The advertisements put so much stress on the apparently umbilical connection between listening to the Walkman and roller-skating that an early component of the legend of Princess Diana, who married into the Royal Family in the summer of 1981, was her habit of roller-skating around the highly polished corridors of Kensington Palace listening to Elton John and George Michael. Twenty years after her death a box of Diana's favourite cassettes was used as part of an exhibition. One of them was marked 'Diana', presumably in case any light-fingered courtier was getting any ideas.

The Sony Walkman changed the way we consumed recorded music. Although the machine had been originally developed to fulfil the dream of Sony boss Akio Morita that he might be able to settle back and listen to his favourite Brahms symphony on a long airplane flight, the Walkman quickly became associated in the public mind with the act of moving about, whether as showily as roller-skating, as improvingly as jogging, or merely blocking out the sounds of a busy tube train. This had an immediate effect on the music they bought and how they listened to it. The majority of the LPs made in the mid-seventies were listened to in bedrooms, living rooms and student dormitories. They were designed to turn your living quarters into an intimate theatre. That context had gone. With the Walkman, the experience of listening to music became like taking part in a movie.

On 1 August 1981 MTV launched in the United States. In the same way that the Walkman meant that you could use your favourite music as a way to fend off the more irritating features of daily life, MTV meant you never had to watch anything that demanded any more of you than a four-minute clip. In the same way that the Walkman seemed inconceivable before it happened and inevitable once it had happened, it seemed staggering that nobody had previously thought of providing pop videos twenty-four hours a day. Selling MTV was like selling the Walkman. It was pushing on an open door. All that was required was to promote it as if it were some sort of civil right from which the grown-ups couldn't keep you. 'I want my MTV.'

American talk show host Conan O'Brien remembered: 'I was a freshman at college and a friend of mine was staying at her grandfather's apartment in New York. She said, "Come over and hang out." When I got there, she said, "I'm watching this new channel, MTV." What a weird thing. What do you mean, they're showing music videos? What's a music video? Why would you show that? I can't stop watching. We watched for six hours. It's one of those things you can't describe to anyone who's younger than you . . . it was like a comet streaking across the sky.'

I was in New York later that year, pounding the streets during the day and looking up at the buildings listening to Grace Jones's *Nightclubbing*, Echo & the Bunnymen's *Heaven Up Here* and the tracks I liked from Heaven 17's *Penthouse And Pavement* on my Walkman, and then going back to my hotel where there was MTV in my room, and if I gave it an hour the video for 'Rapture' by Blondie, which featured Fab 5 Freddy and Jean-Michel Basquiat and had Debbie Harry doing this thing called 'a rap', was bound to show up.

All this stimulation, all this distraction, all this ambient entertainment perfectly structured to your attention span – all this would have been inconceivable to my flatmate when, nearly a decade earlier, he was fighting his way home on the tube, his spirits kept buoyant by the thought of his copy of ZZ Top's *Tres Hombres* revolving on his much-loved turntable in his much-loved room. The Walkman had arrived, and in its wake came the unbundling of the LP and the colonization of every spare moment of our lives with music. The pleasure society was upon us.

1982

'We're here to save the recording industry'

The writer who reported on the year just past in the annual publication *The Rock Yearbook* began his summing up as follows: 'I spent most of the year home taping. The home-made compilation offered the most efficient way of capturing the brightest and best of the year, as well as the only means of making sense of it all. With nearly every week seeing the release of three striking singles, who had forty minutes to spare for albums?

'My in-car tapes were a particular joy: Kim Wilde's "Water On Glass" shooting across the wake of Yazoo's "Only You"; "Genius Of Love" by Tom Tom Club slithering into "Hand Held In Black And White" by Dollar; Heaven 17 followed by Mari Wilson; Madness filling the gap between Haircut 100 and Kool and the Gang; Simple Minds paving the way for Pigbag, Bow Wow Wow, the J. Geils Band, Altered Images, Roxy Music, Grace Jones, Orchestral Manoeuvres,

Bananarama, ABC, Soft Cell and the Police. In Britain at least, the best of the year's music was artful and wide-awake and it poured from the radio in a sparkling stream.'

I believe the writer of that summary of the year had a point. This is just as well since the writer was me.

By 1982 the LP was on the slide. Total shipments of albums in the USA had gone from 344 million in 1977 to under 244 million in 1982. In the UK in the same period they had declined from 81 million a year to fewer than 58 million. At the same time sales of singles had steadily grown, driven by a burgeoning interest in flamboyant pop acts such as Adam and the Ants, Dexys Midnight Runners and the Human League. The market for chart singles boomed. While the teenagers bought singles, put them on tape and played them on their Walkmans, the middle market preferred its Barbra Streisand's *Love Songs* or *The Kids From 'Fame'* on the cassette format, which had doubled in popularity in the same time.

It was around this time that record companies began to manipulate demand at point of sale by introducing new features to their products, features that had been largely unknown in the previous decade. There were bonus singles and free posters to encourage people to buy a record soon after its release. These would be distributed largely to chart return shops, thus ensuring that their sales appeared to count on a national scale. Then there was the vogue for records pressed on coloured vinyl. Although the black pigment was an ingredient added in the production process to hide any imperfections in the surface, music on coloured vinyl never seemed to sound as proper, as final, as definitive as black. Then there were the picture discs. In 1982 Meat Loaf's *Bat Out Of Hell* was reissued with the sleeve artwork pressed on to the record's surface.

Record buyers didn't actually want these additional features. Once they were available, however, a significant minority of people felt compelled to have them. For some, this would be the beginning of a long and needlessly costly marriage to just one record, a record that had a habit of turning round every few years and demanding to be purchased again in a previously unsuspected form, and always at a higher price. The people who succumbed liked to consider themselves victims of unscrupulous marketeers when in fact they were largely the victims of their own weakness for shopping. None of these gimcrack extras or unsought enhancements dealt with the basic problem. The LP was losing its lustre. There were too many of them and they weren't good enough.

The two top-selling albums in the United States in 1982 were John Mellencamp's *American Fool* and the first album by Asia. Even they only just about managed to sell three million copies each. Blondie, who only two years earlier had seemed ready to graduate to the top level of American bands, put out an album called *The Hunter*, the cover of which featured Debbie Harry in a science-fiction fright wig, which failed to even go gold. They cancelled tours and by the end of the year had broken up.

The bands that arrived at the same time as MTV were doing better. By the end of its second year the station was already in profit and was proving that it could break the kind of music that would never have been strong enough on its own to punch through on the radio. In a report in *Rolling Stone* at the beginning of 1983, retailers noted that thanks to the appearance of MTV in their market they had started doing well out of acts such as Duran Duran and ABC, 'who would otherwise be shelf death'.

At the same time the new fashion for dance-mixes of electronic pop tunes on twelve-inch singles was yielding good business for the most unlikely people. With over forty weeks on the chart, Soft Cell's 'Tainted Love' was the longest-lasting single in the history of *Billboard*'s Top 100 but it still didn't result in a hit album. The distant thunder was the coming hip hop revolution, which would take everybody by surprise. Reporting on his year's best-sellers, the man from Kief's Music told *Rolling Stone* that his store 'sold the living shit out of Planet Rock by Afrika Bambaataa and The Message by Grandmaster Flash'. This would not have been surprising if Kief's Music had been in Queens or Compton. The fact that it was in Lawrence, Kansas, right in the heart of the country, hinted that something big was already happening.

Despite the fact that the major record companies are often owned by the same people who own the major oil and gas firms there has never been any tradition of business planning in the record business. It's the only consumer business that doesn't spend any money on asking its consumers what they want. Its unchallenged wisdom is that only two things move the dial of the business: one is a big hit record and the other is new technology.

In 1982 the blank cassette was getting the blame for the underperformance of the LP. The American record business launched a hearts-and-minds campaign that spring, touting their estimate that home taping was costing them $3.3 billion a year in lost revenue. They felt they had a chance that year of getting Congress to give them the right to the proceeds of a levy on the sale of both tapes and tape machines. They presented the results of their research, glossing over anything that didn't help their case, such as the clear finding that the people who did the most home taping were also the people who bought the most recorded music. In the end they were unsuccessful because no legislator was going to bat for a business which was seen by many as greedy and wasteful.

In August 1982 Columbia Records in the USA fired three hundred employees and closed nine regional sales offices around the country. This was their somewhat belated response to what was widely regarded as the post-disco slump. In the United States total sales of all forms of recorded music had fallen from 726 million in 1978 to 578 million in 1982. All the major companies were looking at the same sort of decline and wondering where they could save money.

Their biggest outgoings went under the column marked 'independent promotion'. In the United States, independent promotion meant something characteristically American. It denoted a system whereby huge sums were disbursed to burly gentlemen who for some reason felt the need to employ their own bodyguards. These men were part of a network of specialists who between them controlled all the most powerful radio stations in the country. This network operated more like a protection racket than a network of promoters. If you paid them, your record would magically appear on the playlist of certain stations. Of course that was no guarantee it would be a hit. The only thing you could guarantee was that if you didn't pay these men your record would certainly never be a hit. In 1981, Dick Asher of Columbia Records had organized a boycott of the Network. Fredric Dannen's book *Hit Men* details how the Network responded by abruptly cutting off airplay of the Columbia act Loverboy, who were a personal priority of Asher's, just to show they could.

Within weeks the boycott had come to an end. Some of the executives objected to their bonuses being affected by what they saw as moral grandstanding from another executive. The people who really objected to all these millions no longer being diverted to these shadowy, unaccountable figures in bowling shirts were the people who in every other respect presented themselves as fearless crusaders for virtue and justice. It was the artists who objected most of all to the plan to stamp out independent promotion. It was the artists who wanted to make sure that if anyone was getting an unfair advantage it was them. When the boycott fizzled out and the company went back to paying at an increased rate of $10,000,000 a year, Asher discovered that one of Columbia's labels had been continuing to pay the independents by giving their acts' managers money under the name of 'tour support' and then telling them where to pay it on. The label was Epic. The head of promotion at

Epic was a short, immovable figure who favoured shirts that were forgiving at the waistline and smoked a cigar at all times. His name was Frank DiLeo, and he would play a crucial role in the album that would save Columbia and the record business.

Michael Jackson's previous album, *Off The Wall*, released in 1979, had transcended the disco category, sold nine million copies and won numerous awards. Still Jackson was dissatisfied with its impact. The follow-up album would have greater ambitions. Jackson, whose prime motivation was to impress his father, his brothers, his former boss Berry Gordy, his musical peers Stevie Wonder and Paul McCartney and anyone else who had ever so much as thought of slighting him, needed to prove that he was the big dog now. He embarked on this new record with a simple aim in mind: he wanted it to be the most popular record ever made.

Nobody had ever thought like that before. They had thought about being more popular with their fans or maybe even extending a little beyond their fan base. They hadn't thought of establishing an entirely fresh empire of success. More even than that, the people making this record intended to reverse the decline of an entire business. The engineer Bruce Swedien recalled later that on the day he, Jackson, British songwriter Rod Temperton and producer Quincy Jones first assembled in the studio in 1981 to begin work, Jones said, 'OK, guys, we're here to save the recording industry.'

In every sense, *Thriller* was all about scale. Rather than trying to represent his range or provide listeners with a journey, Jackson wanted to do an album whose every song could be a single. 'If you take an album like the Nutcracker Suite,' he told *Ebony* magazine, 'every song is a killer.'

The process of making the album was hard work. It could never be confused with fun. Jackson talked about it like a movie director getting a little above his station. On a song like 'Billie Jean', he said, 'the bass is the protagonist of the situation and getting that bass to sound right takes a lot of time. You're hearing four basses on there, doing four different personalities, and that's what gives it the character. But it takes a lot of work.'

The final nine songs were chosen from a long list of hundreds of compositions. Many of them were cast into available slots where Jackson was looking for a song that would do a job for him in the market. The first track recorded was 'The Girl Is Mine', his duet with Paul McCartney, which was a way to ensure that he would get radio play beyond the outlets that dealt with disco and pop. Quincy Jones's attitude was that they needed songs that would ingratiate them with all America's ironclad radio formats. Everyone who was trying to get a track on the album knew that commercial considerations trumped creative ones. The record started with a view of what might appeal to the market and then proceeded from there. It was reverse-engineered from the market backwards.

Rod Temperton, who had played such an important role in Jackson's solo success, initially came up with no fewer than two hundred titles for songs. One of them was 'Midnight Man'. He slept on it and by the morning it was clear it had to be called 'Thriller'. Why? 'You could visualize it at the top of the charts. You could see the merchandising for this one word.' They thought it would be good to have a famous horror movie actor saying something at the end of the track. Vincent Price was booked, but it wasn't until the night before he was due to record that they realized actors need a script.

Jackson was almost hysterical in his insistence that *Thriller* had to be the biggest thing ever. At one stage Quincy Jones, no doubt trying to release some pressure by damping down expectation, told him that if all went well he might sell two million copies. Jackson was so dismayed by this apparent lack of faith that he rang Walter Yetnikoff, the boss of his record company, and threatened not to put it out at all.

All through the recording Bruce Swedien had been warning that they had too much playing time for a long-playing record. At a proposed twenty-eight minutes a side the quality and loudness were bound to suffer. The final track on each side would be distorted. When they first played it back in the studio 'I saw Michael sneak out of the control room and go to the other studio, across the hall. He was crying, he was heartbroken. I felt like shouting, "I told you so!"'

The solution was to go back to the master tapes, lose a couple of songs and remix and edit what was left. This they did at the rate of one track a week while nervous record executives and even lawyers looked over their shoulders. Among the tracks that found their way on to the running order late in the day was 'Beat It'. Jones felt it would be a good idea to have something that could be played on rock radio and told Jackson, 'We need a song like "My Sharona".' Jackson wasn't particularly keen on rock but was alive to the desirability of having at least one rock track, so he went away and wrote 'Beat It'. Jones and the album's engineer spent weeks trying to find the right guitar tone for that record. They wanted something that would be soft enough for disco fans and raw enough for rock fans. Finally they asked Eddie Van Halen in to play them a solo. This might help the record get some traction in the white rock radio market. Nothing could be left to chance. As Jones said, 'If a record's going to really penetrate like this record did you have to go for the throat in five or six different areas. You do rock and roll, your adult contemporary thing, your dance stuff and your r&b thing.'

The final album, with a cover featuring a shot of the artist with his new nose (which had recently undergone a remix of its own), came out just before Christmas 1982. It went on to become the biggest-selling album in history. It made fortunes for everybody involved. It broke the heart of anyone not involved. Spare a thought for songwriter Michael Sembello whose composition 'Carousel' was left off the record at the last moment to make room for 'Beat It'.

Jones said, 'It hit everybody from eight to seventy all over the world. It had never happened before. Anybody who tells me they know how to make a record like this is lying. You can't plan it.'

If ever there was a record that didn't appear to be in need of any promotional help it was *Thriller*. Seven out of the nine tracks on the record eventually came out as singles and went top ten. Following Jackson's unveiling of his moonwalk during a twenty-fifth anniversary salute to Motown watched by fifty million TV viewers, he became America's national obsession. That didn't make Frank DiLeo, Epic's head of promotion, any more relaxed about taking Jackson's new records to radio. Each single was eventually backed to the tune of more than a hundred thousand dollars in independent promotion. DiLeo, who died in 2011, waved away any suggestion of criminal involvement, telling reporters there had been no organized crime in America since the death of Al Capone. Nobody has yet managed to explain how you could legitimately spend a hundred thousand dollars mailing copies of a new single by Michael Jackson to every radio station in the USA.

If there had been, DiLeo would surely have known. In between working as a promotion man he had a job taking illegal bets on college football games. This suggested he was either given special dispensation to do this by the people who traditionally control unsanctioned gambling or he was unusually reckless. He left the record business for a while, returning in 1979 soon after all his worldly goods had been lost following a mysterious electrical fire at his home. For some reason the insurance company failed to honour the claim. On the grounds that my bastard should be meaner than your bastard, Jackson became a big admirer of DiLeo, eventually hiring him as his manager. He fired him in 1989 following the disappointing sales of the next album, *Bad*. It had sold a mere twenty million. This was nothing like the hundred million Michael had in mind.

Michael Jackson's album was a product of the Los Angeles studio system. It used the best studio musicians that money could buy. It used the very latest technology. No expense was spared at any point in its making to ensure that its chances of success were maximized. In the years after it came out even more money would be spent on it, on a series of videos that were without precedent and which would take it into an entirely new category of success. Even as music alone it had far more calculation than inspiration. At the same time as it was coming out a record was being made at Ardent Studios in Memphis, Tennessee, previously the home of mavericks such as Big Star, that was every bit as calculated, albeit on a fraction of *Thriller*'s budget. The record was being made by a band that had previously been a byword for making music in the rootsiest, most apparently 'authentic' manner, a band who were now, thanks to the sudden availability of technology that had once been prohibitively expensive, finding a whole new way to make the sausage.

ZZ Top, who billed themselves as 'the best little band in Texas', had been operating since the late sixties. Theirs was the raucous boogie my flatmate would de-compress to in the early seventies. Ten years later their leader Billy Gibbons was looking at a wholly different way of doing things. A different way of making music. A different way of recording music. A different way of presenting yourself. A different way of being a band. In this he would have far more in common with the likes of David Byrne and Brian Eno and the mad scientists of hip hop than the rootsy blues bands with whom he was traditionally bracketed. The story of what he did is included here to illustrate the fact that Michael Jackson wasn't the only one who could calculate his way to the top of the charts.

The transfiguration of ZZ Top began with the visuals. There had been a time when a band like ZZ Top could afford to give no particular thought to what they looked like. It's unlikely that the Doobie Brothers or Little Feat ever gave the subject much thought.

But things had been different in those days for two reasons. The first was that in the seventies all bands were in their twenties. This meant that more often than not they looked naturally fabulous. The other thing that had changed was that whereas in those days TV was an optional extra, now there was MTV. MTV was suddenly the place you were most likely to find new fans and get people to buy your record. The members of ZZ Top had never been love gods to begin with and now, halfway through their thirties, they could no longer guarantee that the camera would love them.

Billy Gibbons didn't seek to remedy the depredations of age with hairpieces or a punishing gym regime. Instead he decided that they would make a virtue of their incipient geezerdom by turning it into that thing they had never previously had: an image. They wouldn't resist an image, like so many bands of their age and status had done. They wouldn't shrug it off as being the work of the devil. They wouldn't make the mistake of saying, 'It's all about the music.' They would have a look. Two of them would grow long beards. The other one, whose surname was Beard, wouldn't. They would wear sunglasses at all times, thereby drawing more attention to the beards. They were no longer just a band. Suddenly ZZ Top were a brand.

Whereas many of their contemporaries had to be dragged towards the MTV revolution, ZZ Top embraced it. They didn't put themselves front and centre in their videos. The prime position was likely to be occupied by somebody young and beautiful. The three members of the band would instead appear in the background like bushy spirits of mischief. The main star of their videos became the ZZ Top Eliminator Car, a fire-engine red 1933 coupé with yellow lightning symbols on the doors which they had built partly for fun after Gibbons had seen a similar one in the 1974 film *The California Kid*, and partly to be the representation of their brand.

Having changed their image they also souped up their sound. Like most groups in 1982 ZZ Top were suddenly being excited by the possibilities of working with devices that blurred the division between music and machines. In a *South Bank Show* in 1982 Peter Gabriel was filmed recording his new album. Viewers were enthralled to watch him record the sound of a glass smashing, store it on a floppy disc, and then play it back via the keyboard of his new Fairlight CMI. At the time effects like that, which the average mobile phone is capable of matching today, required a £30,000 investment. That was beginning to change. Gabriel correctly predicted that the combination of access to music from non-European cultures and the advent of cheap electronic equipment would usher in a new age of 'electronic skiffle'.

Billy Gibbons of ZZ Top was doing something similar in Memphis, albeit with less exalted intentions. Gabriel could save the world if he wanted. All Gibbons wanted was a hit record. Instead of going into the studio with his two fellow members of ZZ Top or starting off in a rehearsal studio trying to get them to play the song as he heard it in his head, as was the traditional way they would make a new album, he could now begin in the studio without their help. The only person whose assistance he needed, as would be the case with an increasing number of bands, was a technician-musician, somebody who could make all these inscrutable little boxes do his bidding. His particular amanuensis was called Linden Hudson. Hudson was the man who could set up the drum machine to play the tempo Gibbons wanted and also programme the bass to play along. Furthermore – and here the twenty-first century was arriving early – Hudson had done some desk research into what tempo was most likely to produce a hit record. The research told him that 120 beats per minute was the optimum. Thus Gibbons made the majority of the next album, which was called *Eliminator*, at 120 beats per minute – what came to be known as 'the People's Tempo'. It was a dance record. It was a container for hit singles. It was the audio version of the audio-visual product that had made them a success.

In late 1986, when *Eliminator* had gone on to sell ten million copies, the band agreed an out-of-court settlement with Hudson whereby he got $600,000 in exchange for relinquishing any claim he might have had on ownership of the song 'Thug' from the album. After the settlement Hudson decided to throw in his job with computers and try to become a musician, which proves once again the truth of the old saw that this is less a job than an incurable disease.

Even for a group as apparently traditional as ZZ Top the LP was changing. It was no longer a question of musicians in a studio simply playing their music and having it captured. It was no longer a question of people in their homes simply listening. It was no longer a question of the music on the record sparking pictures in the listener's imagination because the videos had provided all those pictures for them. Already in August 1982 a new product had been manufactured that would appear at first to be the salvation of the long-player but would ultimately be something else altogether.

AFTER 1982

'Who cares about the box?'

On 17 August 1982 the very first commercial compact disc was produced at Langenhagen in what was then still known as West Germany. The factory was owned by the Dutch electronics giant Philips. The CD in question was *The Visitors* by Abba, the Swedish group who recorded for CBS. As had been the case with the development of the long-player thirty years earlier, the CD had come to fruition because those two giant companies had developed it together, agreeing a common standard of manufacture in 1980 in order to avoid the VHS-Betamax wars that had slowed the rise of the video market. The name, borrowed from the Philips-developed Compact Cassette, was intended to stress the sheer amount of information that could be stored on this new medium.

The CD arrived with a lot of science talk behind it. Unveiling the new technology on BBC's popular science programme *Tomorrow's*

World in 1981, the presenter claimed there were no fewer than six billion microscopic pits on the disc representing the music and that if there was a track on a CD it would in effect be two and a half miles long. From the start the CD was presented as a miracle of science rather than an achievement of craft. Its manufacture called for particle-free environments, a world away from the smell and heat of the pressing plants in which records had traditionally been wrestled into life. How the CD actually worked was as much of a mystery to people as how record players worked, but they were convinced it was an advance. The presenter never did actually spread jam on the surface of the CD and then put it into the player to demonstrate that it still worked, nevertheless the idea took root early on that these discs were at the very least resistant to the thousand scratches and skips that vinyl was heir to and at the very best indestructible. This was much to the chagrin of the people who developed the CD. They felt its actual sound quality should be stressed over its durability. They knew that the latter was in any case still unproven.

Although some record companies were slow to embrace the CD and some felt another format so soon after cassette would only confuse the market, by March 1983 the *New York Times* was cautiously raising the possibility that compact discs might eventually replace the LP record. On the other hand, they noted that since the players still cost almost a thousand dollars, the discs were priced between sixteen and twenty, and only sixteen CBS titles were currently available, this might take a while. The records that companies chose to release on CD in the early days were skewed in favour of classical and other titles, such as Billy Joel's *52nd Street* and the Bee Gees' *Living Eyes*, that appealed to the older, more audiophile end of the pop market. By October of the following year the format had taken off enough for Columbia in the United States to open their first CD manufacturing plant, in Terre Haute, Indiana. Business had been brisk even before the introduction of the CD. Sales of recorded music across the market were 17 per cent ahead of where they had been the previous year, thanks in the main to cassette sales going up by 45 per cent. Retailers were expanding their stores in order to have more room to stock CDs alongside LPs and tapes. RCA announced that it was looking at changing the way it accounted for recording costs in order to encourage more pop acts to follow their classical artists by recording digitally.

The first CD manufactured in Terre Haute was *Born In The USA* by Bruce Springsteen, which was battling at the time for the number one LP spot with *Purple Rain* by Prince, Tina Turner's *Private Dancer* and the first album by Madonna. There was no better example of how the world had changed since *Thriller* than Bruce Springsteen's *Born In The USA*, which was released in the summer of 1984. *Thriller* had changed the way people made records. Jackson's videos had changed the way they promoted them. The unprecedented success of the entire project had further changed their ambitions for those records.

Years of touring had made Springsteen into a hugely popular act who could fill theatres and arenas everywhere he went. Nevertheless he was still a cult. To get him to the next stage he needed something altogether bigger. He needed a giant hit record, something that would put him in the front rank of American entertainers. Jackson had raised the stakes for everyone, and at the same time he made everyone else as calculating as he had been. While they were recording the new album, Springsteen's manager and producer Jon Landau told him that this album wouldn't even be coming out until he had written a big hit single to go on it. This was pressure he had never been under before. Eventually Springsteen wrote just such a song, but it was all about the impossibility of doing that kind of writing to order. The song 'Dancing In The Dark' said you couldn't possibly start a fire without a spark. It proved to be the hit song he needed. The lyrics were just the first of the ironies. What made the record eventually climb to the number two spot in the United States was not the bar band sound that had made Springsteen's name. What made the record was a dance beat as crunchingly discofied as Prince's 'When Doves Cry', Frankie Goes to Hollywood's 'Relax' and anything else that was filling club floors in 1984. That and a hook line that was delivered not by a guitar but by a synthesizer. To drive the point home, Arthur Baker was hired to produce a remix of the song purely for club play. Baker had become famous for his remixes of 'Walking On Sunshine' by Rockers Revenge, which had been the 'Jailhouse Rock' of the dance revolution, and he had gone on to turn Cyndi Lauper into a dance favourite with his remix of her 'Girls Just Wanna Have Fun'. If ZZ Top could make dance records then Bruce Springsteen would have to.

The dance message was further sealed with a video that featured Springsteen plucking a luscious girl out of the audience to dance with him – this was the first big break for *Friends* star Courteney Cox – a move that so successfully melted the hearts of the mass audience that Springsteen has been unable to play the song in public ever since without re-enacting the same ritual with everyone from small children to his elderly mother. Ten years on the road had made Bruce Springsteen rock famous. It took that video, painstakingly choreographed and rehearsed, about as raw and instinctive as a number from *West Side Story*, brought to the screen by Hollywood's Brian De Palma, to make him a different kind of famous – to make him shopping mall famous. The sheer power that MTV had in the middle of the eighties meant that it also established an idea of who Bruce Springsteen was that nothing he did subsequently could ever shift.

I interviewed him early in the tour that followed *Born In The USA* and asked him how he felt about that video. It was a problem, he said, because he didn't want to just act out the story of the song in the video because that didn't allow people to use their imaginations, but nor did he want to superimpose another narrative on the song other than the one that was there in the first place. However, commercial success has a habit of making such concerns evaporate. The video for 'Dancing In The Dark' was what most videos amounted to, simply an advert for the song. As a result more people listened to Bruce Springsteen's *Born In The USA* album than had listened to all his previous albums put together. It is doubtful that any of them listened in quite the same way people had listened to *Born To Run* or *Greetings From Asbury Park, N.J.* MTV took acts like Springsteen and put them in front of the vast, unhip audience that they had always craved. In so doing they changed the nature of the relationship between the fans and the mysterious figures behind the albums. Thanks to MTV their secret love was no secret any more.

The Columbia boss Al Teller recalled his feelings when he first became aware of the potential of MTV in the early 1980s. 'I thought two things: what a great marketing tool and this can prove to be a disaster. Unfortunately, number one is true and number two is true.' One of the reasons big seventies acts like the Who and Led Zeppelin were rarely seen on television was they considered it good business not to be on television. These groups were only available to you if you bought their album or a ticket for their show. Their records were bought by the kind of people who made it their business to go into record shops. Their tickets were bought by those who were sufficiently committed to queue up all night or send off their stamped addressed envelopes. These people would also be the people who bought music papers. Bands were not particularly in the business of trying to reach out to people beyond their following. The pursuit of music was a demanding activity. It was not for the uncommitted.

MTV changed all that. In 1981, the first year of its operation in the USA, the channel had 2.1 million subscribers. By 1983 it had over sixteen million. MTV's marketing slogan placed a plea in the mouth of teenagers all over the nation to the parents who paid the cable bill: 'I want my MTV'. Its appeal went far beyond the traditional core of a youth-oriented product. TV ensured that Michael Jackson's music spread far beyond the youth audience. By the time *Thriller* had been out a few months grandparents knew about the moonwalk, small children had learned the significance of Jackson's magic glove, and even businessmen could discuss the scale of his success. Once something becomes this popular the scale itself takes on a momentum of its own. Eventually even the people who weren't particularly drawn to his music began to feel that they ought to be. At the same time his videos, the spectacular nature of which echoed the values of Busby Berkeley or Gene Kelly, carried the spoor of his music far beyond the narrow confines of the United States and Western Europe.

In bald business terms, video provided the record companies with a way of reaching people they didn't normally reach with their products. It also gave them a way of prolonging the commercial life of the most profitable of those products, the album. Whereas record companies had previously been worried that releasing more than three tracks from an album as singles risked making the artists over-familiar, after the success of *Thriller* they were quite happy to release five or six. When they auditioned a new record from an established artist what they were looking for was something that might, as they put it, go 'six-deep'.

Often they were looking for singles that could be used as tools to prise open new sectors of the market. They wanted something they could take to rock radio, something else that might appeal to the country market, possibly even a ballad for the MOR moms or a hot dance tune that they could remix, and absolutely anything, like the title track of *Thriller*, that was largely an excuse for a blockbuster video. They were no longer worried about saturating the market. They wanted to saturate the market and then saturate it again with a different version of the same thing. Their plan was to market a record and keep on marketing it until the last remaining holdouts came staggering out of their homes with their hands up, falling to their knees and agreeing to buy the album.

Inevitably for this vastly increased audience the album became an audio memento of a visual experience rather than an entertainment in itself. Although *Thriller* hadn't been planned as a video album its life in the marketplace made it every bit as much a visual concept as it was a musical one. This had cost implications for Jackson and for everybody who came afterwards. When he made the video for 'Billie Jean' in early 1983 the budget was $50,000, which was top dollar at the time. On that occasion a request to hire some extra dancers was turned down by his record company because they would have cost $5,000. By the time he hired Bob Giraldi, an old-school TV commercials man, to shoot the video for 'Beat It', just a month later the budget had gone up to $200,000. MTV, still a little shaky in their early days, finally decided they were going to relax their policy of not programming videos by black artists – although at the time there weren't that many videos by any artists – and ran Jackson's videos. By the time he called movie director John Landis to make a fourteen-minute film of the title track of his album the budget was $500,000 and Jackson was paying for it out of his own pocket. In the course of that year Michael Jackson made MTV and MTV made Michael Jackson.

Following this the boom was on. That meant the sums of money being spent started to reflect the sums of money that could potentially be earned. John Taylor remembered 'for our first two albums, Duran Duran shot on video and worked very cheaply. After Michael Jackson, when American artists got a sense of a well-thought-out video, they started shooting on film and it became much more expensive.' The record business was suddenly a major customer of the film business. Increasing sums had to be spent every week on directors, cameramen, stylists, models, make-up artists, runners, drivers, scene makers, party people, weird-looking extras, Winnebagos and wind machines. The drugs it took to keep an exhausted band awake during an all-night shoot on some God-forsaken salt flats or in some derelict power station would be charged back under 'fruit and flowers'. Inevitably as they became more expensive the videos started to look more like commercials, aping the quick cuts and lip-smacking close-ups of Madison Avenue. Music had suddenly become a hard-sell business.

Nobody appeared to be bothered about The Man any more. ZZ Top hired the director Tim Newman to do their videos because his show reel included Coca-Cola. The first one they shot together was 'Gimme All Your Lovin''. It was done over a weekend to avoid paying union rates. This proved so popular that the record company told him to do exactly the same again. That was 'Sharp Dressed Man'. By the time they called him again to direct the video for 'Legs', Newman was asking for royalties on sales of their records, which was some indication of how a business which was supposed to be about music was increasingly about pictures. Billy Gibbons is acutely aware that MTV changed ZZ Top's career. They used to refer to their audiences as their 'sea of dudes'. Video changed all that. 'I still sign autographs for girls who say, "I was just thirteen and I couldn't wait to dress up like the girl in 'Legs'."'

Even as early as 1983 the video was beginning to overwhelm the music. In that year Pat Benatar's 'Love Is A Battlefield' became the first video to add dialogue that wasn't part of the original song in order to have the video make more sense. The singer Irene Cara didn't get to appear at all in the video for her big hit 'Flashdance . . . What A Feeling' because the film's star Jennifer Beals was tauter and more toned. Bonnie Tyler's 'Total Eclipse Of The Heart' was illustrated by a film which proposed her as a teacher at a boys' school, entertaining fantasies about her young pupils. Duran

Duran's 'Hungry Like The Wolf' took them to Sri Lanka and allowed them to indulge their fantasies of being Indiana Jones. Each new video had to become a story in itself. Magazines and newspapers, many of which had not previously had much interest in music, began devoting space to the storyboards of these videos and making minor personalities of the people with walk-on parts. Videos were suddenly the story. They were the kind of showbiz that everybody could understand.

Much as *Star Wars* changed the cinema from a stories business to a franchise business, the success of *Thriller*, which was indivisible from the success of MTV, changed music from a fast-moving world of small bets to a slow-moving world of giant wagers where the upside was huge and the downside was buried deep in the accounts. Now each album aspired to go six-deep and the act that made it would be kept on the road around the world for the better part of two years while the record company worked the record from every angle. Albums now came out every year or eighteen months and would not be let go until they had been wrung dry. By the time later buyers of an album came aboard, early adopters would never want to hear the damned record ever again.

By 1989 cassettes were the most popular music carrier in the United States with 65 per cent of the market. CDs came second with 26 per cent. Vinyl was a poor third with 9 per cent. As early as 1985 CD players had effectively replaced record players in the homes of the kind of people who would have regarded themselves as music fans. They were also beginning to appeal to a wider audience. No visit to a large store was complete without the sound of Dire Straits' *Brothers In Arms*, the first million-selling CD, being used to demonstrate the new player's crisp separation of the music and the almost eerie silence between notes. The CD player was one of those products that sold itself. Even the people who might have had trouble explaining what it was about the sound of CD that was supposed to be an improvement could point to the things it didn't have.

CD held out the promise of 'perfect sound for ever' but the thing that clinched it for most people was that you no longer had to put up with the accidental scratches, impurities in the vinyl and short-comings in the reproduction equipment which had combined throughout the age of the LP to produce what we all called surface noise. Surface noise was a fact of life. Reflecting on any large record collection that had undergone the standard amount of weathering and collateral damage was much like reflecting on one's own teen-age children. You love them unconditionally, of course, but you can never entirely suppress the thought that they were nicer when they were new. Nevertheless, wear and tear is what life is all about. As the DJ John Peel was fond of observing, 'Life has surface noise.'

Perfect sound is a chimera because recorded sound is in itself an illusion. It involves the conversion of a musical performance into a series of electrical impulses which are subsequently decoded by a machine in the home. It can never be perfect. It can only ever be pleasing. CD was pleasing because it didn't have any of the obvious sounds of imperfection, it didn't require a steady hand to start it or finish it (in fact you barely needed to touch it at all), and you could put it on and leave the room, knowing that when it came to the end your precious stylus would not be in danger of colliding with the label. Contrast this with a record, which could no more be left on its own in a room than a puppy or a toddler. What's more it was digital, a transformation that everybody agreed was a massive improve-ment without entirely understanding why.

The early CDs were expensive, which didn't put anyone off. Actu-ally people expected to pay more for such a great leap forward. Many of the CDs they spent their money on were not the new thing. They were the old thing. Some record companies, suddenly faced with a completely unsought bonanza of North Sea oil proportions, made terrible errors in their rush to put out all the old favourites on CD. In many cases these were manufactured from unsatisfactory fifth-generation tapes which in turn had been generated from crudely panned stereo versions. They were mostly disappointing. I had been enjoying the Rolling Stones' *Aftermath* in unapologetic mono ever since it came out in 1966 and I could listen round the scratches on 'Mother's Little Helper'. The first CD version that appeared seemed to put the entire band in one channel, leaving the other one for Mick Jagger's heavy breathing and a single tambourine. It sounded clear, clean and pristine. It also sounded preposterous.

Not every record company appeared to appreciate that the records which had made small fortunes for them at the time of their initial release might yet make far more money for them in this new world where they could suddenly command higher prices. They didn't yet fully believe, as the book business already did, in the value of catalogue. They were still obsessed with the new thing. The independent company Rykodisc set itself up as a CD-only company in 1984 and managed to get the rights to back-catalogue albums by David Bowie, Jimi Hendrix and Frank Zappa because the major companies that would normally have had the rights didn't consider the artists big enough priorities to get behind or believe that their old fans would ever be interested in buying them on CD.

At one end the growth in the CD market was driven by the former LP buyers who simply had to have the very latest and apparently best form of musical reproduction. At the other end of the spectrum it appealed to the same cassette buyers who regarded music as a convenience. CDs were easier to handle and store than LPs and they fitted easily into the average UK living room, which had been getting smaller since the middle of the 1970s.

The problem was – and nobody thought about this at the time – CD as a medium never had any charisma about it. Nobody ever flaunted a CD. Nobody walked down the street with one. Nobody went round to somebody's house and asked to look through their CDs. Whereas the fabulous creation that those engineers and executives had come up with in the late 1940s had the happy effect of making the music it carried seem more important than it was, the CD did the opposite. It reduced the music much as it reduced the package. Compact disc demystified music and in so doing reduced the status of those who made it.

The long-playing record seemed a minor miracle even to the people who made them. That's why so many of them were named after the form itself. The Beatles' *Revolver* is the most famous but there are many others: in 1969 the Welsh rock group Man put out a record called *2 Ozs Of Plastic With A Hole In The Middle*; Keith Moon, Dave Van Ronk, Dick Gregory and T. S. McPhee were just a few of the hundreds of artists who had something called *Two Sides Of*; Bob Dylan, Marvin Gaye, Ella Fitzgerald and Ronnie Laws are four of the many who have gone for variations on *In The Groove*. *Plastic Letters* by Blondie, *Fragile* by Yes and Public Image's *Metal Box* were other records that celebrated the form's materiality in their titles.

In the same way that the majority of people wouldn't care to back their ability to detect a qualitative difference between one recording and another in a blind test, our perception of the quality of sound is always influenced by what we are told about it and what we can see with our eyes and feel with our hands. When we listened to long-playing records on vinyl we were looking at something large and soulful while feeling in our hands paper and cardboard. When we listened to the same records on CD we were looking at something small, where the images were tiny and unimpressive and the words were often illegible, and there was nothing more than cold, unyielding plastic in our hands.

In 2010, on the occasion of the sixtieth birthday of Elektra Records, I spoke to the label's founder Jac Holzman. Elektra was the label most often associated with the virtues of good taste where the product was concerned and sensitivity where the artists were concerned, virtues which all record labels big and small like to feel that they are continuing. Looking back on his unique experience, which encompassed the LP era, the CD era and, by 2010, the download era, Holzman was clear there was one thing he regretted more than any other. 'I cannot believe,' he said, 'that the record business threw away its most powerful tool, which was the jacket of the twelve-inch album.'

Martin Young is a dealer in recorded music of all kinds. In the eighties and nineties he watched the CD tide come in and then go out. As a music fan he wasn't immediately converted to CD but eventually had to give in. 'The annoying thing about CDs is that eventually they always had extra tracks like remixes or duff B-sides and completists didn't want to be left out. Therefore you bought the CD and then played the extra track once and never again. It's like most things. You don't want it but you do want it.' Young remembers the tipping point for CD coming in 1988. By then the major record companies were refusing to accept vinyl returns from retailers. 'The big event was the big HMV sale in 1988. They just virtually dumped vinyl from all of their stores. Everything was 99p.'

On both sides of the Atlantic the retailers couldn't wait to see the back of the LP (although twelve-inch vinyl singles were still the music carrier of choice for dance DJs) and refit their shops so that they could sell larger quantities of this smaller, significantly more profitable format. In the USA the switchover took longer to achieve and involved a five-year period during which CDs were all sold in the controversial 'long box' format. This was a six-inch-by-twelve-inch presentation box that was twice the size of the CD. This satisfied the retailer's requirement for something that could fit into their old record racks and also be big enough to discourage theft.

Each of these long boxes had to be ripped apart before you could get to the CD inside. This meant that the container the music came in, which had previously been of equal value to the record itself, was now the first thing you destroyed and threw in the nearest bin. It would be difficult to imagine a chore more calculated to degrade the mystique around and the value accorded to any product. 'Who cares about the box?' says one shopper interviewed outside Tower on Broadway in 1990. 'I only care about the music.'

Much was made of the fact that the CD could accommodate a playing time of over seventy minutes, which was almost twice that of an LP record. In some cases, such as the 1987 CD issue of Bob Dylan's *Blonde On Blonde*, CBS faded tracks earlier when first remastering the record for CD, in order to get a short double album on to a single disc. As time went by the available playing time increased gradually, which meant there was a temptation to include extra tracks, which suited the marketing effort, rather than leave them out, which could enhance the listening experience. This temptation to long-windedness, which might have been expected to be appealing only to the artistically incontinent, turned heads far beyond the precincts of progressive rock. The first CD to boast that it was offering more than eighty minutes of music was from Mission of Burma, a post-punk band most of whose songs struggled to get to four minutes.

The addition of extra tracks, usually B-sides, live versions or remixes, may have nudged a few waverers at the checkout but after the first couple of plays they were as injurious to the integrity of the original album experience as an extra chapter would be if placed in a Jane Austen novel. The problem is that people always think they want more even when experience teaches that they don't. I have a French edition of Miles Davis's music for the film *Ascenseur pour l'échafaud* which includes all the outtakes. Therefore at the end of the mood-setting opening track you get another version of the same thing, which is about as irritating as it would be if you read a book where chapter one was followed by a less polished version of the same chapter. All through the eighties almost all albums came with stickers offering extra this or bonus that to try to convert the consumer at point of sale. By the end of the decade this kind of thinking had entered the business's bloodstream to such an extent that the marketing tail was now gleefully whirling the industry dog above its head.

When the long-awaited Springsteen live box set was released in 1986, causing unprecedented hysteria at retail, people's excitement at simply being able to buy it made headline news all over the world. Millions of people who in all truth could live without a Bruce Springsteen live album were stopping the traffic in their efforts to get hold of it. The album release story became a regular feature of the record retailing landscape into the next decade with mega retailers like HMV, Tower and Virgin keeping their increasingly enormous premises open at special hours on the day of a new one from U2 or Oasis. It was invariably the case that the greater the fuss made at the time of release the less enthusiastic everybody was about it a few weeks later. Suddenly album release dates were big stories that made the national news. This was because the rock generation were now in power. Rolling Stones fans had grown to be captains of industry. The people who had sat through Pink Floyd doing 'Careful With That Axe, Eugene' now sat astride the wheels of the media. The sub-culture was now the dominant culture. Scale became a story in itself.

When the Springsteen box came out it was available on record, cassette, CD and even eight-track, but things were starting to move decisively in the direction of CD. The major companies moved over to manufacturing CDs rather than vinyl. In time this manufacture would be outsourced to low-wage economies where it could be done more cheaply. CD manufacture didn't call for the same old craft and engineering skills that Roy Matthews had been so proud of when he ran EMI's pressing plant at Hayes. In fact the record companies weren't actually record companies any longer. They no longer made records. Instead they were in the business of exploiting intellectual property. Once you had the machinery, making a CD was an easy business, and, as the record business was to discover, making a copy of a CD was even easier. Once everyone had a personal computer, sharing that copy was easiest of all. CD had raised the price of the album while reducing its value. It was about to be reduced as far as it could be reduced: the same technology that had rescued the record business at the end of the twentieth century was about to turn around in the twenty-first century and eat it.

BEYOND 1990

Played Just Once

By the end of the twentieth century sales of CDs in the United States had reached a level which not even the most optimistic boosters of the format could have envisaged. In 1999 almost one billion were shipped in the United States alone. The economic growth throughout the decade had been far greater than anyone expected. People felt wealthier and therefore they spent money more freely. Even though they were more expensive than their forerunner, the LP, people seemed considerably more relaxed about buying CDs. In the UK a CD could be priced as high as fifteen pounds but would be sold at a discount by increasingly competitive high-street retailers fighting for a share of this gold rush. These high profit margins paid for more expensive marketing campaigns and even more extreme indulgences of the egos of the people who made the records. When Michael Jackson released an album in 1995 he insisted his record company mark the occasion by commissioning nine statues of him, each over thirty feet tall. The one that was sent to London was floated on a barge down the Thames.

An increasing number of new releases were promoted via Friday night TV ads exhorting viewers to cut along to Virgin or HMV or Our Price to pick up the latest release. London's Oxford Street was home to more than one megastore, each of which had its entire frontage open to the street so that passers-by seemingly could not help but tumble into the place. Here they would be confronted by stacks of shrink-wrapped copies of the new releases, lined up in intimidatingly large quantities. The sheer plenty on display was at first exciting and then enervating. Buying a CD in this kind of environment seemed more akin to an act of surrender than to an expression of devotion.

I had a friend at the time who was a manager in one of these shops. I would visit him on Friday afternoons as the week was winding down. Some people who had stopped work at lunchtime had been to the pub and were now doing some shopping on the way home. The two of us would watch middle-aged men cruising the racks, a wire basket over one arm into which they would toss CDs, as if in a daze, as much because they could afford them as because they wanted them. Some CDs were old, some were new, others belonged to a new genre that was clearly designed to sound old, such as *Play* by Moby, which combined Alan Lomax's old field recordings of gospel singers with commercials-friendly electronics. They might throw in Sigur Rós, fast becoming the soundtrack of ethereal commerce, or, for old times' sake, David Bowie's twenty-first album, which was called *Hours* and would be forgotten rather more quickly than *Hunky Dory* had been. A CD like this they would probably play just once and never again. Then they might chuck in a box set of old Duke Ellington recordings which were out of copyright and therefore could be purchased for the price of a hamburger;

and then maybe a DVD of one of those smart, knowing, hard-boiled TV series with which people were increasingly beguiling their time. 'Fifty-pound blokes' is how my friend described this tribe. They were the people who had once saved up every penny they had to buy records. Now they could afford to put fifty pounds' worth of them on their credit card without feeling the pinch. It was a different kind of record buying.

By the mid-nineties, when the record business was clearly enjoying such a boom as it had never seen before and would never see again, when all its ancillary industries such as the music press and the video production sector were also enjoying the riches that fell from its table, an increasing number of people were beginning to feel emotionally short-changed by the CD. It was clearly not a medium that you warmed to over time. I heard many variations on the argument about how warm analogue sound trumps the colder digital kind. This argument appeared to be supported by illustrations of wave forms whose sensual rises and falls stood in soulful contrast to the icy peaks and troughs of their digital equivalent. What many people complained of was the feeling that CD was somehow more tiring to listen to. Engineers explained that this was the result of the way increasing numbers of CDs were mastered to sound as loud as possible so that they punched through on the radio. They might also have been more tiring to listen to because they were getting longer and longer. *Jagged Little Pill*, the breakthrough album by Alanis Morissette, was almost an hour long. The follow-up was almost an hour and a quarter, which meant it was over twice as long as Joni Mitchell's *Blue*.

Sound quality is never not subjective. If you are intellectually convinced that something has been done to the sound to make it better you will tend to agree that it has succeeded. In the late seventies a British hi-fi engineer called Peter Belt even argued that it was possible to improve the sound of recorded music in your room by placing specially treated paperclips over some of your album covers or by placing a single sheet of paper beneath your speakers. Those who took his steps convinced themselves they could actually hear the improvement. Since recorded music only sounds good when we are emotionally prepared for it, who's to say that they weren't right?

In 1992 I asked Neil Young, who was promoting his album *Harvest Moon* at the time and had been foremost among the rock names criticizing the quality of digital sound, to explain what he meant. He went through the technical rigmarole and lost me but his most winning point went as follows. 'Remember when you rolled a joint and just put *Harvest* on the deck and had the cover on your knee? Remember how good the music used to feel? I think that's how music should be heard.'

I can't help but sympathize with him. That experience certainly outshone the experience of listening to *Harvest Moon* on a CD player in the office or the car. Some of that may be down to the superior warmth of analogue sound. Some will be down to the fact that when we heard *Harvest* we were all in our twenties and none of us had heard anything quite like it before. You can be thrilled by an artist's fourth or fifth album. It's difficult to imagine being similarly thrilled by the artist's nineteenth. In the 1990s a lot of artists were coming around for the nineteenth time.

In spite of any misgivings they may have had, everybody embraced what seemed like the future. Starting in the middle of the eighties many of the people who'd bought *Harvest* when it first came out in 1972 had begun to dump their vinyl collections. Eventually there were so many that charity shops couldn't cope with the quantities. It was hard to move for all the apparently unloved vinyl copies of Paul Young's *No Parlez*, Phil Collins' *Face Value* or the Human League's *Dare*. Many people simply threw theirs away at the local dump. The DJ Johnnie Walker, then working in San

Francisco, was asked by his ex-wife what he wished to be done with his collection of LPs back in London. 'Sell them,' he said.

The CD boom of the nineties benefited the most unlikely people. America's best-selling album of 1995 was the first record by the singularly anonymous Hootie & the Blowfish. In that year over seven million Americans somehow felt moved to buy Hootie's CD. It seemed nobody could go wrong. The Berlin Wall was down, the world had opened up and more and more countries now had their own market for recorded music. This meant that *Spice*, the first album by the Spice Girls, which came out in 1996, sold over thirty million copies worldwide. It was number one in seventeen countries. Hilariously, this debut by a group that had been unblushingly assembled for the sole purpose of accumulating mountains of cash was on the Virgin label, which had been instituted twenty years earlier to bring the inner-directed works of Mike Oldfield, Henry Cow and Kevin Coyne to the world. At the time prices of CDs were so high that Virgin was earning a clear five pounds in profit for every Spice Girls CD they sold.

The soundtrack for the Whitney Houston film *The Bodyguard*, which was released in 1992, became the first album to sell more than a million copies in just one week. That was in the United States alone. The English musician Nick Lowe, who had been making critically approved but commercially hopeless albums since the early seventies, found that one of his own songs was covered on the album by Curtis Stigers. Its inclusion on that soundtrack earned him more than a million dollars, more than he earned from the rest of his recording career put together. Even *Nevermind*, the album by Nirvana, the group whose ambitions were as modest as any group who thought themselves underground, sold almost ten million copies in the United States. The members of the band went from selling copies of their self-produced single for cash in order to buy food to being millionaires almost overnight. The majority of those copies of *Nevermind* were on CD with a smaller percentage on cassette. None were on vinyl. It didn't come out on vinyl until 1996 when a specialist label released an audiophile version. By then the only people who wanted vinyl were dance DJs and the people who ran jukeboxes. In 1995 the American record industry shipped a total of two million vinyl LPs in the entire year. At that time Alanis Morissette was selling approximately that many copies of her *Jagged Little Pill* on CD every month.

In August 1997 the Manchester rock group Oasis released their third album. Its two predecessors had both been huge successes with the public. This time the media and the music business resolved not to be caught making insufficient fuss. *Be Here Now* came in a cover featuring a Rolls-Royce in a swimming pool. Since the cover was less than five inches across all that money appeared to have been expended in pursuit of a significance the format could no longer sustain. *Be Here Now* was released in the midst of an unprecedented hullabaloo in the pop press. Since the newspapers had discovered that music coverage sold copies, the pop press now meant all the press. The record was released to ecstatic reviews, the kind that records get when reviewers are trying to make up for the fact that they may not have been sufficiently enthusiastic about previous records and are determined not to be remiss this time. Oasis didn't have to hype their record. Britain hyped their record for them.

In his book about Britpop, John Harris says that you would have had to go back to the release of *Sgt Pepper's Lonely Hearts Club Band* to find an album that had attracted 'gushing notices in such profusion'. This is fair, although few of the reviews of *Sgt Pepper* at the time had anything like the same air of certainty as the reviews of *Be Here Now*, all of which seemed convinced that Oasis had made a record that met the expectations that had been raised. This had been made more pressing by the fact that at every stage in their rise to fame in the UK Oasis had encouraged parallels between their career and that of the Beatles, in which many in the media who should have known better had been only too happy to collude. That was because Oasis didn't just sell records. They also sold magazines. They drove ratings on TV and radio programmes. They got people into the record shops. They moved voters. Oasis were invited to Downing Street. It was even argued that they contributed to a renewed sense of national self-confidence. Certainly they seemed to be everywhere. Pop music was far deeper in the national bloodstream than it had ever been in the Swinging Sixties. In its first week, *Be Here Now* sold just under 700,000 copies in the UK alone. It went into the *Billboard* chart at number two.

Oasis never went so high again. In years to come somebody would suggest that an alternative title for *Be Here Now* should be *Played Just Once*. In years to come people would even argue that *Be Here Now* was the record most likely to be found in second-hand bins. There had been clues there in the recording process. Even Liam Gallagher, the singer, thought that the songs, written by his brother Noel, weren't up to much. Noel may have thought the same himself because he had chosen to cover over any shortcomings in the material with up to thirty guitar overdubs. Recorded in a blizzard of cocaine and helmed by a producer who wasn't experienced enough to employ the most valuable word in the producer's lexicon, which is 'enough', *Be Here Now* was a record that was so determined to be a behemoth that it had no inner life, no small charm; it was innocent of all modesty. It was built for victory or surrender. It set out to be a globe-girdling, precedent-setting, era-defining, legend-making success or nothing at all. In the end it turned out to be nothing at all.

At the same time, in Kings Mountain, North Carolina the clock had begun ticking on this apparently unstoppable business. It was here that two employees at a plant producing CDs had worked out a way to smuggle pre-release CDs past the security guards. At first it was done for laughs and beer money. They would take something out – preferably an upcoming release by stars like Mary J. Blige or Eminem – and, using their expensive home computers, rip a copy. Then, using the CD burner which they had bought, they would make a copy and sell it for five dollars to whoever was having a party that weekend. It began to become more profitable when they bought equipment that could make the rip and burn process quicker. When they made contact with the small number of people who were beginning to exchange music via the internet, their hobby became a lot more profitable.

Even in the days when the chosen medium was cassette and the process of copying had to be done in real time with mistakes only undone after a lot of effort, home copying had had its attractions. As soon as it became simply a question of converting the music on a CD back into files and then being able to move around, reshuffle and manipulate those files, it started to feel like a creative act of its own. When CD was first demonstrated to the bosses of the music business one of the few who wasn't convinced was Maurice Oberstein, at the time the managing director of Polygram in the UK. His question was simply, 'Do you realize we're giving away our master tapes here?'

Apparently, nobody did realize. They couldn't imagine that copying a CD would ever be anything but a difficult process calling for special equipment and specialist skills. They couldn't foresee a situation where just about anybody could produce their own CDs, just as the record companies did. When that situation came to pass they couldn't believe it. The general public had never imagined they could make a copy of an LP record that would be an adequate replacement for the real thing. They could easily see how you did that with a CD.

Once you put anything on the hard drive of a computer you

diminish the thing you have imported and elevate the status of the person doing the importing. Once Jackson Browne's 'Late For The Sky', Jacqueline du Pré's performance of Elgar's Cello Concerto and 'Roast Fish And Cornbread' by Lee Perry are lining up alongside your bank statements, some footage of a cat chasing a ball of wool and an email from your office, nothing can ever quite restore the special regard you had for the song when it was a track on a record. As soon as you could see your favourite few moments of music as a neat little waveform it could never be quite the same, much as *Catcher in the Rye* wouldn't be the same if the first time you had read it it had been as a file in a word processing programme. As soon as you could copy a track yourself you felt like God, and the artist was simply one of your subjects.

Some people were ripping and burning for profit. Many more were doing it for fun. They were just people who had a lot of CDs and this seemed like a splendid way to increase the amount of fun they could have with those CDs. One of the first things they did was go to their favourite albums and rip just the two tracks they actually liked from that album to put on their own compilation. They seemed to believe what Phil Spector had believed: an album was two hits plus whatever else was around. Fans of electronic dance music, which was growing in popularity at the same time, thought about music in terms of favourite 'tunes' rather than in terms of favourite musicians. When the DJ, who was beginning to become as big a star as the person whose records he spun, played one they happened to like they held up a card on which was written the single cheery word 'Tune!' Whole generations came to adulthood referring to their music collection as 'my tunes'.

In 2001, when most people were still using a dial-up modem and an iMac had only enough storage space to keep maybe a hundred tracks, this was still something for hobbyists who were prepared to spend time to achieve their results. Most MP3 players had pitifully little storage and were unfathomably hard to navigate. It was then that Steve Jobs decided it would be a priority for Apple to develop a user-friendly player. Jobs talked about music being his passion. This was an expression that was hardly ever heard before the age of computers. We heard it a lot over the subsequent ten years as the value in music was shifted from the people who made the music to the people who moved it around. Nobody who made their fortune in the digital revolution ever uttered the truth, which was that their true passion was computers.

Apple's player was the iPod. 'Rip. Mix. Burn.' said the adverts, stressing the fun you could have while destroying the LP experience. The iPod quickly became a phenomenon even greater than recorded music itself. It reflected the way people wanted to listen to music, which was on the move, and also the music they wanted to listen to, which was as a series of individual tunes rather than in sequences put together for the benefit of a medium that had effectively vanished. There was another thing. Our feelings about music carriers were never exclusively rational and the iPod was no exception. People formed an attachment to their iPods. They liked looking at them, feeling them and spending time with them. The iPod (and subsequently the iPhone) couldn't help but be more exciting than any of the individual items of music that were stored on it. Much as you could refill an empty water bottle from the tap, it was the work of a moment to top up your iPod with fresh tunes. By 2007, when sales of CDs had already halved from their 1999 peak, a story was doing the rounds within the music business about the band who had stopped selling their CD after their gigs because they had discovered that it had eaten into the sales of the item from which they made most money – their T-shirt.

By this time a younger generation who had grown up in the days of the CD were starting to feel some nostalgia for something they had never had. Fifteen years ago, when my son was sixteen, I arrived home to find my work room at the top of the house occupied by him and half a dozen of his fellow sixth-formers. Nothing I possessed had previously been considered worthy of the attention of such a deputation before. The thing that had drawn them was the rumour of a sizeable accumulation of long-playing records. They sat there looking at them with the same slack-jawed amazement with which they had previously regarded vintage sports cars. That was when I began to realize that I had something most people no longer had. Most of their parents would have had something similar in the past but they had all given in to the inevitable and traded it in during the great clear-out of the late eighties. That was my first glimpse of the kind of future that was lining up for the LP. It would take its place alongside the Moleskine notebook as a signifier of how people wished the world was rather than how it actually was.

Nobody seemed to have any qualms about getting rid of their CDs when their time came. In due course DVDs would be let go with similar ease. There was something about this combination of plastic, paper and carbon fibre that failed to engender the same warmth we felt about the combination of plastic and paper which was the long-player. When it came to questions of love rather than utility, the CD's durability actually counted against it. Whereas people would talk about 'my copy' of an LP as if this properly reflected what they saw as its uniqueness, they saw their CD as being much like anyone else's CD, impervious to the marks of ownership and thus infinitely replaceable. Once you knew you could take a CD apart, reorder it or remove the parts you didn't like, it was just another carrier, just another organization of noughts and ones that would ultimately require no carrier at all. Music had been something you could have and hold. Soon you would no longer be able to have and hold it. It would simply be sent down a phone line. Thanks to streaming services you would no longer need to buy. You could simply rent it instead.

There is, of course, a vinyl revival. Stories about the comeback of this plucky old survivor are now a media favourite. This comeback is celebrated by the same radio stations that no longer have either record decks or CD players and only play the music that is on the company's hard drive. This Lazarus-like return from the lip of oblivion is trumpeted by the same newspapers that in the nineties gave away millions of free CDs that nobody played in order to get a 5 per cent uplift on their news-stand sale. The very record shops that were most keen to rip out their LP racking and replace it with CDs, which offered more profit per square foot, now pretend they were in the LP's corner all along. The indie supergroups make sure they put their records out on vinyl because they know there are a proportion of their fans who will demand them and will pay far more for them than anyone would have paid back in the days when vinyl was the leading format. Statistics wheeled out to demonstrate the scale of the comeback usually avoid the fact that the unit sales of vinyl LPs are still tiny compared to the seventies. When you can charge over twenty pounds for an album you don't need to sell that many of them to make your numbers look good.

The vinyl revivalists do well out of the fact that the market they're catering to doesn't actually exist for the majority of people. Since the big companies no longer manufacture, a small pressing plant has a full order book and can charge premium prices. Since the big high-street retailers have gone it's possible for a handful of small retailers to make a living catering to the hardcore. The people who campaign for vinyl to come back would probably resent it if vinyl did come back because the first thing it would do is decimate the value of the things they carefully squirrel away. The vinyl market is something like the market for organic food. It may be growing slightly. It may be able to charge higher prices. It will be lucky if, like the market for organic food, it gets to the point where it accounts for even 2 per cent of the total market.

But what about the album itself? Does it have a future? Does anybody apart from the band who've just spent their money making an album actually want it at all? It never did make any sense to download an album. On the internet, the album appears as a shopping list of songs. Only an idiot wouldn't realize it's an invitation to make your own selection rather than take the selection inside the bag that somebody has pre-packed. There will be a small number of fans who will continue to listen as closely as possible in the way the artist intended them to listen. For them it will be a token of their earnest. There are a handful of artists, such as Tom Waits, who have this kind of relationship with their listeners. The overwhelming majority of people won't listen like that. The overwhelming majority of people don't feel the way the fans feel.

In July 2018 the *New York Times* ran a story about *Scorpion*, the fifth album by the Canadian hip hop star Drake. Drake is arguably the biggest star in popular music today and *Scorpion* was on its way to being his biggest album yet by all the measures the music business uses today. One of those measures is that in the three days following its release it was streamed 435 million times. You will not have seen *Scorpion* displayed in a record shop window because there aren't many record shops left these days. Nor will you have seen a proud Drake fan flaunting his copy of the CD on the top of a bus because, according to the *New York Times* story, there were very few copies around. They called sixteen stores around and about New York and found that only six of them had the CD. In total they found those shops had sold a mere sixteen copies. The shops said that if it came out on vinyl they might order a few but not a whole lot more.

On the same day this story was published the BPI, the body representing the UK music business, announced its first National Album Day. On one hand you have the market signalling loudly and clearly that it no longer has need of something. At the same time the business seeks to persuade the market it is mistaken in feeling this way. You can see why the business wants to do this. The albums were always where their profit was. Ever since the advent of streaming unbundled the album and allowed people to take just the track they wanted and nothing more they have been trying to persuade people back to album buying. The record companies and the artists are on the same page here. They both still want to make albums, even though there is very little indication that people want to buy them. It makes money. It justifies tours. It keeps the business rolling on. Artists also want to make an album for the same reason that most writers think they've got a novel in them. It's the thing that gets them up in the morning. It's the thing that they want to tell their friends about. It proves they're serious. They're the kind of people who make albums. They're in the same trade as REM, the Beatles and Marvin Gaye.

Art can't buck the market. Charles Dickens' novels were the length they were because they were published in twenty monthly instalments. People who could never have afforded to buy his books could afford to pay for those instalments. He didn't know what the ending of the book was going to be when he started out. He was paid per instalment and he had to keep people reading, which is why each of his novels has twenty cliffhangers. As the cinema has declined and Netflix has become the number one customer for the film industry, writers and directors have recovered the same knack for cliffhangers. When Dickens found he couldn't get any royalties out of the American market he went over there and toured, much as the Rolling Stones have done.

There's no earthly reason why music should continue to occur to musicians in units of forty minutes. The early LPs were the length they were because of the technical limitations and the need to accommodate a symphony. The symphony was the length it was because forty minutes was as long as people in the nineteenth century could be expected to listen without needing to stretch their legs. The Beatles devoted the same running time to recording their stage act. Albums continued to be the length they were because that was roughly the amount of material a band could come up with in a year.

Over the last twenty years many of the things we were formerly so attached to have passed from the realm of the physical to the virtual. The LP record has more of a claim on us than, say, the film camera, which has been no less demystified and disintermediated by the smartphone. That's not because of what it is. It's because of what it signifies for us. It's because of the part of our life that it reawakens and makes us yearn for. The LP has a strong appeal to the heart, something which is above and beyond all questions of analogue versus digital, microgroove versus MP3, the big cover or the small cover, the discreet charm of your local record shop versus the frictionless, passionless sensation of downloading something remotely. It's because we're human beings.

Tim Milne's speciality is the relationship between digital and actual objects. Like me, he's a member of the generation who are digital immigrants, who started off doing everything in the real world and have witnessed its transformation into the digital equivalent and have thus been provided with a unique opportunity to see the differences and resemblances between the two. Tim works on the borders between design and digital and therefore has done a lot of thinking about how things which once were physical objects we could hold in our hands are now invisible processes. He thinks we're at a unique point in human history where the physical world has migrated into a million inscrutable machines. We used to be able to see how many of the machines did the things they did. As we watched a record revolve we could see how the expensive cartridge danced on the end of the precisely balanced arm, how the brand-new stylus deciphered the lovingly buffed sheen of the surface of the disc, what label it was on, which side was playing, and how far it had to go before we might turn it over. Now we simply press buttons to command things to be done for us.

As Tim observes, our soul rebels against this. We demand that things still look the way they used to even though there's no earthly reason why they should. Word-processing programs that work their voodoo by reshuffling zeroes and ones at inconceivable speeds are set before us as if they were ancient books with pages and margins and chapter marks in the scriptorium of some Victorian gentleman of letters. The engine of a piece of recording software such as GarageBand works in exactly the same way as the software that sorts out your taxes. That's why we demand that its front end must be designed to look like our sentimental, nostalgic idea of the kind of desk George Martin was looking at when he committed 'I Saw Her Standing There' to tape in 1963. And it's not only digital immigrants like me who want things to look like the things they replaced. There's a sizeable cohort of young enthusiasts who have rebelled against the way the rest of their generation consumes music and think that the LP record represents in some sense the proper way. As Tim Milne says, 'The world has changed the meaning of the LP and we still crave the old meaning.'

A survey in 2017 found that Americans listen to music more than thirty-two hours a week. That was a significant increase on the year before and the year before that. They also spend that time listening to more music, which means they are spending less time on each piece of music and less time on each artist. A lot of the time they're browsing. A Spotify stream has to play for longer than thirty seconds for the artist to be paid. In writing about 2018 releases by Post Malone and Rae Sremmurd, the *New York Times* suggested that the acts that were prospering in the new world of streaming were deliberately obliterating the gaps between tunes so that listeners were given fewer and fewer reasons to click to another stream. Their music intentionally avoided the builds and climaxes of the old medium. They were no longer thinking about people sitting down in their living rooms and engaging in the ceremony of playing a record. They weren't setting out to produce anything that satisfied people. Instead theirs was music built for travelling and never arriving. This, when you think about it, is the natural condition of the internet. We only have to think about our own behaviour online to know how restless the internet has made us. Its defining characteristic is browsing. It's clicking. It's moving listlessly from page to page. What these two acts provide is music that never gives the listener any reason to move away. It proceeds at one pace as if it were all one very long single. It's the ideal solution to the problem of competing in the attention economy. Avoid boredom by avoiding excitement.

If we had possessed thousands of albums back in the days of physical product we would have had difficulty deciding what to play. This is something that unbelievers would point out to us. My mother used to stand over my accumulation of LPs, an accumulation that appeared to her to be a bewildering quantity, and she would plead, 'But you can't play them all.' Now all of us have access to the biggest record collection in the world. We really can't play them all. Her words ring truer than ever. Our dreams have come true. And now, as we're discovering, that's never a good thing.

In 1967, at the dawning of the era of the LP, it seemed that most recorded music was in the present or in the future. It's inevitably the case that as time goes on the bulk of it is in the past. More and more people will be going back as there's more to go back to. It's equally inevitable that the increasing number of people who come to it as the music of the past will be drawn to the form in which it first appeared as if that were special and unique. To a certain extent it was, and the great flowering of popular music between *Sgt Pepper* and *Thriller*, during the imperium of this fabulous creation, wouldn't have happened if there had been a better way for performers to fulfil their artistic ambitions and the business to reach its fiscal objectives at the same time.

Nevertheless, in the end it's not about the vinyl. Nor is it about the cover. It's not even about the unique qualities of the people who made the records that we hold most dear. It's certainly not about being whisked back to some special time in our life.

The LP record retains its symbolic power because it speaks to us of something that has gone from our lives. That's something which has been driven out of our lives at our own urging, as we have eagerly embraced each new technological distraction and declared that we really don't know how we lived without it.

If you're one of those people who let their LPs go, that doesn't have to be the end. In the end you can always get yourself a new record deck. You can fill your room with the very best loudspeakers. You can spend your money on a pristine new copy of your favourite album. It can be produced on the highest-quality vinyl. It can feel reassuringly weighty in your hand. You can afford it. That bit is easy.

The really difficult bit will be convincing yourself that for the next forty minutes you have nothing better to do than listen to that record. Because that's how it was back in the golden age of the LP. It seemed as though we had all the time in the world.

A HIDDEN TRACK

Roy Matthews was born into the record business. He came from Hayes in Middlesex, in the days when that was a company town. His mother, like most people in Hayes, worked for EMI. 'We had no electricity in the house until I left school. We lived on a big estate. We didn't have a radio. Radio came via a cable system. When I started at EMI I was working on 78 presses. At that time we were moving over to 45 rpm singles and 33 rpm LPs. I was trained as an engineer. I could just as easily have been working with pots and pans. I was lucky to be working on something so alive. I had a little while away and then came back in 1967 as General Manager of the factory. At that time we had over eight hundred people there. The factory was running twenty-four hours a day five days a week. We had a hundred men working the presses. They were all men. It was heavy manual work. We were preparing the plastic which was specially mixed on site. We had our own chemists. We even had ink manufacturers working for us. You couldn't use just any paper for the labels. Everything had to be done specially. It was all done by hand at first. During my time there we grew from producing 50,000 LPs a day to 250,000 a day. EMI were making about 70 per cent of the UK production in those days. Back in the seventies a big order might be for half a million of a Beatles Greatest Hits. The lowest order for a new release would be a couple of thousand. When I think I could have had a white label of just about every record ever pressed. I could have had the Beatles' white labels. I never thought of getting anyone to sign anything.'

When Roy retired and EMI stopped manufacturing he didn't think the world would have any further need of his expertise. Then, after a few years, his phone in the West Country began ringing: people wanted his advice on running small pressing plants or making CDs. A few years ago a Polish company that had been making a lot of CDs saw the writing on the wall for that medium and wondered about diversifying into pressing some records to cater for the collectors market. They contacted Roy wondering if he could help them source some record presses. Roy knew this wouldn't be easy. You can't buy record presses off the shelf. Back in the day EMI used to make their own.

'I tried everywhere and got nowhere until somebody said to me, "Don't laugh, but somebody's selling a couple of presses on eBay." I looked, and there they were, and they were exactly the kind of thing we wanted. So I made further enquiries and I ended up taking a long plane trip with the boss of the Polish company to where these presses were. We got there and were driven out to this factory. Nobody had been inside for fourteen years. We opened the door and it was like a mausoleum. But there they were. Four presses plus spares. Plus the equipment for making the stampers. There they were – in Zimbabwe.

'They had belonged to a Polygram company. The presses had been in South Africa but they'd moved them on when they moved over to CDs. Anyway, there they were, plugged in and piped up. I looked nervously at the Polish MD. Had I brought him all this way on a wild goose chase? I took a deep breath, we plugged them in, and turned them on.

'They worked!'

SHELF LIFE – AN APPENDIX

This book was written in a room dominated by shelves full of LPs, many of them dog-eared, scratched, scribbled over and unappealing to the increasingly preposterous collectors' market of today. While writing the book I got these LPs out and played them again. This was not merely to see how many of them lived up to their sometimes inflated reputations. It was also to feel them in my hands and to try to interact with them now in the way I interacted with them back then. Here I've tried to sum up how I felt about them then and how I feel about them now. I've chosen ten for each of the years covered by the book. I've not attempted to be definitive. This is not one of those 'albums you have to hear before you die' articles. It's just a bunch of records that I happen to share some personal history with.

1967

The Beatles: *Sgt Pepper's Lonely Hearts Club Band*

When this came out I listened to it on my own. For the subsequent fifty years it was OK to refer to it and listen to songs from it but you probably wouldn't actually play it all the way through. That would have seemed corny. On its fiftieth anniversary in 2017 there was a recital of the remastered version in Studio Two at Abbey Road. Hundreds of us sat in rows and listened in silence, which is something few do now. Everybody sat there with a dazed look on their faces. You could criticize *Sgt Pepper*. Anyone denying its enveloping charm would merely be saying something about themselves, something it's probably better not to say.

Bob Dylan: *John Wesley Harding*

This may be my favourite Bob Dylan record. At the time it just seemed a bit dull. Where were the fireworks? Why no song about Vietnam? Why nothing florid and extreme? Now I realize it's Dylan's recalcitrance that has kept his career going this long. He was rebelling against psychedelia every bit as much as he'd rebelled against Brylcreem and Fabian. I don't pretend to know what the songs are 'about' but I do know that each of them buries an idea in your subconscious, an idea that may not detonate for years.

Aretha Franklin: *I Never Loved A Man The Way I Love You*

No matter what was happening in rock, the music we danced to in the discos in 1967 was all on Atlantic or Stax. In 1967 bands couldn't get booked in the UK unless they could play 'Respect'. We only took notice of Aretha when she signed to Atlantic. This was her first album on the label. It started with 'Respect'. Aretha sang well for years but all her great records are on Atlantic.

Van Dyke Parks: *Song Cycle*

Everybody should hear this once if only to realize that in 1967, even before *Sgt Pepper*, a major record company like Warner

Brothers allowed a musician like Parks, who was far from a name, to do something as ambitious as this. It wasn't until he'd finished it that they realized there was absolutely nobody they could sell it to. '"Song Cycle"?' said Warner Bros. 'Where's the songs?' It flopped so badly that the company actually took out ads boasting about how much they lost on it. $35,509, to be precise.

The Incredible String Band: *The 5,000 Spirits Or The Layers Of The Onion*

'Incredible' was the adjective of 1967. If they hadn't had it in their name Robin Williamson and Mike Heron would have been just another folkie duo. 'Incredible' suggested their wobbly vocals and strangely gauche songs were deliberate. This is the kind of music that might still exist today, but it would have to be nurtured by independent labels and showcased by the right festivals. In November 1967, however, it actually entered the chart. That's not the alt-folk chart. That's the proper UK album charts. It was between the *Fiddler on the Roof* cast recording and *Tony Bennett's Greatest Hits*. Such was the true world of 1967.

Jimi Hendrix Experience: *Are You Experienced*

I still prefer this to every other album that Hendrix made. Once he starts panning the stereo he loses me. To me, this record still reeks of the small club circuit of the mid-sixties rather than the blasted heath of Woodstock. My favourite is the virtuoso blues 'Red House'. Years later I asked Eddie Kramer, who engineered that session, how people could possibly play things as accomplished as that and do it live. 'First,' he said, 'you've got to be really, really, really, really good.'

Cream: *Disraeli Gears*

Notwithstanding the none-more psychedelic cover designed by Clapton's flatmate Martin Sharp, *Disraeli Gears* is actually short, sharp club-friendly stompers all the way. Cream were interested in hit records. For instance, Ginger Baker couldn't come up with a drum part for 'Sunshine Of Your Love'. Somebody suggested doing it like the Shadows' 'Apache'. And he did. It's that kind of jukebox wisdom that makes it work.

Judy Collins: *Wildflowers*

This was the first time I'd heard Leonard Cohen songs. There are three of them here. The song side two of the album starts with was something she first came across when Al Kooper rang her and told her he'd followed an attractive girl home, that the girl wrote songs and would she like to hear one? He passed the phone to the girl, who sang the song to Judy. The song was 'Both Sides Now'. The girl was Joni Mitchell.

Scott Walker: *Scott*

In its way this was just as revolutionary as *Sgt Pepper*. A scream idol suddenly doing a load of songs about grown-up women, grown-up booze and grown-up issues like death, all to the accompaniment of massive orchestras and a thundering rhythm section. The girls who had his poster on their wall lapped it up. We boys whose actual love lives were hardly off the ground aspired to be as deep and complicated as Scott. We also rushed out to get ourselves a coat like the one he was wearing on the cover and probably slipped a slim volume of the Liverpool poets into its pocket.

Bonzo Dog Doo Dah Band: *Gorilla*

This was a classic case of playing with the LP format. At the end of side one there's a track called 'Narcissus' which is a conversation between two theatregoers at the interval. Side two begins with 'The Intro And The Outro' during which Viv Stanshall free-styles his roll call of the notional musicians contributing to the track: 'Eric Clapton on ukulele . . . Adolf Hitler on vibes . . . J. Arthur Rank on gong'. Makes me oddly proud to be British.

1968

Simon & Garfunkel: *Bookends*

Not long after buying this in 1968 I remember taking it to a pub on a summer evening. I can still see the sun glinting off the Richard Avedon photograph on the front. His picture made them look thoughtful. I too wished to appear thoughtful, which is why I carried the album to the pub. My favourite track, now as much as then, is 'America' for the way it perfectly captures that feeling of being away from home and rather enjoying the homesickness. Listening to it now, hearing the sound effects and the interviews with old people, I can't believe that I didn't detect the signs that the whole record had started life as something more ambitious.

Van Morrison: *Astral Weeks*

A few years ago I was talking to the novelist Jonathan Franzen. He had just finished a book. He told me *Astral Weeks* was the one record he had listened to while writing it. He said he just played it again and again. I could see why. It's the kind of record you can only follow with more of the same. I'm sure Van would hate it to be called easy listening but on one level it is. Earlier this year a Belfast friend took me down Cyprus Avenue, the street where the young

Van used to go to gaze at posh girls. It was funny to be reminded that the street had existed in reality years before it began another life in the imaginations of thousands of people all over the world. And still does.

The Zombies: *Odessey And Oracle*

I didn't buy this at the time. Like everybody else I had bought the sampler album *The Rock Machine Turns You On* and really liked 'Time Of The Season', but at the time buying a Zombies album seemed a backwards step. All due respect, but in 1968 they already seemed to be over. I didn't foresee that almost fifty years in the future their kind of well-mannered rococo pop would come back into fashion and would be celebrated long after bigger names of the time such as Tim Rose and Johnny Winter had been forgotten.

The Rolling Stones: *Beggars Banquet*

The world moved swiftly in those days, so when this came out at the end of 1968 nobody reminded the Rolling Stones of their recent psychedelic misadventure. They seemed to be doing everything in their power to put that behind them. This was meaner and nastier than ever, which was the way we liked it, and it still stands up as such. 'No Expectations' is their best acoustic blues, 'Salt Of The Earth' is Keith's greatest moment, and what I like about 'Stray Cat Blues' is the fact that even those contemporary radio stations that pride themselves on their edginess still wouldn't dare play it. In those days Decca records had a hole in the top corner of the sleeve through which you could glimpse the colour of the inner bag. It was blue for stereo and red for mono.

Leonard Cohen: *Songs Of Leonard Cohen*

I've lived with the music of Leonard Cohen for fifty years. It took me twenty of those years to realize that, far from being miserable, he was often funny. At some point in the seventies he was turned into a form of shorthand for misery. Lots of people who had never actually heard him had an inherited view of him. The girl he wrote about in 'So Long Marianne' appeared, wearing only a towel, on the back of his second album. Oh, how we ached to live Leonard's life. As time went on my admiration only increased. Marianne died a couple of years before Cohen did. He wrote to her when she was on her death bed saying he was so close behind her that if she reached out she'd be able to touch his hand.

The Band: *Music From Big Pink*

It wasn't until their second album that I truly got the Band. All the musicians were dropping the name of this in interviews so I had to get it. It was a bit hard work, starting with Richard Manuel's dirge-like 'Tears Of Rage' (presumably because it was co-written by Dylan) rather than 'The Weight'. However I didn't trade it in because I still liked the idea of being the guy who had the first album by the Band. Recently I was talking to a friend who had just bought a fiftieth anniversary reissue. I worked out he paid twenty times as much for his as I paid for mine. Age has its compensations.

The Beatles: *The Beatles*

My copy's numbered 0389700. I haven't looked but I'm confident if I did there will be entire websites devoted to the study of numbering the White Album. There was a poster inside it. It was one of those montages of shots of the band tooling around which we absolutely devoured. The poster went on the bedroom wall and got lost when I left home. We hardly ever played the side which had 'Revolution 9' on it but we forgave its inclusion just the same. I agree with Paul McCartney when he was asked about it in 1996. 'People say it would have been better if it was a single album. I say, "Get over it – it's the Beatles' White Album."'

Small Faces: *Ogdens' Nut Gone Flake*

The circular design of the cover here was impractical, even by the zany standards of the time. I stretched mine out and put it on my wall at college. The sinews connecting the paper circles weren't meant for this kind of treatment and it didn't take long to fall apart. At the time I thought the Small Faces were all about Steve Marriott. These days I think about Ronnie Lane a lot. I also think of Stanley Unwin, who narrated the story on the second side. Stanley was famous in his day but he's forgotten now. What immortality he has he owes to this record.

The Jeff Beck Group: *Truth*

All the sixties acts who were produced by Mickie Most – Donovan, the Animals and Jeff Beck – had two things in common: the first is that they were very sniffy about Most's contribution and the second is that funnily enough none of them did anything quite so good again. At the time I preferred the Beck Group's hard rock to Led Zeppelin's, particularly since Rod Stewart was a more distinctive lead singer. I think I still do.

Fleetwood Mac: *Mr Wonderful*

This was the high point of what I think of as Fleetwood Mac's rugby shirt years. At the time they weren't just a blues band, they were also a party band. The cover, a fold-out of Mick Fleetwood naked but for a tree, proves it, and foreshadows by a decade his similarly balls-out appearance on the cover of *Rumours*. But they also had, in Peter Green, the most soulful of the British bluesmen. I still think 'Love That Burns' is the best recording to come out of that whole period.

1969

King Crimson: *In The Court Of The Crimson King*

It was the track '21st Century Schizoid Man' that did it. That and the cover. The whole pitch of King Crimson was so steely and fearsomely accomplished you just had to bow down before them whether you actually liked the music or not. Nobody had heard anything quite like it before. On one level it was like a stereo test record. Everybody was buying a stereo and they were looking for records that seemed to put their stereo through its paces. I'm not sure that all the people who bought it actually liked it but you couldn't not be impressed by it.

Creedence Clearwater Revival: *Green River*

John Fogerty's group came along at the point when everybody else was getting more complex and cerebral, playing the kind of music that sounded as though it had always been there. They sang about the South so I assumed they were from the South. Actually they were from Oakland, which was a bit like coming from Southampton. I still play all those classic Creedence albums. They were anachronistic back then, which is one more reason why they haven't dated one bit.

Frank Zappa: *Hot Rats*

I was never particularly a Frank Zappa fan but it was the cover, with that infrared picture of Miss Christine, and the title, which sounded both hard-boiled and hip, that did it. This record goes to show that a strong opening track will get you a long way in the public's affections. I still play 'Peaches En Regalia' regularly and reflect on what a good career Frank Zappa could have had writing themes for cop shows if he hadn't wasted so much of his time trying to impress other musicians.

Captain Beefheart: *Trout Mask Replica*

John Peel would play this all the time, introducing it as 'the good Captain' or 'the mighty Captain'. It's standard to say that the world of music has moved on so much that what once sounded outlandish now makes perfect sense to our ears. *Trout Mask Replica* sounds every bit as strange and jarring now as it did back then. Most days of the year you can do without it. Then there's one day a year when only 'Moonlight On Vermont' will do.

Chicago Transit Authority: *Chicago Transit Authority*

God, we were easily taken in by anything that seemed new. The first Chicago album was a cheap double and we should have known when we saw that a track called 'Free Form Guitar' ran for almost seven minutes that they had padded like crazy to fill up four sides. We also should have known from the way they included recordings of protests at the Democratic Convention in Chicago that they were chancers. We didn't. We were young.

Fairport Convention: *Unhalfbricking*

I loved this record when it came out and I still love it today. I love the cover picture of Sandy Denny's parents in their garden in Wimbledon. I love their recording of 'Who Knows Where The Time Goes?' I love the way they did Bob Dylan in French and got on *Top of the Pops*. Most of all I love 'A Sailor's Life', which singlehandedly vindicates the murky business of the extended jam. Eight years later Nick Kent was commending Television for emulating it on *Marquee Moon*. A great British band at their peak.

The Who: *Tommy*

So much of the Who can be explained by the fact they were managed by Kit Lambert, who had grown up as classical music royalty and therefore always wanted them to do something that was more than pop music. Strange, then, that the bits of this double album that make most sense to me nowadays are the songs, like 'Pinball Wizard' and 'Go To The Mirror!', that sound most like pop. The amazing thing in retrospect is that there was so little controversy at the time around a track like 'Fiddle About', which is, not to put too fine a point on it, about child abuse.

Crosby, Stills & Nash: *Crosby, Stills & Nash*

When they called it 'wooden music' that wasn't a criticism. It was supposed to indicate that by playing this music on acoustic instruments these former Byrds and Hollies were somehow being more true to themselves and to us. It amazes me that they took off the way they did, since they were less a group than three solo artists operating as a trio. I used to think it was the apotheosis of groovy. I now think it's the essence of twee.

Quicksilver Messenger Service: *Happy Trails*

The cover, an illustration from a vintage cowboy comic, made you want to love it. Once you got inside, what did you find but an extended, allegedly live recording of Bo Diddley's 'Who Do You Love', which had been tricked up into an alleged 'suite' where each member of the band got his solo spot. John Cipollina, the star of the group, went to his grave not knowing what the fuss was about. 'It was just a two-chord jam,' he shrugged when asked about it later.

Blind Faith: *Blind Faith*

'In The Presence Of The Lord' still stands up, as does 'Can't Find My Way Home'. I'm not saying they didn't have enough material but the last fifteen minutes of the album were taken up by a jam called 'Do What You Like', which was allegedly composed by Ginger Baker. Nobody talked about the cover at the time. These days nobody talks about anything else.

1970

George Harrison: *All Things Must Pass*

It felt heavy. It sounded heavy. The songs were about matters that were indisputably heavy. He was only twenty-seven when it came out and many of those songs were about dying. It was a remarkable record then and it still is today. Nothing before or since has sounded quite so exquisitely layered. It was the last good thing George ever did. He'd held back his best stuff from the Beatles to make sure his solo album was good. It was so good he made it impossible to follow.

Elton John: *Tumbleweed Connection*

So you take a pub pianist from Pinner and a would-be poet from Lincolnshire, put them together, and what do they do? They indulge their fantasies of being Robbie Robertson and Leon Russell with a bunch of songs about burning missions and father figures who carried guns. Furthermore, on the cover they try to pass off a station on the Bluebell Railway in Sussex as though it's the kind of place where Gary Cooper waited for a man in a black hat. We so badly wanted it all to be true that we were prepared to overlook our misgivings.

Neil Young: *After The Gold Rush*

The patches on the jeans on the back cover of this album were sewn on by the artist's then wife, who got a credit. I had similar patches on a similar pair sewn on by my girlfriend. That cover was the peak of vagabond chic. The apparent frailty of Young's voice seemed to match the pictures exactly. The spidery style of the hand-written lyrics on the poster inside seemed just perfect. We all wanted to be like Neil, inscrutable and sensitive behind our own curtain of hair with somebody to sew our jeans. I interviewed him twenty years later and he entered the room looking largely the same. I've rarely met a musician so aware of his brand values.

Derek and the Dominos: *Layla And Other Assorted Love Songs*

It didn't sell. Serves Clapton right for trying to sink his identity in a band nobody had heard of. Of course eventually whatever success it had was completely down to the singles market being better at spotting a good tune than the hairy albums buyers. I'm still not wholly convinced by it. A lot of the time it seems to have no heft to it. If I want twin guitar duelling nowadays I reach for the Allman Brothers.

Van Morrison: *Moondance*

I always knew this record was good, great even, but it took decades for me to truly appreciate its beauty. Only an Irishman, someone with a grounding in that country's showband tradition, could have done it. Once he'd done it lots of people tried to follow its lead. It turned Bruce Springsteen's head around, led to the hiring of

Clarence Clemons, and indicated a more sensual, soulful direction for an artist who could easily have turned into Pete Townshend.

The Grateful Dead: *Workingman's Dead*

If I could reclaim all the hours of my life I've spent trying to like the Grateful Dead I could have written a big fat novel. I always like the idea of them – never more so than at this point when they were going country-folk – but for me they're always held back by a lack of warm blood. Furthermore, I always thought the people who danced at Dead concerts were the kind of people who really had no business dancing to anything.

Black Sabbath: *Black Sabbath*

I started college in 1968. The guys who started the year after liked different things. They liked Deep Purple, Free and most of all Black Sabbath. I can remember hearing this coming from the room of a new student from the Midlands (of course) and thinking Ozzy Osbourne's 'Oh no, please God help me' had to be a joke, surely? More fool me.

The Who: *Live At Leeds*

The thing that fascinates me listening to this album nowadays is the restraint of the audience. They're witnessing the most impressive demonstration of rock power in the live setting of all time and they sound as impressed as if they were listening to Pete Brown and his Battered Ornaments. Truly, we didn't know we were born.

Traffic: *John Barleycorn Must Die*

Oh, I know the songs aren't up to much but I still love the dappled hippy vibe of 'Glad' and 'Empty Pages'. Jim Capaldi was one of those drummers who didn't rate himself as much as I did. It was only in later years, when people let us in on all their secrets, that I realized this was supposed to be a Steve Winwood album. When he got lonely – they always get lonely – he called up his old mates and it turned into a Traffic album.

Paul McCartney: *McCartney*

I didn't admit it at the time but I was disappointed by this. Except, as everybody noted, by 'Maybe I'm Amazed'. We all liked that because he sounded wholehearted about it. The rest of it just sounded like the stool suddenly only had the one leg. Still, we loved the pictures and the whole domestic contentment vibe projected by the cover. We just wished the record had been as good as the pictures.

1971

Marvin Gaye: *What's Going On*

EMI distributed Motown Records in the UK. The manner in which they did it made it pretty clear they didn't believe Motown was an albums label. In the UK this record wasn't graced with a fold-out, an explanatory sleeve note or even the names of the musicians who played on it. It's the perfect illustration of the hammock effect of having the two best tracks (the title and 'Inner City Blues') placed at the beginning and the end. That's a characteristic it shares with the next LP on my list.

The Who: *Who's Next*

I still insist that the most exciting bit of the most exciting track of the most exciting year in rock occurs around one minute six seconds into the first track here. 'Baba O'Riley' is the Who in excelsis, which means it's as powerful as rock gets. And the key bit is the moment when, after Townshend's Lowry organ-through-a-synthesizer intro has been chased by his own chords on the piano, Keith Moon's rolling thunder drums and Townshend's slashing chords, Daltrey's vocal and Entwistle's bass both enter in the nick of time. *Who's Next* has got a brilliant beginning and in 'Won't Get Fooled Again' it's got a brilliant ending. It can afford all sorts of stuff in between.

David Bowie: *Hunky Dory*

I preferred David Bowie before he was cool. I prefer him when he was cranking out tunes for Peter Noone and glad of the work. Even at the time this struck me as a classic case of reach exceeding grasp. *Hunky Dory* is a bit like his White Album. There's the sentimental song about his son and the faintly desperate dropping of the names of Bob Dylan and Andy Warhol. I find it difficult to believe even he knew what 'The Bewlay Brothers' was all about. It's all so gauche but there's a redeeming warmth to it that I actually prefer to anything else he did.

Sly & the Family Stone: *There's A Riot Goin' On*

I bought this because I loved 'Family Affair' (who didn't?) and I confess I found it all perplexing and impenetrable and not at all the kind of thing designed to take you higher. Nearly fifty years later I still defy anyone not to find it the most challenging, edgy and provocative thing ever to get to the number one spot in the United States album market. Without *There's A Riot Goin' On* there is no hip hop.

The Rolling Stones: *Sticky Fingers*

I remember hearing the DJ play 'Can't You Hear Me Knocking' on a Sunday afternoon gig at the Roundhouse and being knocked out by Bobby Keys' sax solo. When I actually got the record the track I used to play more than any other was 'Moonlight Mile'. It was the moodiness of the whole thing that won me over. And, as one review of the period observed approvingly, if you put the album cover on your shelf the zip on the front of the jeans ripped the cover of whatever LP it was placed alongside.

Yes: *The Yes Album*

One of the reasons this kind of flashy progressive rock was so popular at the time was that it provided the perfect outlet for our fantasies of being a member of a rock band. We would close the curtains, put the record on and then prowl the living room, our fingers tracing out Chris Squire's bass patterns on our hip bones. The common cliché about listeners to progressive rock is that they remained stock still and just listened closely. Not true. For the most part we were a blur.

Joni Mitchell: *Blue*

I find a lot of this funny these days. When her old man's away the bed's too big, the frying pan's too wide, which conjures the unlikely spectacle of Graham Nash waking Joni on a Sunday morning in Laurel Canyon with a traditional Blackpool fried breakfast. What you can't argue with is Joni Mitchell's piercing candour. This record was like an X-ray, as she said afterwards. Nobody had ever done anything quite like it before. She was lucky in a way. When she made it she didn't have Joni Mitchell's *Blue* to compete with. I feel sorry for her successors.

Rod Stewart: *Every Picture Tells A Story*

It's hard for those who grew up with Rod Stewart after 'Do Ya Think I'm Sexy' to understand what a star he was at the time this record came out. He wasn't just a great musical talent. He was also a person-ality, living out the larger life the rest of us could only dream about. I now find some of it a bit hard to take but he's still a genuinely great singer, as 'Seems Like A Long Time' and 'Tomorrow Is A Long Time' prove. There's something in his voice that is beyond faking.

Paul McCartney: *Ram*

Time has conspired to make this record sound better than it did at the time. That slightly unfinished quality that was mildly irritating for those of us still waiting for another Beatles record is now part of its charm. It sounds like somebody trying to get over the Beatles, which applied to him then and has applied to the rest of us ever since. The impersonation of a Trimphone on 'Uncle Albert/Admiral Hal-sey' takes those of us who were there at the time right back to 1971.

Nick Drake: *Bryter Layter*

Ah, the shot on the back cover of him watching the traffic go by on the Westway. We all identified with that idea at the time. For we too were too fine, too soulful for the hurly-burly which was the lot of everyone else. Truth to tell I didn't buy Nick Drake. Nor did most people. There were other, crisper things competing for our atten-tion. This seemed too pallid, too watercolour back then. All these years later it's the very quality I treasure the most.

1972

Roxy Music: *Roxy Music*

There was certainly something in the air in 1972: an appetite for something a bit more plastic, something belonging to the new dec-ade rather than the last one. Roxy Music supplied it. Half the heavy lifting was done by the cover. It was the first LP I remember being a hit because it was hip. I think it's surprising it sold as well as it did, considering that in the original version it didn't contain 'Virginia Plain'. That song changed the whole picture with Roxy Music. From then on they were hitmakers.

David Bowie: *The Rise And Fall Of Ziggy Stardust And The Spiders From Mars*

I remember buying this in the summer vacation and then taking it back to the flat I shared in north London. The first thing we all did when reassembling at the beginning of a new term was play each other the new albums we had bought. One of my flatmates didn't like this. He reckoned it was cold. I think it was the coldness I responded to at the time. I think 'Starman', which was added at the last minute when the record company wanted a single, and 'Suffragette City' are the tent poles that hold it up still.

Stevie Wonder: *Talking Book*

This was the new version of Stevie Wonder. Newly grown-up and making the kind of records he felt like making. He toured in 1972 supporting the Rolling Stones. *Talking Book* was aimed at the white rock market, because these people bought albums. You could tell he'd produced it himself because there was nothing obvious or reassuring about it. The track everyone focused on was 'Superstition'. This seemed to be a harbinger of an entirely new kind of dance music.

Todd Rundgren: *Something/Anything?*

'I Saw The Light' was the first case I remember of something being too good to be a hit. This double began with winning pop tunes and culminated in a fourth side called 'Baby Needs A New Pair Of

Snakeskin Boots (A Pop Operetta)'. On the way there was a track where he demonstrates the studio noises that can mar recordings. It was that kind of record. Its most 1972 touch is 'Duds by Granny Takes A Trip' among the credits. Apparently this is Axl Rose's favourite record. If so, he's not a bad judge.

Randy Newman: *Sail Away*

I bought this on a Saturday morning after staying up all night to see the J. Geils Band at the Lyceum. If I'm honest I was slightly disappointed by its dryness. I now think it's a masterpiece. It's the dryness that has made it endure. When I first heard 'Political Science' I thought it was a zany lampoon of American ignorance of the wider world. Over forty-five years later there's a President who would agree with most of it.

Little Feat: *Sailin' Shoes*

In the cover's small print, every inch of which we scanned, it says, 'People don't make good albums for 15 grand. I'll give you ten.' Everything Little Feat did was a joke about themselves. Their name. The album's title. The cover featuring a cake on a swing à la Fragonard. The whole thing was like a private joke which we wanted in on. And they even took a second swing at Lowell George's song 'Willin'', which they'd already done on their last album. We thought they were the best band in the world.

Dr John: *Dr John's Gumbo*

This was a history lesson as well as a party. It was Mac Rebennack doing the songs he'd grown up with in New Orleans. The whole project was a deliberate attempt to dignify that heritage. Inside the cover was a leaflet with a couple of thousand words explaining it. It was here I first read of Professor Longhair, Cow Cow Davenport and Poppa Stoppa. It was here I first heard 'Tipitina' and 'Mess Around'. I love this record for the joy it gives me still.

Richard Thompson: *Henry The Human Fly*

The cover featured the young ex-Fairport Convention genius wearing a bug-eyed mask, a leotard and tights. The sleeve note began with the words ' "Bugger," said God, "raining again." ' Rarely has a record been made with so little evident thought for its likely commercial success: Jimmy Shand dance tunes, songs about racehorses, no flash guitar solos. No wonder this died like a louse in a Russian's beard. I got it out to write this and played it all the way through. Twice. 'I was looking for trouble to tangle my line / But trouble came looking for me.'

The Rolling Stones: *Exile On Main St*

This got lukewarm reviews at the time. There was one that said, 'The only person doing his job is Charlie Watts.' People thought it was light on songs, which it is. It tries to make up for the material by cranking up the noise. We used to play 'Rocks Off' and 'Tumbling Dice' but four sides were just too much. It was only when we heard the albums that came after it that we went back to it and belatedly counted our blessings.

Ry Cooder: *Boomer's Story*

I've still got the white label copy of this I plucked out of a north London bargain bin in 1972. This is one of those records which was an education as well as a pleasure. Ry Cooder's genius is his ability to tap into America's rich history of strange music on the borders between folk and entertainment and to bring it into the present with much of its strangeness intact. I've learned more from Ry Cooder than just about any other musician.

1973

Pink Floyd: *The Dark Side Of The Moon*

Funny to think there was a time when the cover needed to have a sticker on it so that people would know the name of the band and the title of their record. I can't claim this was ever a favourite of mine but I could see how people were attracted to its solemnity, its stately pace. A couple of years ago I spent an entire weekend at Abbey Road with Alan Parsons as he demonstrated for a paying audience how the record came into being. Among that audience were people who had travelled thousands of miles and paid thousands of pounds just to be there. This would have been thought hilarious at the time of its original release.

Mike Oldfield: *Tubular Bells*

I bought it. Because it had no track marks you couldn't leap ahead to my favourite bit where Viv Stanshall announced the instruments and in doing so gave it the drama it otherwise lacked. You just had to sit there, eat your greens and wait. I was certainly not immune to the faintly snobbish hope that some way could be found of rock music meeting up with classical music. Now I don't believe that's possible, nor do I think it would be even desirable.

Paul McCartney and Wings: *Band On The Run*

The cover features Paul, Linda and Denny Laine with their top showbiz pals Michael Parkinson, Kenny Lynch, James Coburn, Clement Freud, John Conteh and Christopher Lee. What nobody suspected at the time was that forty-five years later people would be looking at the cover and asking, 'Who are these people with Paul and Linda?'

Marvin Gaye: *Let's Get It On*

One of my favourite moments in the whole of recorded music comes on the fade-out of the title track when he sings 'I've been sanctified' and then there's the first of a series of hand-claps. On the single you only hear one and then it fades. This may still be the apogee of boudoir soul but it's no longer the kind of thing you can actually put on in a public situation. Not without somebody asking you what you think your game is.

Roxy Music: *For Your Pleasure*

This is still the Roxy Music album I reach for more than the others because the first side starts with 'Do The Strand', a song that more than lives up to the promise of the cover picture of Amanda Lear leading a panther on a leash, and ends with 'In Every Dream Home A Heartache', a drama about a man and a blow-up doll.

The Wailers: *Catch A Fire*

I can remember hearing this in one of those old-fashioned listening booths at a shop in Wood Green. Of course what attracted everyone was the cover, which was specially fashioned, at ridiculous expense, to resemble a Zippo lighter. Chris Blackwell had insisted there be no more than nine tracks to make it seem like a rock album and had overdubbed a few more rock-friendly instruments. What clinched it was the stealthy, sensual opening to 'Stir It Up', a Marley composition pop singer Johnny Nash had already recorded.

Paul Simon: *There Goes Rhymin' Simon*

When the roll is finally called up yonder and there is a definitive reckoning about who were the greatest of the singer-songwriters, I fancy Paul Simon will be in the top three and this record will be introduced in evidence. Really clever ideas like 'Kodachrome'. Heartfelt songs like 'Something So Right'. Great tunes like 'Tenderness'. And it all adds up to more than the sum of its parts. He's made lots of great records in the course of his career but I think this is the best.

Steely Dan: *Countdown To Ecstasy*

If you looked at the picture on the back, in which the band slouched around the mixing desk, there was a mysterious extra hand. Steely Dan were full of pranks like that. I could tell from the reviews that their fellow Americans thought they were irritatingly clever. We just thought they were clever and, although nobody ever used this word, cool with it. Steely Dan were probably the most played band of the LP era because they had that combination of catchiness and mystery. They never wore out their welcome. This album still hasn't. Furthermore, a lot of it has come true. 'Showbiz kids, making movies of themselves, they don't give a fuck about anybody else.'

Nilsson: *A Little Touch Of Schmilsson In The Night*

He wanted to make an album of standards. The kind of thing that nowadays we call the Great American Songbook. So they did. Derek Taylor produced it. Gordon Jenkins arranged it. But Nilsson had been drinking, drugging and smoking so much that, as he later recalled, his 'incredible, flexible, rubber-band voice' was all but shot. But before it went completely he managed to pull together this, a record that introduced a new generation to the beauty of songs they were previously sniffy about and also played a vital part in securing his legacy.

ZZ Top: *Tres Hombres*

We used to dream that there was a land where there were bars where bands like this one played. For ZZ Top, blues was music to dance to, not just a structure on which to drape your instrumental virtuosity or parade your pain. We lived above a noisy thoroughfare at the time and would turn up 'La Grange' as loud as it would go. It was a song about a cathouse just outside a little town in Texas. I know the chorus by heart. It goes 'a haw haw haw, a haw haw haw' . . .

1974

Joni Mitchell: *Court And Spark*

Before this album she struggled to find musicians who could grasp her songs. Tom Scott's bunch of pop-jazzers were the perfect solution. They were accustomed to the world of TV themes. You can hear that here. You can imagine some of these arrangements setting the scene for an episode of *Taxi*. 'Everything comes and goes, marked by lovers and styles of clothes,' as she sings in 'Down To You'. That may be true but this has retained every atom of its flavour and complexity.

Randy Newman: *Good Old Boys*

At the time this came out people were aware it was controversial. But nobody tried to stop it. Newman even launched it with a concert in Atlanta, Georgia and invited Governor Lester Maddox. In the twenty-first century I no longer dare play this record in my house for fear that it reaches the ears of anyone under the age of forty who wouldn't be able to hear beyond the language it uses to detect its intention. It's the only concept album in rock that delivers.

Jackson Browne: *Late For The Sky*

The cover, inspired by Magritte, shows a car outside a house on a street at night time. The last track on the first side is called 'The Late Show'. It's about a man trying to get a woman to go away with him. At the end of the song there's a minute gap in the music, a gap which is filled with the sound of a car door slamming. You wait to hear if there's somebody getting in the passenger seat. Go and listen. Bruce Springsteen said there was 'no more searching, yearning, loving music for and about America'.

Steely Dan: *Pretzel Logic*

Dan fans, who were already establishing themselves as the maniacs' maniacs, all agreed that, since with this they ditched the lead singer and started bringing in the session men, this was the first example of the Dan in their maturity. Side one, which starts with the peerless 'Rikki Don't Lose That Number' and finishes with their note-perfect tribute to Duke Ellington's 'East St Louis Toodleoo', is rendered even more perfect by the fact it's only seventeen minutes long.

Neil Young: *On The Beach*

When this came out *Rolling Stone* called it 'one of the most despairing albums of the decade'. They only said that because they didn't know that the next six years would produce plenty more contenders for that title and they were unaware that coming next was *Tonight's The Night*, which would make this seem like *Please Please Me*. In fact this LP remains the perfect bridge between homespun early Neil Young and the apocalyptic tendencies of his later stuff. Its mystique was increased immeasurably by the fact that Canada's Mr Awkward made it unavailable for years.

Richard and Linda Thompson: *I Want To See The Bright Lights Tonight*

Just a couple of years after his abortive solo record Thompson came back with his wife Linda and a record which is as bracing and British as a cold shower in August. It's a bunch of songs about poverty, drink and the profound importance of going into town on a Saturday night all delivered with the coiled power of virtuosity kept on a tight leash. It remains one of the genuine masterpieces of folk-rock.

Bryan Ferry: *Another Time, Another Place*

It's his version of 'Smoke Gets In Your Eyes' that does it for me. That and his driving version of Dylan's 'It Ain't Me Babe'. And also his take on Dobie Gray's 'The In Crowd'. There's a tragic dimension to Ferry's singing that only his cover versions properly bring out.

Van Morrison: *It's Too Late To Stop Now*

Some of this live double was recorded at the Rainbow during his triumphal return to the United Kingdom after his self-imposed exile in the USA. Here he mixes rhythm and blues classics with the best of his own albums and even throws us a bone in the shape of old favourites from Them. It's as much of a joy now as it was then.

Robert Palmer: *Sneakin' Sally Through The Alley*

This was the first, and in many ways the best, of Island's attempts to get a hit with Robert Palmer by putting him in a studio with the hippest American musicians (in this case Little Feat) and packaging him as an incurable ladies' man. If you came out with this album today you could write your ticket.

Gram Parsons: *Grievous Angel*

There are few artists whom death became more winningly than Gram Parsons. This was put together from material he had been working on when he died and then given a name and a cover treatment which perfectly expressed his legacy. When an album finishes with a song like 'In My Hour Of Darkness' it helps immeasurably if it's the artist's last one.

1975

Bob Dylan: *Blood On The Tracks*

Pete Hamill won a Grammy for best sleeve notes for his essay on the back of the original LP. By that time the essay had been taken off and replaced by one of Dylan's drawings. Maybe he decided this record was one of the few that didn't benefit from further explanation. In which case he would have been right.

Led Zeppelin: *Physical Graffiti*

For all kinds of reasons – specifically 'Kashmir', 'Trampled Under Foot', 'In The Light' and 'Boogie With Stu', the die-cut representation of a New York brownstone that comprises the cover, the rumbling funk of John Bonham's drums, and the fact that it's a double and therefore none of these sides is overloaded with signal – this is still my favourite Led Zeppelin record.

Bruce Springsteen: *Born To Run*

Here is the wellspring of Springsteen's myth. This is what people still buy tickets to get near. The handsome boy from the wrong side of the tracks who turns up outside the home of the nice girl, promising to whisk her away for a night that could be transformational for both of them. It's planned like a movie: 'Thunder Road' its pre-titles sequence, 'Jungleland' its epic denouement, and halfway through there's the title track which is the breathless action sequence everybody remembers. The best bit on the whole record is Ernest 'Boom' Carter's drumming on 'Born To Run'. Amazingly, it was the only thing he ever recorded with them.

The Eagles: *One Of These Nights*

As this book was being finished the Eagles' *Greatest Hits* album passed Michael Jackson to become the best-selling album in history. This in itself is remarkable because it features nothing recorded after 1975. There are three tracks from *One Of These Nights* on that compilation – the title song; 'Lyin' Eyes', pretentious apostrophe and all; and 'Take It To The Limit' – which is quite a strike rate. My personal favourite track is 'Hollywood Waltz', which perfectly captures their delicious self-pity. 'She looks another year older,' they warble. Poor girl doesn't have access to the expensive airbrush the Eagles used to fend off the march of time.

Dr Feelgood: *Down By The Jetty*

Here began the counter revolution. 'Back to mono' badges had been circulating since the most recent reissue of Phil Spector's Christmas Album and therefore when Dr Feelgood announced they were putting out their first album in mono they were chiming with the prevailing 'back to basics' mood. Listened to again at this distance you wish they hadn't been quite so intent on self-denial. They made better albums when they opened themselves up to production.

Burning Spear: *Marcus Garvey*

When know-nothings parrot the 'nothing was happening until punk rock' line they gloss over all sorts of things and certainly never think of a magisterial masterpiece like this, which hasn't dated one iota. I play Burning Spear almost as often as Steely Dan.

Elton John: *Captain Fantastic And The Brown Dirt Cowboy*

My feelings about this album, which was all about his and Bernie Taupin's struggles to make it, were always somewhat coloured by the fact that Elton chose to mark its summer release by playing the whole of it to an audience who'd spent all day in the burning sun at Wembley Stadium and would really have preferred 'Crocodile Rock'. We only perked up for 'Someone Saved My Life Tonight', which was a damned good suicide song. Still is.

Rod Stewart: *Atlantic Crossing*

I resented this album at the time. I resented its cover. I resented its title. I resented its production, which seemed to acquiesce to all the worst instincts of American radio. I'm a lot less dogmatic now and can open myself up to 'It's Not The Spotlight', 'Three Time Loser' and, of course, Danny Whitten's 'I Don't Want To Talk About It'. 'Sailing' is a recording I still associate with the expansion of radio in the UK. Ten years earlier you hadn't heard your favourites enough on the radio. Suddenly you were hearing them too much.

Patti Smith: *Horses*

This still does very little for me. It always sounded like people who were all in favour of rock and roll but couldn't actually play it. I was however aware that there were people a couple of years younger than I was who found it life-changing. I tried it again and haven't changed my views.

Bee Gees: *Main Course*

This is where they came back to claim their place in the sun. It wasn't intended that way. They started off with standard ballads in their old style, and then some combination of their love of recent Stevie Wonder records, the Miami location, Blue Weaver's use of synthesized bass and their manager's pressure on them to come up with hits resulted in 'Nights On Broadway', 'Jive Talkin'' and the strangely alluring 'Fanny (Be Tender With My Love)'.

1976

Stevie Wonder: *Songs In The Key Of Life*

The four sides of this double were still organized as though people remained in the habit of stacking their LPs on their auto-changer deck. The booklet copy actually says, 'Stevie Wonder is the necessary vehicle on which Stevland Morris must be carried on his mission to spread love mentalism.' Fortunately the records inside, two plus a bonus 45, include 'Pastime Paradise', 'Isn't She Lovely', 'Sir Duke' and 'I Wish', which is more than enough to make up for any shortcomings on the outside.

Peter Cook and Dudley Moore: *Derek And Clive (Live)*

Wasn't all that funny then. Even less funny now.

David Bowie: *Station To Station*

'It's not the side-effects of the cocaine. I'm thinking that it must be love.' Cocaine has been responsible for some terrible records. It has also been responsible for some good ones. This still feels the way it felt at the time, as the harbinger of a new form of music which was mostly about the groove. It got a new lease of life with the arrival of the portable tape player.

Ramones: *Ramones*

Whereas the Bowie record had just three tracks a side, this had seven a side. We would play it in the shop and the standard reaction from most people was hilarity. One of the things they found hilarious was that every song was shorter than they expected it to be and was immediately followed by another song that sounded roughly the same. It was one of the best jokes ever played at the expense of the dignity of the LP record. They should have quit as soon as they finished this because they could never hope to improve on it.

ELO: *A New World Record*

Jeff Lynne had been the coming man since the Idle Race in 1968 but he had to wait until 1976 for his long-term plan to prove that rock and strings could go together to be finally vindicated, thanks to 'Rockaria!', 'Livin' Thing' and, my favourite of his many heart-tugging ballads, 'Telephone Line'. Plus there's a concession to his old fans in the shape of yet another version of 'Do Ya', which by then had become a bit of a punk rock classic.

Peter Frampton: *Frampton Comes Alive!*

You can trace the dawning of the age of hype by the increasing volume and hysteria of the audience noise on live recordings. According to this, the people of San Francisco greeted Peter Frampton as though it was the second coming of the Beatles. The performances of all the songs that had made him a popular staple of American FM radio are all authentic enough but it was the sizzle of ersatz hysteria that sold this record rather than the steak of the music. It was an enormous success from which he never recovered.

Boz Scaggs: *Silk Degrees*

Of all the people who jumped on the already full-to-capacity disco bandwagon, Boz Scaggs was the one who managed to do it with the greatest possible taste. He made this record, which was his first and greatest commercial success, with the guys who were eventually to make up Toto. Their Rolls-Royce performances of songs like 'What Can I Say', 'Lowdown' and 'What Do You Want The Girl To Do' must have pricked the ears of Quincy Jones because a lot of it turned up two years later on *Off The Wall*.

Genesis: *A Trick Of The Tail*

When Peter Gabriel left the group after *The Lamb Lies Down On Broadway* few thought they could ever replace him. At first they considered carrying on as a purely instrumental band. Then they decided that drummer Phil Collins had a strong enough voice to handle the songs. This was their first try at proving he could sing. I actually preferred them when they were led by Collins, as they are here on 'Dance On A Volcano', 'A Trick Of The Tail' and 'Los Endos'.

The Rolling Stones: *Black And Blue*

When this album came out Mick Jagger was quoted by *Rolling Stone* saying, 'Girls say to me, "Don't use girls on the record – we really don't like it."' In the same issue the magazine ran the ad in which a model sat astride the Stones record while appearing to have been beaten black and blue. The reaction to the advert marked the first time anyone had challenged the casual sexism of standard rock behaviour. It rather distracted attention from one of the more sinewy and appealing albums of the Stones' interminable middle-age.

Bob Dylan: *Desire*

People fell back in love with Bob Dylan around the middle of the seventies because he seemed to be doing the sort of things that had made him famous: songs about gangsters and pugilists who had been wronged by the state, songs that seemed to lend themselves to being sung along to, songs in which his voice was snaked by the violin of Scarlet Rivera or the harmonies of Emmylou Harris. I think people liked the idea that they could put this on and leave it on to provide a sustained mood. It made everyone's living room seem like a Greenwich Village dive.

1977

Fleetwood Mac: *Rumours*

Things had changed since their last album. Now they had their own logo on the record label. Suddenly Fleetwood Mac could have anything they wanted. They repaid Warner's indulgence with a bunch of songs that were even better than its predecessor. You have to go back to *Rubber Soul* or *Revolver* to find a long-player where each track seemed to be if anything slightly better than the one before. It's since sold twenty million copies in the United States alone and it's hard to imagine any of those twenty million feeling they've been short-changed.

Ian Dury: *New Boots And Panties!!*

Only in rock could Ian Dury's talent have been so perfectly showcased, and only on the LP record could he have made such a profound impression on as many people as he did with this surprise best-seller. Here are songs about early-morning erections, Gene Vincent, Dury's chauffeur father and social climbers from Essex called Dickie, all set to arrangements that married danceable funk with punk rock aggression. A genuinely unique and brilliant long-playing record.

Television: *Marquee Moon*

I like the tracks on this album that sound like Country Joe & the Fish ('Venus', 'Marquee Moon' and 'Torn Curtain'); I'm less bothered about the rest, which sound like the Buzzcocks. The best is still as majestic as it sounded at the time of its release and I still get a frisson when hearing that line 'Broadway looked so medieval – it seemed to flap like little pages'. Listening to this record you can feel the decade tensing up.

Kraftwerk: *Trans-Europe Express*

The thing about the LP record is you could get an idea of what it was going to sound like by looking at the surface of the vinyl. Classical boffins could work out which symphony it was by looking at the width of the bands. You could also get an idea of the dynamic range by looking at how crowded the grooves were. This looked smooth and regular and was barely broken by gaps between tracks. Because what it offered was a brilliant celebration of losing yourself in the tedium of a journey.

Meat Loaf: *Bat Out Of Hell*

Composer Jim Steinman and Meat Loaf shopped this around all the record companies and were laughed out of just about all of them. Nobody could imagine that anything which was so madly over the top in both its writing and performance could ever be popular with the mass market. The only person who saw anything in it was the producer of *The Old Grey Whistle Test*, who aired a clip of the band performing all nine minutes of the title song and got a hugely favourable reaction. The album started to go mad and stayed on the charts for years, suggesting there was a huge audience for just about anything that was too vulgar for the tastemakers.

Steely Dan: *Aja*

After years of hiding from view and refusing to discuss what they were all about, this seemed to offer not one but two sets of sleeve notes. The first, supposedly by a frustrated journalist, was actually by Becker and Fagen. You could tell because it used the word 'legerdemain', which is beyond journalists. The second was actually written by the president of their label, with whom they were in the process of falling out. The music, which features the likes of Steve Gadd and Wayne Shorter, is arguably the most sophisticated ever pressed into the service of pop music. Its proudest achievement is that its sophistication doesn't get in the way of its enjoyment.

David Bowie: *Low*

My copy has a sticker on the back with the names of the songs on it. Bowie presumably planned to release it with just his name and the title on it on the basis that if you needed any more information you weren't likely to care for the record. This was probably true. The first side was made up of very similar-sounding songs united by the same crunching beat. The second side was all doom-sounding synthesizer instrumentals. In that sense it was like one very big single. As such it still works.

The Clash: *The Clash*

My feeling about this is the same as it was in 1977. 'Janie Jones' is a cracking opener which they simply can't sustain.

Elvis Costello: *My Aim Is True*

George 'Porky' Peckham was the mastering engineer people asked for by name. If he was particularly pleased with his work in cutting the master from which LPs would be made, he would inscribe the words 'A Porky Prime Cut' in the run-out groove around the label. That's the signature on my copy of Elvis Costello's first album. Since just about everything on the record was done using the same technology that would have been used ten years earlier, since the record was in every sense hand-made, this seems doubly appropriate.

Al Green: *The Belle Album*

This has no right to be as good as it is. It was the first time he'd written the songs himself and played the guitar. It was the first he'd made without producer Willie Mitchell, with whom he'd had a string of hits. The title track was the most transcendentally blissful thing he'd ever done and the rest is no disgrace either. There's a sound in the rhythm section on this record, a sound which has subsequently vanished from the earth.

1978

Blondie: *Parallel Lines*

In 1978, when there was so much musical division, it would have been hard to find many people who didn't find something to like in Blondie's marriage of pop yearning and downtown cool. Obviously nobody predicted just how big 'Heart Of Glass' was going to be.

Otherwise they wouldn't have put it in the middle of the second side, traditionally where LPs hid their weaker compositions.

The Band: *The Last Waltz*

This is the first sign of rock getting a rather inflated sense of its own importance. The Band retire from playing live, as if they'd been doing one-nighters for the previous ten years rather than just doing some quite comfortable gigs with Dylan and on their own, play a New Year's Eve farewell show and then get Martin Scorsese to blow smoke up their fundaments in a special film, of which this is the soundtrack. It was all very grand but, as we can see now, somewhat premature.

Kate Bush: *The Kick Inside*

This might have too many moments of showing off for teacher about it but it nonetheless still beggars belief that she was only nineteen when she pulled off this debut, containing as it does 'The Man With The Child In His Eyes', 'Wuthering Heights' and 'Moving', her tribute to dance and mime teacher Lindsay Kemp, who died while I was writing this.

Talking Heads: *More Songs About Buildings And Food*

On the back cover is a photomosaic of the United States made up of 569 photos taken from space. This was presumably inspired by the last song 'The Big Country' in which Byrne blankly describes what he can see when he looks down from the airplane and announces, 'I wouldn't live there if you paid me.' Listening to it again after a long time, what's striking is how important the inclusion of Al Green's 'Take Me To The River' is to ensuring the listener doesn't go mad with the accumulated tension. Side note: Andy Partridge says he made up the album's name and gave it to David Byrne in a sports hall in Holland.

Tom Waits: *Blue Valentine*

In the first half of his recording career, before he met his wife and collaborator, Waits hammed up the character side of what he did and made less of the musical side. This made for some absorbing albums that were never likely to appeal to anyone but fans. *Blue Valentine* starts with 'Somewhere' from *West Side Story* and then goes even further out. 'Kentucky Avenue' describes the efforts of one adolescent to run away with another adolescent. The major logistical problem is the second boy's in a wheelchair. Not a dry eye.

Todd Rundgren: *Hermit Of Mink Hollow*

The record company rejected the original running order of this as being too haphazard. Todd solved the problem by making the first side 'the easy side' and putting the hit single 'Can We Still Be Friends' there, and the second side 'the difficult side' and putting all the songs there that radio wouldn't be likely to programme. It works.

The Police: *Outlandos D'Amour*

At the time this was a huge hit, thanks to the singles success of 'Roxanne' and 'Can't Stand Losing You'. The fall-off between the Police's singles and the rest of the material was so steep it's difficult to imagine anyone playing it now.

Marvin Gaye: *Here, My Dear*

This ran into an unprecedented panning at the time it came out. Here was Marvin, who was never known for taking a 'chin-up' attitude to anything that life threw at him, doing an album about his divorce from Berry Gordy's sister Anna and offering his earnings from the record as part of the divorce settlement. I'm not saying it's self-pitying but it does contain the line 'Why do I have to pay lawyers' fees?' If you want to see inside the psyche of a spoiled superstar you won't get a better opportunity.

Bob Seger: *Stranger In Town*

Seger had been a local hero in Michigan for years before he achieved his place on the national stage. This was probably the high point. Songs like 'Hollywood Nights' and 'Old Time Rock & Roll' were perfect for mirror miming. The latter was the number Tom Cruise chose to dance around to in his underpants in the 1983 film *Risky Business*. Other songs like 'Still The Same', 'Till It Shines' and 'We've Got Tonite' underline Seger's claim to be the great closing time balladeer of his generation.

Brian Eno: *Music For Airports*

When Eno first introduced the idea of making background music respectable I'm not sure that many of us saw that he was just a few years ahead of a technological and creative wave that would make all music to some extent 'ambient'.

1979

The Cure: *Three Imaginary Boys*

Three kids, barely out of their teens, present their first album, which is made up of quietly ticking, slightly disturbing anthems of suburban anomie like '10:15 Saturday Night', and see themselves represented on the cover by a lamp, a fridge and a vacuum cleaner. It was the beginning of a forty-year career.

The Clash: *London Calling*

'Give them a good opening number and they'll forgive you a lot,' said Oscar Hammerstein, who could have been talking about the way the opening title track here still carries the whole first side. Listening to their previous two albums it's difficult to believe that somewhere between the first album and this, the third, they learned how to walk it where they had previously merely talked it.

Rickie Lee Jones: *Rickie Lee Jones*

She had straddled Tom Waits on the cover of his *Blue Valentine*, released the previous year, and she had written 'Easy Money' from Lowell George's solo album, also released in 1979. This was her debut, and it's still a joy. 'The Last Chance Texaco' is the best female-penned automotive metaphor I've ever come across.

Michael Jackson: *Off The Wall*

It's all dance tunes on the first side. The pace doesn't slacken until halfway through side two. The music on tunes like 'Don't Stop 'Til You Get Enough' and 'Rock With You' was worth listening to closely while you were dancing to it. There he is on the cover, thumbs in his pockets, funkily elegant, clearly both black and beautiful, with a magic aura glowing from the region of his dancing feet. Was it really all so simple then?

Tom Petty and the Heartbreakers: *Damn The Torpedoes*

Petty and Springsteen are similar, both second-generation rock stars trying to emulate the music of their own idols. Petty spent years reaching for that yearning note in the music of the Byrds and the dam-bursting explosions of the Who, and here, on songs like 'Refugee' and 'Even The Losers', he brings it all off.

Elvis Costello and the Attractions: *Armed Forces*

There's a brief period in the careers of rising bands when they think they can't do wrong. Then something misfires and they're never quite the same again. During the tour following the release of this, Elvis had his run-in with Bonnie Bramlett which clipped his wings. This Nick Lowe-produced third album is the apogee of that period as both pop star and provocateur when everything they did seemed to be both catchy and clever. 'Free EP inside!' as well.

Chic: *Risqué*

Nile Rodgers has a simple motto: 'Don't bore us, get to the chorus.' He was the man who told David Bowie that 'Let's Dance' had to start with the chorus. All but one of the tracks here obey that simple rule. It turned out to be a very influential album. Tony Thompson was certainly a very influential drummer. Can't imagine actually getting it out and playing it today but hats off nonetheless.

Fleetwood Mac: *Tusk*

One of the things I've learned while working on this book is that Fleetwood Mac are even better than I thought they were. Another thing I've learned about albums is that when you grow tired of liking the obvious albums you can throw yourself into the arms of the not-so-obvious ones. Compared to its predecessors *Tusk* was a bit of a mess, but messiness has its own appeal.

Ry Cooder: *Bop Till You Drop*

I interviewed Ry Cooder around the time of this album and he was very excited that it was the first rock record that had been digitally recorded. It's a perfectly good Ry Cooder record but you can't help thinking that in removing some of the imperfections of the old way they lost some of the spirit as well.

Neil Young & Crazy Horse: *Rust Never Sleeps*

At the time, Neil Young didn't know he would spend the rest of his career railing against the cult of perfection promised by digital delivery. He just wanted to record his band live and then work on the recordings in the studio. This wasn't a live recording smoothed out in the studio. It was a studio recording roughed up in the live arena. It's still fascinating and still exciting.

1980

Grace Jones: *Warm Leatherette*

This was the first of the excellent series of albums the former model made with producer Chris Blackwell and the Compass Point band at the beginning of the eighties. It was the first time she did edgy songs like Daniel Miller's title tune and Chrissie Hynde's 'Private Life' rather than the standard disco fare. There was something about her stern delivery, the band's relentless groove and the challenging graphics that was a better guide to where music was going next than either the Gang of Four or Donna Summer.

Joy Division: *Closer*

Although you wouldn't have found any of their boosters in the music weeklies saying it at the time, this second and last Joy Division album had more in common with dance records like Jones's than you might think. Both were tough, sure of themselves, not given to ingratiation and entirely rhythm-driven. This has stood up well over the intervening four decades.

Pete Townshend: *Empty Glass*

My favourite sleeve credit of all time is here: 'Thanks to Remy Martin Cognac for saving my life by making the bloody stuff so expensive'. In years to come all rock superstars would undergo therapy and make albums that were thinly disguised attempts at mending fences with their nearest and dearest. This is the first one I remember and it's still a pretty good one.

Bob Dylan: *Saved*

It always seems to me that what gets Bob Dylan out of bed every morning is his desire to prove to his most devoted fans that they don't understand him anything like as well as they think they do. His Christian period is a perfect illustration of this deep-seated cussedness. Many Dylan fans think this is the nadir of his entire career. I would still never part with any Dylan record because experience has taught me that, though it might take years, you always find something to love in all of them. In this case it's 'Solid Rock', which is the craziest rock shakedown he's ever recorded.

Roxy Music: *Flesh And Blood*

Roxy Music are like the Rolling Stones. All their best records have the best covers. When Roxy Music returned in the late seventies they made records that were good rather than great and packaged them in album covers that anybody could have come up with. This was not the same old Roxy Music. For a start it didn't have the great Paul Thompson on drums. Instead it was mixed by Bob Clearmountain at the Power Station and seemed far more eager to please than they had ever been in the past.

Echo & the Bunnymen: *Crocodiles*

The interesting thing about the bands making their first albums in those days is how they went out of their way to avoid giving the impression of being young and enthusiastic. They arrived at a similar style to the one that had been arrived at by the Cure because they were avoiding guitar solos and lyrics you could easily latch on to. Their key quality as makers of albums was that they could establish a mood of elegant hopelessness and then sustain it for almost forty minutes.

XTC: *Black Sea*

XTC weren't ones for looking at their feet and hiding behind their fringes. They looked straight at you and sang songs that people could understand: about the threat of nuclear war ('Living Through Another Cuba'), about suburbia ('Respectable Street') and even about the deaths of navvies building Victorian cities ('Towers Of London'). Of all the albums they made in the early days when they were still touring this is the strongest.

U2: *Boy*

Steve Lillywhite, who produced this and the XTC album, told me that U2 were so much their own invention that they didn't know how to play a twelve-bar blues. This was a feature of many of the bands coming through after punk. They had one style and it was their own. Nearly forty years later it doesn't sound like enough. What's most interesting is to be reminded of the fact that there was a time when you could put a picture of a naked boy on the cover of an album and not be accused of pederasty.

Bruce Springsteen: *The River*

Springsteen is well known for his idea that a live show should be a little bit of everything; dance party, political rally, revival meeting, comedy show and confession session. With this record he brought the full range of what he did and successfully spread it across a double album.

John Lennon & Yoko Ono: *Double Fantasy*

Some records are made poignant. Others have poignancy forced upon them. This is at the head of the latter category.

1981

The Pretenders: *Pretenders II*

Suddenly it seemed like everything was a tribute or a pastiche. The cover, with its white border and the members of the band in half-shadow, is a direct pinch from the second Rolling Stones album. It's a pleasant surprise to play it for the first time in decades and find chart singles like 'Talk Of The Town' and 'Message Of Love' popping up between the 18-certificate stuff like 'Bad Boys Get Spanked' and 'The Adultress'. Then there's her version of Ray Davies's 'I Go To Sleep'. It was to be the last record made with the original line-up, two of whom died drug-related deaths.

Phil Collins: *Face Value*

I know he's the butt of jokes from wiseacre comics on panel shows who have no opinions of their own. I won't have a word said against Phil Collins the musician. This is where he set out the template of his solo albums – big, breezy funk numbers, songs about his personal life and well-chosen cover versions – and it still stands up far better than most of the records that probably turned up in the best of the year. Best song? 'I Missed Again'. Nobody else could have done that.

Pat Metheny & Lyle Mays: *As Falls Wichita, So Falls Wichita Falls*

This is one of those records I bought purely because of the title. I have absolutely no regrets.

Eno and Byrne: *My Life In The Bush Of Ghosts*

Nine out of ten movies nowadays have some flashback sequence in which our hero relives some harrowing episode that took place in the Middle East in the wars that followed 9/11. The music used will marry the urgency of clubbing music with the sounds and textures of the music of the Third World. This tradition of wordless abstract music for the modern day began here and makes more sense with every passing year.

Rosanne Cash: *Seven Year Ache*

Maybe they're right when they say that the story-telling tradition of rock and roll has vanished into country music. A lot of people driven away from pop music by hip hop fled into the arms of country. People like Rosanne Cash are worthy heirs to that tradition and the title track here was one of the best songs of the decade.

Kraftwerk: *Computer World*

I worked in magazines when this came out. Our copy was still sent to the typesetters by courier. Pages were wrestled into being from Letraset and glue. There were just three TV channels. All the reviews of this record, like all the records talked about in this book, were written on manual typewriters. This still seemed to belong to a place called the Future. We were only a few years away from the day when the future arrived.

Stevie Nicks: *Bella Donna*

She started working on this while the sessions for *Tusk* seemed to have no end. She completed it with Benmont Tench as musical director and Jimmy Iovine, the master of the full-fat rock and roll sound beloved of American radio, as producer. It was a huge success and went on to establish brand values ('Leather And Lace', 'Edge Of Seventeen' and 'Stop Draggin' My Heart Around') which have endured to this day.

Black Uhuru: *Red*

My copy is pressed on red vinyl, a reminder of the priorities of the record business back in the waning days of vinyl. Produced, driven and shaped in every respect by Sly & Robbie, this was taut, forceful reggae from a new generation who had grown up under the spell of Bob Marley. You can hear this record all over Grace Jones's *Nightclubbing*, which came out the same year.

Heaven 17: *Penthouse And Pavement*

Seventy-five per cent of this record is in the cover, which is given over to an illustration of the three members of the group dressed up as businessmen. This time they hoped to emulate the executive lifestyle rather than satirise it, which was a big change. It depicted a working environment for musicians which would soon look the same as the working environment for technocrats because they would both be working at screens. They didn't know how right they were.

Human League: *Dare*

Phil Oakey didn't want 'Don't You Want Me' on the album at all. He thought it was too corny. He eventually relented and it was put at the very end of side two. It went on to be the biggest hit of the entire second British Invasion which was going on at the time. It's paid their mortgages ever since.

1982

Donald Fagen: *The Nightfly*

'The songs on this album represent certain fantasies that might have been entertained by a young man growing up in the remote suburbs of a northeastern city during the late fifties and early sixties, i.e. one of my general height, weight and build.' This is one of the last masterpieces of the golden age of the LP.

ABC: *The Lexicon Of Love*

There is no way this Sheffield group could have hoped to make a record as advanced as this without the help of producer Trevor Horn and also the Fairlight CMI, a magical and at the time prohibitively expensive machine that enabled them to fly in any sound they wanted from the past and the future. Soon the new technology would become cheaper, enabling everyone to make their record sound equally expensive.

Bruce Springsteen: *Nebraska*

These songs were first recorded on a very crude cassette-based Porta-studio with the intention that they would be re-recorded with the E Street Band. In the end he decided he couldn't improve on them and so they should master the record from the cassette. There was so much surface noise on the tape that at first they couldn't get it to actually cut a groove in the master disc. No wonder his next record, *Born In The USA*, was the brightest, loudest, splashiest thing he ever did.

Prince: *1999*

This hardly warrants a double. The first side is only about fifteen minutes long. By this time that could have been the playing time of a twelve-inch single. It was also front-loaded. The first two tracks were the title track and 'Little Red Corvette'. It sold well but you can't help suspecting that most listeners weren't there by the time 'All The Critics Love U In New York' rolled around on side four.

Neil Young: *Trans*

This is a perfect illustration of what happens to artists when they find themselves making more than ten albums. They can either try to repeat themselves, inevitably finding themselves a pale shadow of their former selves. Or they can strike out, as Neil Young did here, with new instruments like the vocoder, and end up being sued by their own record company for making records that no longer sound like people have a reasonable expectation that they should sound.

Richard and Linda Thompson: *Shoot Out The Lights*

He sits in the corner of a room from which the furniture has recently been stripped. The only sign of her is a picture on the wall. The songs include one called 'Did She Jump Or Was She Pushed?' That's what you call a divorce album.

Culture Club: *Kissing To Be Clever*

For about a year Culture Club were truly the biggest thing in the world. They were provocative but popular. No comedian in the world was allowed to leave the stage without making one crack about Boy George. And then they faded away, leaving millions of copies of this album to go unplayed and then, in time, to make their way to the charity shop. I'd be amazed if anyone has played this in the last ten years.

Dexys Midnight Runners: *Too-Rye-Ay*

At the dawn of the video age Kevin Rowland's band seemed to point to a new version of pop success, in which a band would effectively reinvent themselves with new members and new clothes for each new album. On the cover of this he was pictured as a Depression-era gypsy, just as on the first one he'd been seen as devoted soul boy. Again the huge single, 'Come On Eileen', is relegated to last in the running order, served up after you've worked through 'Liars A To E' and 'Until I Believe In My Soul', which seems at the very least hubristic.

Grace Jones: *Living My Life*

The first side of this, which starts with 'My Jamaican Guy', develops through 'Nipple To The Bottle' and climaxes with her version of Melvin Van Peebles' 'The Apple Stretching', is one of the most playable sides of popular music of the eighties. The other side's OK as well, but I tend to just play the first side again.

Michael Jackson: *Thriller*

The Beatles generation of musicians were all the children of Buddy Holly. The people who made it in the seventies and eighties were all the children of Dylan and the Beatles. The people who made it in the nineties and in the present century are all, for good or ill, the children of Michael Jackson's *Thriller*. This is where this story ends.

SELECT BIBLIOGRAPHY

Albertine, Viv, *Clothes, Clothes, Clothes, Music, Music, Music, Boys, Boys, Boys* (Faber & Faber, 2013)

Baker, Danny, *Going to Sea in a Sieve* (Weidenfeld & Nicolson, 2013)

Barfe, Louis, *Where Have All the Good Times Gone?* (Atlantic Books, 2004)

Blake, Mark, *Pigs Might Fly* (Aurum, 2007)

Bracewell, Michael, *Roxy: The Band that Invented an Era* (Faber & Faber, 2007)

Cartwright, Garth, *Going for a Song* (Flood Gallery, 2018)

Coe, Jonathan, *The Rotters' Club* (Viking, 2001)

Cornyn, Stan, *Exploding* (Harper Entertainment, 2002)

Costello, Elvis, *Unfaithful Music & Disappearing Ink* (Viking, 2015)

Curtis, Deborah, *Touching from a Distance* (Faber & Faber, 2005)

Dannen, Fredric, *Hit Men* (Muller, 1990)

Davis, Clive, *Clive: Inside the Record Business* (William Morrow, 1975)

Difford, Chris, *Some Fantastic Place* (Weidenfeld & Nicolson, 2017)

Egan, Sean (ed.), *Fleetwood Mac on Fleetwood Mac* (Omnibus, 2016)

Fagen, Donald, *Eminent Hipsters* (Cape, 2013)

Fleetwood, Mick, *Play On* (Hodder & Stoughton, 2014)

Forster, Robert, *Grant and I* (Penguin, 2016)

Goodman, Fred, *The Mansion on the Hill* (Vintage, 1997)

Gorman, Paul, *Reasons to Be Cheerful* (Adelita, 2010)

Greenfield, Robert, *The Last Sultan* (Simon & Schuster, 2011)

Hagan, Joe, *Sticky Fingers* (Canongate, 2017)

Harris, Carol Ann, *Storms: My Life with Lindsey Buckingham and Fleetwood Mac* (A Capella, 2009)

Harris, John, *The Last Party* (Fourth Estate, 2003)

Helm, Levon, *This Wheel's on Fire* (Chicago Review Press, 2000)

Holzman, Jac, *Follow the Music* (First Media, 2000)

Hook, Peter, *Unknown Pleasures* (Simon & Schuster, 2012)

Hoskyns, Barney, *Waiting for the Sun* (Viking, 1996)

Hoskyns, Barney, *Small Town Talk* (Faber & Faber, 2016)

Houghton, Mick, *Becoming Elektra* (Jawbone, 2016)

Houghton, Mick, *I've Always Kept a Unicorn* (Faber & Faber, 2016)

Hynde, Chrissie, *Reckless* (Ebury, 2016)

Johns, Glyn, *Sound Man* (Plume, 2015)

Kastin, David, *Song of the South* (Turntable Publishing, 2014)

Martland, Peter, *Since Records Began* (Batsford, 1997)

Mason, Nick, *Inside Out* (Weidenfeld & Nicolson, 2004)

McLeod, Kembrew, *Parallel Lines* (Cassell, 2010)

Milner, Greg, *Perfecting Sound Forever* (Granta, 2009)

Murphy, Gareth, *Cowboys and Indies* (Serpents Tail, 2015)

Rice, Tim, *Oh, What a Circus* (Hodder & Stoughton, 1999)

Robertson, Robbie, *Testimony* (Crown Archetype, 2016)

Scher, Paula, *Make It Bigger* (Princeton Architectural Press, 2005)

Simmons, Sylvie, *I'm Your Man* (Harper Collins, 2012)

Sinclair, David, *Tres Hombres: The Story of ZZ Top* (Virgin, 1986)

Springsteen, Bruce, *Born to Run* (Simon & Schuster, 2016)

Stafford, David and Caroline, *Fings Ain't Wot They Used t' Be: The Lionel Bart Story* (Omnibus, 2011)

Steinweiss, Alex, *For the Record* (Princeton Architectural Press, 2000)

Taraborrelli, J. Randy, *Michael Jackson: The Magic, The Madness, The Whole Story* (Pan, 1991)

Taylor, Derek, *As Time Goes By* (Davis Poynter, 1973)

Thompson, Harry, *Peter Cook – A Biography* (Hodder & Stoughton, 1997)

Thomson, Graeme, *George Harrison: Behind the Locked Door* (Omnibus, 2013)

Townshend, Pete, *Who I Am* (Harper Collins, 2012)

Trucks, Rob, *Fleetwood Mac's Tusk* (Continuum, 2011)

Webb, Jimmy, *The Cake and the Rain* (Omnibus, 2017)

Womack, Kenneth, *Sound Pictures* (Orphans, 2018)

ACKNOWLEDGEMENTS

During the time I'm working on a book like this, almost every conversation with a friend or colleague sparks off a line of thought. Thanks very much to the people who were aware their brains were being picked – Andrew Collins, Brian Cooke, Bruce Findlay, David Howells, Chris Johnson, Steve Lewis, Eugene Manzi, Roy Matthews, Tim Milne, Jonathan Morrish, Neil Storey, Chris Topham, Tony Wadsworth, Johnnie Walker and Martin Young – and also to the many others who weren't. Into this latter group I would like to welcome the LP lovers I follow on social media, many of whom I've never actually met. They've given me more ideas than they could ever know.

Thanks once again to Mark Ellen for wise counsel and encouragement and to Bill Scott-Kerr, Sally Wray, Darcy Nicholson, Eloisa Clegg and Richard Shailer of Transworld and Charlie Viney of the Viney Shaw Agency.

PICTURE ACKNOWLEDGEMENTS

Although every effort has been made to trace copyright holders and clear permission for the photographs in this book, the provenance of a number of them is uncertain. The author and publisher would welcome the opportunity to correct any mistakes.

First section

Page 1: CBS chief engineer Dr Peter Carl Goldmark: CBS via Getty Images

Page 2: [top] Cover of album *Sgt Pepper's Lonely Hearts Club Band* by the Beatles: Jeff Morgan 04/Alamy Stock Photo; [bottom] Sgt Pepper launch: © Mark and Colleen Hayward/Getty Images

Page 3: [bottom] Joni Mitchell and Leonard Cohen at Newport: David Gahr/Getty Images

Page 4: [top] Bruce Findlay: sourced from *The Scotsman*; [bottom] King Crimson album: CBW/Alamy Stock Photo

Page 5: [top] The Band in 1968: Elliott Landy/Redferns/Getty Images

Page 6: [top] 1960s USA Sony magazine advertisement: courtesy of The Advertising Archives; [bottom] Jack Nicholson: Elliott Landy/Redferns/Getty Images

Picture Acknowledgements

Page 7: Mick Jagger: David Montgomery/Getty Images

Page 8: [top] Cream recording session: Michael Ochs Archives/Stringer/Getty Images

Second section

Page 10–11: [bottom left] Roxy Music album window display: Brian Cooke/Redferns/Getty Images

Page 12: [top] Donna Summer cake: Michael Ochs Archive/Getty Images; [bottom] David Geffen: Julian Wasser/The LIFE Images Collection/Getty Images

Page 13: [top] Patti Smith: Richard McCaffrey/ Michael Ochs Archive/ Getty Images; [bottom] Elton John: Michael Putland/Getty Images

Page 14: [bottom] Pink Floyd: Mick Gold/Redferns/Getty Images

Page 15: [top left] Stevie Nicks and Fleetwood Mac: Fin Costello/Redferns/Getty Images; [top right] *Rumours* cover: sjvinyl/Alamy Stock Photo; [bottom right] Blondie in a recording studio: Roberta Bayley/Redferns/Getty Images

Page 16: [top left] USA Sony Walkman magazine advert: courtesy of The Advertising Archives; [main middle] 26th Annual GRAMMY Awards: Ron Galella/WireImage/Getty Images; [bottom right] Cover of album *Thriller* by Michael Jackson: f8 archive/Alamy Stock Photo

INDEX

A

A-tom-ic Jones 2
Abba 124, 156, 199
   The Visitors 235–6
Abbey Road studios 98, 106–7, 215, 272, 292
ABC Television 140
ABC 224
   The Lexicon Of Love 319
Acoustic Research 94
Adam and the Ants 223
Afrika Bambaataa, *Planet Rock* 225
Akai 94
Albertine, Viv 23, 137–8, 159
album covers/ art 4–5, 6–7, 13–14, 37–8, 44–6, 76–91, 130, 135–7, 183–4
albums, 78s xiii–xiv
All the President's Men 218
Allman, Gregg 156
Allman Brothers Band 283
   At Fillmore East 64
   Eat A Peach 84
Alpert, Herb 9
Altamont 32
Altec 94
Amazing Rhythm Aces 156
Amboy Dukes 52
American Bandstand 28
Antonioni, Michelangelo 46
Apocalypse Now 194
Apple iPod 260
Apple label 63

Archies, 'Sugar, Sugar' 33
Ardent Studios 231
Are You Being Served? 89
Area Code 615 52
Arista 110
Armatrading, Joan 158
'artists', musicians as xvi, xviii–xix
Asher, Dick 226
Asia 224
Aspinall, Neil 9
Astral Weeks 216
Asylum 117, 118
Atlantic 110
Avedon, Richard 275
Ayers, Kevin 100

B

Bacall, Lauren 194
Bach, J. S., Mass in B Minor 9
Back to the Future 219
Baker, Arthur 238
Baker, Danny 97
Baker, Ginger 37, 274, 282
Band, The 40–6, 62
   'Across The Great Divide' 46, 77
   'Basement Tapes' 40
   Band, 'Darktown Strutters' Ball' 45
   live album 177
   Music From Big Pink 42–4, 277
   'Tears Of Rage' 277
   The Band 43–6

Band The – *Cont.*
  The Last Waltz 308
  'The Night They Drove Old Dixie Down' 41
  'The Weight' 42, 277
  'Whispering Pines' 46
Bangs, Lester 60–1
Banks, Peter, *Flash* 83
Barnard, Stephen 122
Barrett, Syd 98
Basquiat, Jean-Michel 221
Bates, Blaster 69
BBC Light Programme 3
BBC Radio 1, launch 20
BBC2 *Film Night* 96
Beach Boys 100, 66
  'Belles Of Paris' 175
  M.I.U. 174–5
  Pet Sounds 6
  Surf's Up 64
Beals, Jennifer 242
Beatles 100, 114, 184, 264, 265
  albums xvi
    Abbey Road 38, 55, 85–6
    Hard Day's Night 4, 7, 62
    Help! xvi, 4
    Magical Mystery Tour 16
    Revolver 246, 304
    Sgt Pepper's Lonely Hearts Club Band
      xvi–xvii, 3–16, 19, 39–40, 42, 101,
      108, 111, 146, 256, 267, 271–2
      buying 3, 5–8
      cover art 4–5, 6–7, 13–14
      influence 10–16
    The Beatles (White Album) 24, 53,
      277–8
    With The Beatles 4, 115
  Apple label 63
  bootlegs 53, 55
  songs
    'A Day In The Life' 11
    'All You Need Is Love' 16
    'Hello Goodbye' 16
    'I Saw Her Standing There' 266
    'Lovely Rita' 59
    'Lucy In The Sky With Diamonds' 3
    'Penny Lane' 4, 7
    Rubber Soul 304
    'Strawberry Fields Forever' 4, 7
    'Twist And Shout' 208
    'You Know My Name (Look Up The
      Number)' 16
Be-Bop Deluxe, *Modern Music* 140
Beck, Jeff 70
Becker, Walter 84, 306
Bee Gees 166, 169, 178

  'Fanny (Be Tender With My Love)' 301
  'Jive Talkin'' 135, 301
  Living Eyes 236
  Main Course 301
  'Nights On Broadway' 301
Bell, Max 155
Belt, Peter 253–4
Benatar, Pat, 'Love Is A Battlefield' 242
Benson, George, *Give Me The Night* 205
Berg, John 84
Berkeley, Busby 240
Berry, Chuck, *Rockin' At The Hops* 79–80
Beyond the Fringe 149
Big Ben 139
Big Brother 29–31
  Cheap Thrills 29–31, 45
Big Star 83, 231
Billboard xiv, 9, 31, 103, 112, 176, 190, 206,
  224, 257
Birkin, Jane, 'Je T'aime . . .' 125
Black and White Minstrel Show 3
Black Sabbath
  Black Sabbath 284
  Master of Reality 64
Black Uhuru, *Red* 318
Blackburn, Tony 20
Blackwell, Chris 76, 87, 151, 212, 293, 313
Blake, Peter 13
Blige, Mary J. 258
Blind Faith
  Blind Faith 35–6, 282
  'Can't Find My Way Home' 282
  'Do What You Like' 282
  'In The Presence Of The Lord' 282
Blodwyn Pig 67
Blondie 163, 178–81
  'Heart Of Glass' 180, 181, 307–8
  'Once I Had A Love' 179–80
  Parallel Lines 179–81, 307–8
  Plastic Letters 246
  'Rapture' 216, 221
  The Hunter 224
Blood, Sweat & Tears 28
  Child Is Father To The Man 28
Blue Oyster Cult, live album 177
Blues Project 28
Blume, Judy, *Forever* 126
Bodyguard, The 255
Bogart, Neil 126, 128
Bonham, John 298
Bonzo Dog Doo Dah Band
  Gorilla 275
  'Narcissus' 275
  'The Intro And The Outro' 275
Booth, Connie 129

bootleg LPs 53–8
Born To Run 239
Bose 94
Boston, 'More Than A Feeling' 140
Bow Wow Wow, 'C30, C60, C90 Go!' 212
Bowie, David 3, 127, 245
   'Fame' 135
   Hours 252
   Hunky Dory 65, 72, 85, 286
   Let's Dance 189
   'Let's Dance' 312
   live album 177
   Low 156, 203, 306
   'Starman' 289
   Station To Station 301–2
   'Suffragette City' 289
   The Man Who Sold The World 50, 202
   The Rise And Fall Of Ziggy Stardust . . . 85,
      86, 289
   Young Americans 124, 135
Boy George 321
Boyd, Joe 9
Boylan, John 115
BPI, *National Album Day* 263
Bradbury, Malcolm, *The History Man* 126
Brady, Mathew 45
Bramlett, Bonnie 312
Branson, Richard 51, 101
Brass Construction 178
Britannia Row 202, 203
British Electric Foundation, *Music For
   Stowaways* 212
Brown, Pete 23
Browne, Jackson 71, 116
   'The Late Show' 296
   Late For The Sky 80, 82, 117, 296
   'Late For The Sky' 259
Bruce, Lenny, *The Berkeley Concert* 147
Bryon, Dennis 135
Bubbles, Barney 183–4
Buckingham, Lindsey 184, 185, 186–95
Buckley, Tim
   Goodbye And Hello 15
   Greetings From L.A. 82–3
   'Morning Glory' 28
Burchill, Julie 155, 159
Burdon, Eric, *Winds Of Change* 14
Burning Spear, *Marcus Garvey* 300
Bush, Kate 216
   Hounds Of Love 216
   'Moving' 308
   The Kick Inside 308
   'The Man With The Child In His Eyes' 308
   'Wuthering Heights' 308
Butch Cassidy and the Sundance Kid 46

Byrds 11, 40
   'Eight Miles High' 44
Byrne, David 214–16, 231, 308–9
   and Brian Eno, *My Life In The Bush Of
      Ghosts* 215, 216, 317

C
Cadence Records, *The First Family* 144–5
Caillat, Ken 194
California Kid 232
Callaghan, James 139
Cannon, Geoffrey 36
Capaldi, Jim 284–5
Capitol 41, 100
Captain Beefheart and His Magic Band 20
   Trout Mask Replica 39, 280
Car Wash 142
Cara, Irene, 'Flashdance . . . What A Feeling' 242
Caravan, *In The Land Of Grey And Pink* 72
Carlin, George, *Class Clown* 149
Carlin, Peter 11
Carpenters 199
Carson, Johnny 129
Carter, Ernest 'Boom' 299
Carter, Jimmy 203
Casablanca Records 126, 128, 176
Cash, Rosanne, *Seven Year Ache* 317
cassettes/ players 196–202, 210–16, 243
Catcher in the Rye 163, 259
Cato, Bob 44–5
Cavaliere, Felix 114
Cavett, Dick 120
CDs 235–50, 251–65
Chambers, Marilyn, *Behind the Green Door* 129
Chapman, Mark 208
Chapman, Mike 179–80
Chappell shop 68
Charlie's Angels 140
Cheech and Chong 147
Cherry Red 201
Chic, *Risqué* 189, 312
Chicago 84
   Democratic Party convention 56
   rioting 32
Chicago Transit Authority 56–7
   Chicago Transit Authority 280
   'Free Form Guitar' 280
   'It Better End Soon' 57
Chichester, Francis 3
Chinn, Nicky 179
Chrysalis Records 179
Ciccone, Madonna 119
Cipollina, John 281–2
Citizen Kane 8
Clapton, Eric 13, 36, 42–3, 274, 283

Index

Clash 160, 163, 165
Clash, 'Janie Jones' 307
   London Calling 165, 190, 311
   The Clash 307
Clearmountain, Bob 189, 314
Clemons, Clarence 284
Clift, Montgomery 14
Coburn, James 292
cocaine 192–3
Cocker, Joe 62
   Grease Band 34
Cockney Rebel, *The Best Years Of Our Lives* 124
Cohen, Leonard 18–20, 274
Cohen, Leonard, 'Hey, That's No Way To Say
   Goodbye' 19
Cohen, Leonard, 'Sisters Of Mercy' 19, 20, 22
Cohen, Leonard, 'So Long Marianne' 19, 277
Cohen, Leonard, *Songs Of Leonard Cohen*
   19–20, 23–4, 277
Cohen, Leonard, 'Suzanne' 19, 33
Cohn, Nik 166
Colbert, Stephen 148
Cole, Marilyn 90
Collet's, New Oxford Street 68
Collins, Jackie 136
Collins, Judy 33
   Wildflowers 9, 274
Collins, Phil 303
   Face Value 254, 316–7
   'I Missed Again' 317
Columbia xiii, 18–23, 27–31, 44, 110, 166,
   225–6, 239
   and The Man 56–7
   Rock Machine 21–3
comedy LPs xiv, 145–53
Comfort, Alex, *Joy of Sex* 88
Commander Cody and His Lost Planet
   Airmen 113, 115–16
Common Market (EU) 33
Como, Perry 51
compact cassettes 166
Compass Point 313
Conkling, Jim 144
Conniff, Ray 94
Conteh, John 292
Cooder, Ry 158, 65
   Boomer's Story 291–2
   Bop Till You Drop 188–9, 312–13
   Into The Purple Valley 84
   Paradise And Lunch 80
Cook, Peter 149–53
   and Dudley Moore, *Derek And Clive (Live)*
   142–3, 149–53, 301
Cooke, Brian 76, 90
Cooper, Alice, *School's Out* 83

Cooper, Michael 13
Copeland, Stewart 196–7
Cordet, Ester 137
Cornwell, Hugh 170
Cornyn, Stan 57
Cosby, Bill
   Revenge 9
   Why Is There Air? 148
   Wonderfulness 148
cost of living 1970 48–9
Costa Sam 20
Costello, Elvis 123, 184–5
   'Accidents Will Happen' 182
   'Big Boys' 183
   My Aim Is True 307
   'Oliver's Army' 183
   This Year's Model 172, 184
   and the Attractions, *Armed Forces* 182,
   183–4, 312
Country Joe & the Fish 159
Cox, Courteney 238
Coyne, Kevin 255
Crackerjack 96
Cream
   Disraeli Gears 13, 43, 274
   'Mother's Lament' 13
   'Sunshine Of Your Love' 274
Creedence Clearwater Revival 62
   Green River 279
Criss, Peter 176
critics 102–3
Crosby, Bing 58
Crosby, David 11
   'Almost Cut My Hair' 49
Crosby, Stills & Nash, *Crosby, Stills & Nash* 281
Crosby, Stills, Nash & Young, *Déjà Vu* 49
Crumb, Robert 30, 44–5
   Keep On Truckin' 54
Culture Club, *Kissing To Be Clever* 320–1
Cure, '10:15 Saturday Night' 310
Cure, *Three Imaginary Boys* 310
Curtis, Debbie 202–3
Curtis, Ian 202–3, 204, 206
Curved Air 196
Czukay, Holger 215

D
Dakota Building 206, 207
Daltrey, Roger 14, 286
Damned, The 163, 184
Dan Hicks and the Hot Licks, *Striking It Rich* 82
Dandelion 54
Danko, Rick 41, 43, 45
Dannen, Fredric, *Hit Men* 226
Dansette xv, xviii

Davies, Ray 169, 316
Davies, Rhett 38
Davis, Clive 21, 27, 29, 110–11, 122
Davis, Miles, *Ascenseur pour l'échafaud* 248–9
Davis, Richard 25
Davis, Sammy Jr 43
Dawson, Pete 72
Days of Rage 32
De Palma, Brian 238
DeShannon, Jackie 133
Dean, Roger 84
Decca 37
Dee, Simon, *Dee Time* 3
Deep Throat 129
Denny, Sandy 9, 280
Denon 94
Denselow, Robin 153
Derek and the Dominos, *Layla* 164, 182–3, 283
Derek, Bo 194
Dexys Midnight Runners 223
    Too-Rye-Ay 321
Diana Princess of Wales 219
Dickens, Charles 264
Diddley, Bo 44
    'Who Do You Love' 281
Difford, Chris, *Some Fantastic Place* 134
DiLeo, Frank 227, 230
Dire Straits, *Brothers In Arms* 243
disco boom 125–38
Dobell's, Charing Cross Road 68
Don Ellis Orchestra 21
Donovan 25
    In Concert 42
Doobie Brothers 231
    Toulouse Street 84–5
Doors, The 44, 159
    L.A. Woman 64
Douglas, Carl, 'Kung Fu Fighting' 135
Dr Feelgood 155
    Down By The Jetty 299
Dr John
    Dr John's Gumbo 290–1
    Gris-Gris 22
    'Mess Around' 291
    'Tipitina' 291
Drake
    Scorpion 263
Drake, Nick 39
    Bryter Layter 65, 288
Draper, Don 21, 57
Driscoll, Julie 40
drug culture, heads 47–8
du Pré, Jacqueline 259
Dual 94
Duran Duran 224, 241

'Hungry Like The Wolf ' 242–3
Dury, Ian
    Do It Yourself 184
    New Boots And Panties!! 206, 304–5
Dylan, Bob 17–18, 19, 22, 40, 53, 118, 133,
    170, 246
    albums
        Blonde On Blonde xvi, 40, 59–60, 248
        Blood On The Tracks 128–9, 137, 183, 298
        Desire 304
        Hard Rain 142
        John Wesley Harding xviii, 17–18, 85–6,
            272
        live album 177
        Nashville Skyline 39, 53
        Planet Waves 117, 118–19
        Saved 314
        Self Portrait 58–9
        Slow Train Coming 60
        Street Legal 174
    bootlegs 55, 58
    songs
        'All Along The Watchtower' 17
        'I Pity The Poor Immigrant' 17
        'Mr Tambourine Man' 174
        'Sad Eyed Lady Of The Lowlands' 58
        'Solid Rock' 314
        'This Wheel's On Fire' 40
        'You Ain't Going Nowhere' 40
        'You're Gonna Make Me Lonesome
            When You Go' 183

E
E Street Band 319
Eagles 169
    Eagles: Their Greatest Hits 116, 143, 299
    'Hollywood Waltz' 299
    Hotel California 183
    'Lyin' Eyes' 299
    One Of These Nights 299
    'Take It To The Limit' 299
    'Wasted Time' 183
Earth Records Aylesbury 69
Easy Rider 46, 54
Ebony 227
Echo & the Bunnymen
    Crocodiles 315
    Heaven Up Here 220
Edgar Broughton Band 23
Electric Flag 22
Electric Ladyland 164
Electric Light Orchestra 65, 96
    A New World Record 142, 302
    'Do Ya' 302
    'Evil Woman' 135

Index

Electric Light Orchestra – *Cont.*
  'Livin' Thing' 302
  'Rockaria!' 302
  'Telephone Line' 302
Electric Prunes, *Release Of An Oath* 24
Elektra Records 22, 246–7
Ellington, Duke 252
  'East St Louis Toodle-oo' 296
Elliot, Cass 9
Ellis, Terry 178–9
EMI 64, 145–6, 151, 250, 285
  factory 269–70
  Music for Pleasure 66
  pressing plant 109
Eminem 258
Emmanuelle 129, 142
Eno, Brian 127, 215, 231
  Music For Airports 310
  and Byrne, *My Life In The Bush Of Ghosts* 215, 216, 317
Entwistle 286
Epic 226–7, 230
Epstein, Brian 4, 11, 16
Ertegun, Ahmet 110
Eurythmics 215
Evening Standard 209
Everett, Kenny 3
Exorcist, The 101

F
Fab 5 Freddy 221
Fabian album 80
Factory Records 203–5
Fagen, Donald 84, 306
  The Nightfly 319
Fairlight CMI 319
Fairport Convention 9, 39, 44, 159, 291
  'A Sailor's Life' 280–1
  Liege & Lief 75
  Unhalfbricking 280–1
  'Who Knows Where The Time Goes?' 280
Fall and Rise of Reginald Perrin 140–1
Family, *Bandstand* 82, 168
Farren, Mick 154–5, 162
Fawlty Towers 129
Ferry, Bryan 87, 90–1
  Another Time Another Place 297
  'It Ain't Me Babe' 297
  'Smoke Gets In Your Eyes' 297
  'The In Crowd' 297
Fiddler on the Roof 273
5th Dimension 11
Fillmore Auditorium 30
Findlay, Bruce, Edinburgh record shop 34–7

Fisher, Alan 152
Fitzgerald, Ella 246
Five Easy Pieces 48
Five Live Yardbirds 2
Flanders, Michael, and Donald Swann
  At the Drop of a Hat 145
  'I'm A Gnu' 145
  'Song Of Reproduction' 145
  'The Gas Man Cometh' 145
Fleetwood Mac 44, 166
  'I Know I'm Not Wrong' 192
  'Love That Burns' 279
  Mr Wonderful 278–9
  'Over And Over' 195
  Rumours 166, 172, 183, 185, 186–7, 192, 195, 304
  'Sara' 195
  'The Ledge' 195
  Tusk 184, 186–95, 312
Fleetwood, Mick 187–95, 278–9
Flying Burrito Brothers 52
Footloose 218
Forbert, Steve 173
Forster, Robert 80
45rpm records xv–xvi
Forum 125
Frampton, Peter 178, 185
  Frampton Comes Alive! 302–3
Frank Comstock Orchestra 130
Frank, Robert, *The Americans* 81–2
Frankie Goes to Hollywood, 'Relax' 238
Franklin, Aretha, *I Never Loved A Man The Way I Love You* 272
Franzen, Jonathan 275
Frehley, Ace 176
Freud, Clement 292
Friedkin, William 101
Friends 238
Fury, Billy 87

G
Gable, Clark 131
Gabriel, Peter 233, 303
Gadd, Steve 306
Gainsbourg, Serge, 'Je T'aime . . . ' 125
Gallagher, Liam 257
Gallagher, Noel 257
Galuten, Albhy 135
Gang of Four 313
GarageBand 266
Garcia, Jerry 110
Garrard 94
Garrod and Lofthouse 77
Gaye, Marvin 246, 264
  'Inner City Blues' 285

Here My Dear 168, 309–10
   Let's Get It On 133, 293
   What's Going On 64, 285
Gaynor, Gloria 135
Geffen, David 116, 117, 118, 206
Genesis
   A Trick Of The Tail 303
   'A Trick Of The Tail' 303
   'Dance On A Volcano' 303
   'Los Endos' 303
George, Lowell 311
   'Willin'' 290
Gershwin, George, 'Summertime' 30
Gibbons, Billy 231–4, 242
Giles, Johnny 140
Giraldi, Bob 241
Gleason, Jackie 131
Go-Betweens 80
Godber, Barry 37
Goldstein, Richard 10
Good Life, The 140
Goodwin, Ron 146
Gordon, Shep 83
Gordy, Berry 227, 310
Gormé, Eydie 21
Grable, Betty 87
Graduate, The 26
Graham, Bill 30
Grand Funk Railroad 114
   Phoenix 168
Grandmaster Flash, *The Message* 225
Grateful Dead 29
   Live/Dead 110
   Workingman's Dead 110, 284
Grayson, Larry, *Shut That Door* 89
Grease 172
Grease Band 34
Great White Wonder (bootleg LP) 53
Green, Al
   'Take Me To The River' 308
   The Belle Album 307
Green, Peter 158, 279
Greene, Graham, *Travels With My Aunt* 96
Greetings From Asbury Park, N.J. 239
Gregory, Dick 246
Grossman, Albert 31, 40, 41
Grundy, Bill 152–3
Guardian 36, 153
Gutbucket 22–3
Guthrie, Arlo 63
   'Alice's Restaurant' 33
   Running Down The Road 33
   wedding 32–3
Guthrie, Woody 33

H
Haight-Ashbury 3, 30
hair as culture 49–50
Hair 'tribal love rock musical' 36, 125
Hall, Daryl 114
Hall, Jerry 90
Hamill, Pete 298
Hammerstein, Oscar 311
Hammond, John 18
Hammonds of Hull 35
Hampton Grease Band 52
Hancock, Tony, *The Radio Ham* 147
Hands and Feet 76
Hannett, Martin 203–4
Hardin, Tim
   'Don't Make Promises' 24
   'The Lady Came From Baltimore' 24
Harlequin Records 71
Harley, Steve, *Hobo With A Grin* 178
Harman Kardon 93
Harris, Emmylou 304
Harris, John 256
Harrison, George 42
   All Things Must Pass 63–4, 282
   'My Sweet Lord' 64
Harry, Debbie 169–70, 180, 221, 224
Hawkins, Ronnie 41
Hayward, Justin, and John Lodge, *Blue Jays* 124
Head 76
heads 47–61
Healey, Denis 141
Heaven 17, *Penthouse And Pavement* 221, 318
Helm, Levon 41
Henderson, Joe 'Mr Piano' 68
Hendrix, Jimi xi, 37, 245
   Axis: Bold As Love 14
   'Red House' 273
   Experience 20
      Are You Experienced 273
Henley, Don 116, 191
Henry Cow 255
Heron, Mike 273
higher education 23–4
Hird, Thora 3
hit singles importance 111–12, 115–16, 182–3, 237
HMV 68, 247, 249, 252
   Oxford Street shop 70–1, 109
Ho Chi Minh 14
Holiday, Billie 18
Hollies 11
Holly, Buddy xvi, 8
Holy Modal Rounders 52
Holzman, Jac 246–7
Home Box Office 149

Index

Hook, Peter 203, 206
Hootie & the Blowfish 255
Hope, Bob 129
Hopper, Dennis 46
Hormel, Geordie 187–8
Horn, Trevor 319
Houston, Whitney 255
Howells, David 18–23
Howerd, Frankie, *Up the Front* 88
Hudson, Garth 40, 45
Hudson, Linden 233
Human League 212, 223
Human League, 'Don't You Want Me' 319
    Dare 254, 319
Humperdinck, Engelbert 23
Hunter, Ian 80
Hunter, Robert 110
Hunter, Tab 143–4
Hyde, Jackie 32–3
Hynde, Chrissie, 'Private Life' 313

I
Iggy Pop 122
Incredible String Band, *The 5000 Spirits Or
    The Layers Of The Onion* 273
independents 200–6
Inman, John 89
International Times 38
Iovine, Jimmy 318
Iron Butterfly, *In-A-Gadda-Da-Vida* 22, 42, 128
Island and Chrysalis, *You Can All Join In* 22
Island Records 35, 37, 76, 87, 89, 151, 212, 297
Isley Brothers 135
IT 54

J
J. Geils Band 290
    Full House 167
    Sanctuary 168
Jackson Five, 'Never Can Say Goodbye' 135
Jackson, Michael 240
    Bad 230
    'Beat It' 229, 241
    'Billie Jean' 227–8, 241
    'Don't Stop 'Til You Get Enough' 194, 311
    Off The Wall 227, 311
    'Rock With You' 311
    statues 251–2
    'The Girl Is Mine' 228
    Thriller xvii, xviii, 227–31, 237, 240–1,
        243, 321
Jackson, Millie, *Caught Up* 136
Jagger, Mick 12–13, 79–80, 82, 174, 245, 303
    'What a drag it is getting old' 182
Jam 163, 165

James, Elmore 44
JBL 94
Jeff Beck Group, *Truth* 278
Jefferson Airplane, *Surrealistic Pillow* 9
Jenkins, Gordon 294
Jethro Tull 170
    Thick As A Brick 84
Jewell, Derek 102
Jobs, Steve 260
Joel, Billy, *52nd Street* 172, 236
jogging 211–12
John, Elton 199, 219
    *Captain Fantastic And The Brown Dirt
        Cowboy* 300
    Madman Across The Water 65, 68
    'Philadelphia Freedom' 135
    'Someone Saved My Life Tonight' 300
    Tumbleweed Connection 282–3
Johnny Howard band 20
Johns, Glyn 12–13, 15–16, 116
Johnson, Lyndon 14
Jones, Brian 37
Jones, Grace
    Living My Life 321
    'My Jamaican Guy' 321
    Nightclubbing 220, 318
    'Nipple To The Bottle' 321
    'The Apple Stretching' 321
    Warm Leatherette 313
Jones, Mick 138, 159
Jones, Quincy 227–30
    Off The Wall 303
Jones, Rickie Lee
    'Easy Money' 311
    Rickie Lee Jones 311
    'The Last Chance Texaco' 311
Jones, Tom 23
Joplin, Janis 29–31
journalism 154–66
Joy Division 202–6
    Closer 204–6, 313
    'Love Will Tear Us Apart' 202
    Unknown Pleasures 203, 205
    see also New Order
Jude, Dennis 151
'Just Released' rack 167–9

K
Kahn, Susan 132
Kari-Ann 87
Kaye, Stubby 3
Keats, John 14
Keegan, Kevin 140
Kelly, Danny 163–4
Kelly, Gene 240

Index

Kemp, Lindsay 308
Ken and Betty (Record Bar) 2, 74
Kent, Nick 122, 156, 158–60, 162–4, 281
Kenwood 93
Kerouac, Jack 24
Kids From 'Fame' 223
Kief's Music 225
King, Carole
  Tapestry 64
  'You've Got A Friend' 64
King Crimson 86–7, 89
  '21st Century Schizoid Man' 279
  In The Court Of The Crimson King . . . 35,
    36–9, 279
King Kong 140
King, Stephen, *Carrie* 140
Kingston Trio 144
Kinks 66, 170
Kiss 176
Kojak 140
Kooper, Al 28, 274
Kraftwerk 180
  Autobahn 128
  Computer World 317–18
  Trans-Europe Express 305
Kramer, Eddie 273
Kramer vs. Kramer 203
Kristina, Sonja 196

L
LA Express 118
La Rue, Danny 89
LaBelle, Patti, and the Bluebells 135, 136
Laine, Denny 292
Lake, Greg 37
Lambert, Kit 281
Landau, Jon 237
Landis, John 241
Landy, Elliott 45
Lane, Ronnie 278
Lange, Jessica 140
Larkin, Philip 102
Lauper, Cyndi, 'Girls Just Wanna Have Fun' 238
Lawrence, Steve 21
Laws, Ronnie 246
Lear, Amanda 90, 293
Led Zeppelin x, 108, 151, 205, 239, 278
  'Boogie With Stu' 298
  'In The Light' 298
  In Through The Out Door 194
  'Kashmir' 298
  Led Zeppelin IV 65, 86
  Physical Graffiti 124, 137, 298
  'Trampled Under Foot' 298
Lee, Christopher 292

Lefort, Albert 49
Leigh, Mike, *Abigail's Party* 136
Lennon, John 55, 206–8
  Imagine 64
  Toronto show record 58
  & Yoko Ono, *Double Fantasy* 206–8, 316
Let It Bleed 38
Let It Rock 121–2
Lewis, Steve 51, 53
Liberty, *Gutbucket* 22–3
Lightfoot, Gordon 58
Lillywhite, Steve 315
Listener 101
listening booths 34
Little Feat 64, 231
  Sailin' Shoes 71, 84, 290
live albums 176–7
Lloyd Webber, Andrew
  Jesus Christ Superstar 33–4
  Joseph and the Amazing Technicolor
    Dreamcoat 33
Logan, Nick 154
Lomax, Alan 252
Long, Huey 119
Louvin Brothers 44
Love Affair (group) 18
Love Unlimited Orchestra 134
Loverboy 226
Lowe, Nick 255, 312
Lownds, Sara 174
LPs complete work xvi–xvii
  carrying 50, 79–81
  cover art 4–5, 6–7, 13–14, 76–91, 130,
    135–7, 183–4
  easily damaged 77–81
  introduction xiii–xvii
  survival xvii–xviii
Lubov, Arthur 132
Lynch, Kenny 292
Lynne, Jeff 302
Lynott, Phil 177

M
M*A*S*H 194
MacManus, Declan *see* Costello, Elvis
Maddox, Lester 120, 295
Madonna 247
Majors, Farrah Fawcett 211
Man, *2 Ozs Of Plastic* . . . 246
Manhattan Transfer 124
Mann, Herbie, *Push Push* 198
Mann, Manfred 37
  Manfred Mann's Earth Band, *The Roaring*
    Silence 143
Mann, William 10

Manor studio 101
Manson, Charles 54
Manuel and His Music of the Mountains 68
Manuel, Richard 41, 277
Mao Tse-tung 139
Marantz 94
Marcus, Greil 25, 55, 58, 60–1
Marley, Bob 137, 293, 318
  live album 177
Marriott, Steve 278
Marsh, Dave 192
Martin, George 8, 28, 115, 145–6, 183, 266
Martyn, John 65, 76
  Inside Out 77
Mason, Dave 54
  Alone Together 67
Matthews, Roy 109, 250, 269–70
Mayall, John, *Bare Wires* 23
Mayfair 88
MCA record company 33–4, 113
McCartney, Linda 292
McCartney, Paul 53, 64, 85, 114–15, 227, 228, 278
  'Maybe I'm Amazed' 285
  McCartney 285
  Ram 64, 288
  'Uncle Albert/Admiral Halsey' 288
  and Wings, *Band On The Run* 292–3
McLane, Daisann 192
McLaren, Malcolm 212
McLean, Don, *American Pie* 65
McLennan, Grant 80
McNay, Iain 201
McPhee, T. S. 246
McVie, Christine 191, 192, 195
  'Songbird' 183
McVie, John 191
Meat Loaf, *Bat Out Of Hell* 166, 223, 305–6
Mellencamp, John, *American Fool* 224
Melody Maker 121, 157
Men Only 88
Merlis, Bob 147–8
Merseybeat 172
Metheny, Pat, & Lyle Mays, *As Falls Wichita* 317
Michael, George 219
Midnight Cowboy 46
Miller, Daniel 313
Miller, Mitch 21, 110
Miller, Steve 15–16
Mills, Mrs 68
Milne, Tim 81, 265–6
Milner, Greg, *Perfecting Sound Forever* 189
Mitchell, Joni
  Blue 64, 253, 287
  'Both Sides Now' 274

Clouds 39
Court And Spark 117–19, 120–2, 295
'Down To You' 295
For The Roses 83
'Free Man In Paris' 118
'Help Me' 121
Ladies Of The Canyon 57
Song To A Seagull 22
Mitchell, Willie 307
mixtapes 214–16
Moby Grape 20
  'Can't Be So Bad' 22
Moby, *Play* 252
'Modern Adventures of Plato, Diogenes and Freud' 28
Mojo 121
Mom's Apple Pie 83
Monck, Chip 63
Monkees 9
  Headquarters 4
Monterey Pop Festival 21, 30
Monty Python, Cheese Shop sketch 123
Moody Blues 20, 37
  Days Of Future Passed 14
Moog, Robert, synthesizer 28
Moon, Keith 174, 246, 276, 286
Moore, Dudley 149–53
Moore, Nick 142
Moore, Rusty
  Knockers Up 148–9
  SinSational 148–9
Moore, Thurston 214
Morgan, Marabel, *The Total Woman* 126
Morissette, Alanis, *Jagged Little Pill* 253, 256
Morita, Akio 219
Moroder, Giorgio 125–30, 135
Morrish, Jonathan 133
Morrison, Van
  Astral Weeks 24–6, 275–6
  'Caravan' 61
  'Into The Mystic' 61
  It's Too Late To Stop Now 297
  Moondance 61, 283–4
  St Dominic's Preview 85
  'Sweet Thing' 25
  Veedon Fleece 117
Morrissey, 'We Hate It When Our Friends Become Successful' 160
Most, Mickie 278
Motown 70, 230, 285
  Motown Chartbusters 2
Mott the Hoople 76
Mountain 62
MP3 players 259–60
MTV 220–1, 224, 232, 238, 239–43

Muller, Martin (Neon Park) 84
Murphy, Elliott 173
Murray, Charles Shaar 155, 159
Music Centre Cornwall 35
musicals albums xiv
Musicland 71
Muslim Council of Great Britain 216

N
Nash, Graham 11, 287
Nash, Johnny 293
Nashville 17
National Lampoon, *Lemmings* 147
Nesmith, Michael, *And The Hits Keep On Coming* 85
Netflix 264
Network 226
New Dylans 173
New Order *see* Joy Division
New York Rock and Roll Ensemble 42
New York Times 10, 32, 100, 103, 132, 186, 210–11, 236, 263, 266
Newhart, Bob 147
    The Button-Down Mind Of Bob Newhart 144, 149
Newman, Randy 119–22
    'Every Man A King' 119
    Good Old Boys 119–21, 295–6
    Johnny Cutler's Birthday 121
    'Just One Smile' 28
    'Kingfish' 119
    'Political Science' 290
    'Rednecks' 120
    Sail Away 290
Newman, Tim 242
Newton-John, Olivia, 'Physical' 212
Nichols, Mike 26
Nicks, Stevie 191, 193, 195
    Bella Donna 318
    'Edge Of Seventeen' 318
    'Leather And Lace' 318
    'Silver Springs' 190
    'Stop Draggin' My Heart Around' 318
Nile, Willie 173
Nilsson, Harry 113
    A Little Touch Of Schmilsson In The Night 294–5
    'Without Her' 28
Nirvana, *Nevermind* 255–6
Nitty Gritty Dirt Band 52
Nixon, Richard 119
NME (New Musical Express) 99, 137
    writers 154–66
    cassettes 214
    reviews 59

Not Only . . . But Also 149
NRBQ 52
nudity 35–7

O
O'Brien, Conan 220
O'Driscoll, Gerry 98
O'Neill, Terry 174
Oakey, Phil 319
Oasis 249
    Be Here Now 256–7
Oates, John 114
Oberstein, Maurice 258
Observer 102
Ohio Express 42
Ohio Players, *Honey* 137
oil crisis 1973 109–10
Old Grey Whistle Test 306
Oldfield, Mike 100–1, 104, 255
    Tubular Bells 101, 102, 103–4, 111, 292
Oldham, Andrew Loog 12
Olympic Studios 34
Omega Records, *Bedside Companion For Playboys* 130
One Plus One series 212–13
One Stop Records 34, 68, 71, 97
Ono, Yoko 206–7
    Plastic Ono Band 55
Orwell, George, *1984* xvii
Osbourne, Ozzy 284
Otis, Shuggie 65
Our Miss Fred 89
Our Price 252
Oz 54

P
Pacific Gas and Electric 52
Page, Jimmy 133
Palmer, Robert, *Sneakin' Sally Through The Alley* 297–8
Palmer, Tony 102
Parkinson, Michael 292
Parks, Van Dyke, *Song Cycle* 272–3
Parliament, *Chocolate City* 124
Parlophone 145
Parsons, Alan 98, 106–7, 292
Parsons, Gram 122
    'In My Hour Of Darkness' 298
    Grievous Angel 117, 298
Parsons, Tony 155
Partridge, Andy 308–9
Pastor, Terry 86
Pavel, Andreas 198
Peanut Butter Conspiracy 21
Peckham, George 'Porky' 307

Peel, John 20, 25, 48, 101, 140, 244, 280
   Dandelion 54
Pekar, Ron 83
People 211
Perry, Lee,'Roast Fish And Cornbread' 259
Perry, Richard 113
Petty, Tom
   'Even The Losers' 311
   'Refugee' 311
   and the Heartbreakers, *Damn The*
      Torpedoes 311
Philips 235
Piblokto! 23
Picnic (A Breath Of Fresh Air) 23
Pink Floyd 23, 66, 92, 202
   A Saucerful Of Secrets 23
   Atom Heart Mother 50
   'Careful With That Axe, Eugene' 249
   'Money' 99
   'On The Run' 98
   The Dark Side Of The Moon 96–100, 101,
      102, 103–7, 108, 111, 129, 190, 204,
      292
   The Wall 190
   'Time' 98
   Ummagumma 39, 73–5
Pioneer PL 12D deck 93
Plastic Ono Band 55
Playboy 129–30
Poco, 'Rose Of Cimarron' 140
Pointer Sisters 124
Police 196–7
   'Can't Stand Losing You' 309
   Outlandos D'Amour 309
   Reggatta De Blanc 194
   'Roxanne' 309
Polydor 35
Polygram 258, 270
Pop, Iggy 202
Pop Shopper 20
Post Malone 266
Powell, Nik 51
Powell, W. David 84
Power Station 189, 314
Pratt, Andy, *Records Are Like Life* 67
Presley, Elvis xvi, 87, 144, 207
   Aloha from Hawaii 103
   first LP xiv
Pretenders
   'Bad Boys Get Spanked' 316
   'I Go To Sleep' 316
   'Message Of Love' 316
   'Talk Of The Town' 316
   'The Adultress' 316
   Pretenders II 316

Pretzel Logic 218
Price, Antony 88
Price, Vincent 228
Prince
   'All The Critics Love U In New York' 320
   'Little Red Corvette' 320
   1999 320
   Purple Rain 237
   'When Doves Cry' 238
Prine, John 65, 173
Private Eye 150
producers, role 113–16
Pryor, Richard, *Bicentennial Nigger* 149
psychedelic revolution 15–16
Public Image, *Metal Box* 246
Pure Prairie League 83
Pye, Marble Arch 66

Q
quadraphonic sound 103
Quatro, Suzi 179
Queen 152
   The Game 205
Quicksilver Messenger Service 52, 160
   Happy Trails 281–2
Quintessence, *In Blissful Company* 184

R
Radio London 3
radiograms xv
Rae Sremmurd 266
Rafferty, Gerry, *City To City* 172
Rainbow Theatre 92
Ramones 172, 178
   Ramones 302
RCA xiii, 103
   Pop Shopper 20
Rebennack, Mac 290–1
record covers 4–5, 6–7, 13–14, 37–8, 44–6,
      76–91, 130, 135–7, 183–4
record shops 1–2, 65–75
Record Bar 2, 4, 6, 13, 74
Record Mirror 157
Record Mirror, reviews 59–60
Record Plant 115
Record Retailer 35, 36
Record Store Day x
records industry
   and blank cassettes 225–6
   finance 109–16
   pressing 269–70
Redd Foxx 149
Reed, Lou 202
   Street Hassle 168
Reeves, Martha 113

REM 264
Renaldo and Clara 174
Revolver 164
Rice, Tim
  Jesus Christ Superstar 33–4
  Joseph and the Amazing Technicolour
    Dreamcoat 33
Richard, Cliff
  and the Shadows 215
  'Wired For Sound' 219
Richards, Keith 12, 80, 82, 156
Rifkin, Joshua 9
Riley, Terry, *A Rainbow In Curved Air* 100
Risky Business 310
Rivera, Scarlet 304
Rivers, Johnny 11–12
Riviera, Jake 184
Robertson, Robbie 17, 40, 41–3, 46, 118, 282
Rock Machine 21–3
Rock Machine Turns You On, The 22–3, 276
Rock Yearbook 222–3
Rockers Revenge, 'Walking On Sunshine' 238
Rockford Files 194
Rockwell, John 186
Rockwell, Norman 83
Rodgers, Nile 189, 312
Rolling Stone 25, 36, 54, 116, 185, 192, 194,
  224, 225, 296, 303
  Reviews 54–61, 64
Rolling Stones 12–13, 29, 37, 53–4, 80, 82,
  151, 158, 249, 264
  albums
    Aftermath 245
    Beggars Banquet 276
    Black And Blue 303–4
    Exile On Main St 291, 81–2
    Get Yer Ya-Ya's Out! 57–8
    It's Only Rock 'n' Roll 60
    LIVE-r Than You'll Ever Be (bootleg) 55
    Some Girls 174
    Sticky Fingers 64, 286–7
    Their Satanic Majesties Request 13
  bootlegs 55
  songs
    'Can't You Hear Me Knocking' 286
    'Moonlight Mile' 287
    'Mother's Little Helper' 245
    'No Expectations' 276
    'Rocks Off' 291
    'Salt Of The Earth' 276
    'Shattered' 174
    'Sing This All Together' 13
    'Stray Cat Blues' 276
    'Tumbling Dice' 291
Ronettes, 'Be My Baby' 163

Rose, Axl 290
Rose, Tim 21, 22, 276
Rossiter, Leonard 140
Rossner, Judith, *Looking for Mr Goodbar* 126
Rotel RX150 amplifier 93
Rotten, Johnny 152–3, 185
Rough Trade 201
Rowland, Kevin
  'Come On Eileen' 321
  'Liars A To E' 321
  'Until I Believe In My Soul' 321
Roxy Music 86–91
  Country Life 90
  'Do The Strand' xi, 182, 293
  Flesh And Blood 314
  For Your Pleasure xi, 90, 293
  'In Every Dream Home A Heartache' 293
  Roxy Music 288–9
  Siren 90
  Stranded 90
  'Virginia Plain' 89, 288, 289
Roy C 136
Rundgren, Todd 114, 133
  'Baby Needs A New Pair Of Snakeskin
    Boots . . . ' 289–90
  'Can We Still Be Friends' 309
  Hermit Of Mink Hollow 309
  'I Saw The Light' 289
  live album 177
  Something/ Anything? 134, 289–90
  Todd 114
Russell, Leon 282
  Americana 178
Rykodisc 245

S
sampler albums 21–3
Santana 39, 62
  Abraxas 50
Saturday Evening Post 83
Saturday Night Fever 136, 166, 172
Saville, Peter 204
Scaggs, Boz 39, 185
  'Lowdown' 303
  My Time 168
  Silk Degrees 303
  'What Can I Say' 303
  'What Do You Want The Girl To Do' 303
Schwarz, Brinsley, *Silver Pistol* 72
Scofield, Paul 203
Scorsese, Martin 308
Scott, Tom 118, 295
Scott-Heron, Gil 65
Searchers 172–3
  'Needles And Pins' 172

Sedaka, Neil, 'Love Will Keep Us Together' 202
Seger, Bob
  'Hollywood Nights' 310
  'Old Time Rock & Roll' 310
  'Still The Same' 310
  Stranger In Town 310
  'Till It Shines' 310
  'We've Got Tonite' 310
Seidemann, Bob 36
Sellers, Peter
  Songs For Swingin' Sellers 146
  The Best Of Sellers 146
Sembello, Michael, 'Carousel' 229
Sex Pistols 140, 152–3, 163
  Never Mind The Bollocks . . . 185
Shadows, 'Apache' 274
Sham 69 165
Shand, Jimmy 68
Sharp, Cecil 44
Sharp, Martin 13, 274
Shorter, Wayne 306
Sigue Sigue Sputnik 162
Sigur Rós 252
Sill, Judee 65
Simmons, Gene 176
Simon & Garfunkel
  'A Hazy Shade Of Winter' 27
  'America' 27, 275
  Bookends 26–8, 275
  'Mrs Robinson' 27
  'Old Friends' 27
  'Save The Life Of My Child' 27, 27–8
Simon, Carly, *No Secrets* 85
Simon, John 18, 28–31, 39, 41, 42–3, 46
Simon, Paul 26–8, 122
  'Kodachrome' 294
  'Something So Right' 294
  'Tenderness' 294
  There Goes Rhymin' Simon 294
Sinatra, Frank xiv, 100, 111, 144, 205
  Songs For Swingin' Lovers! 146
Singing Postman 67
Sire 172
Six-Day War 3
Sly & the Family Stone, *There's A Riot Goin'*
  On 65, 286
Small Faces, *Ogdens' Nut Gone Flake* 278
Smith, Delia 38
Smith, Giles, *Lost In Music* 105–6
Smith, Joe 29
Smith, Maggie 96
Smith, Patti 158, 162
  Horses 137–8, 159, 160, 300–1
Soft Cell, 'Tainted Love' 224
Sonic Youth 214

Sony Walkman xviii, 196–8, 210–15,
  218–21
sound engineering 187–9
sound equipment 93–6
Sound of Music 23
Sounds 157
Soundstream 188
Sousa In Stereo 144
South Bank Show 233
South Pacific xiv
Spector, Phil xvi, 259, 299
Spencer, Jeremy 193
Spice Girls, *Spice* 255
Spirit 20
  'Fresh Garbage' 22
Spizzenergi, 'Where's Captain Kirk?' 201
Spotify 266
Springsteen, Bruce 45, 166, 173, 283,
  296, 311
  Born In The USA 189, 237–8, 320
  Born To Run 137, 160, 298–9
  'Dancing In The Dark' 237–9
  Darkness On The Edge Of Town 172
  live box set 249
  'Jungleland' 299
  Nebraska 214, 319–20
  The River 190, 316
  'Thunder Road' 299
Squire, Chris 287
Stanley, Paul 176
Stanshall, Viv 275, 292
Staples Singers 135
Star Wars 217, 243
Starr, Ringo 63, 113
Status Quo 66
Steeleye Span, *Below The Salt* 168
Steely Dan
  Aja 306
  Can't Buy A Thrill 84
  Countdown To Ecstasy 294
  Pretzel Logic 109, 296
  'Rikki Don't Lose That Number' 296
Stein, Phyllis 211
Steinman, Jim 305–6
Stevens, Cat
  Tea For The Tillerman 70
  Teaser and the Firecat 65
Stevens, Guy 165
Stevens, Ray, 'The Streak' 121
Stewart, Al
  'A Long Way Down From Stephanie' 26
  Bed-Sitter Images 26
  Love Chronicles 26
  'Swiss Cottage Manoeuvres' 26
Stewart, Dave 215

Index

Stewart, Rod 185, 278
   An Old Raincoat Won't Ever Let You Down 36
   Atlantic Crossing 300
   'Do Ya Think I'm Sexy' 287
   Every Picture Tells A Story 64, 287–8
   'I Don't Want To Talk About It' 300
   'It's Not The Spotlight' 300
   'Sailing' 300
   'Seems Like A Long Time' 288
   'Three Time Loser' 300
   'Tomorrow Is A Long Time' 288
Stiff label 184
Stigers, Curtis 255
Sting 196
Sting, The 121
Stokes, Geoffrey, *Starmaking Machinery* 112–13, 115–16
Stone, Jesse, 'Don't Let Go' 115
Stooges 39, 159
Stranglers 158, 170
streaming services 261–8
Streisand, Barbra 113
   Love Songs 223
studio time costs 111
Studio D 187–8, 191
Summer, Donna 180, 313
   Bad Girls 190
   Live And More 177
   'Love To Love You Baby' 125–30, 135, 136
Summer of Love xi, 3, 43–4
Summers, Andy 196
Sun 88
Sunday People 26
Sunday Times 102
Supremes Sing Rodgers & Hart, The 3–4
Swamp Dogg, *Total Destruction To Your Mind* 67
Swedien, Bruce 227, 229

T
T. Rex 20
   Electric Warrior 65
   My People Were Fair . . . 23
   Zinc Alloy . . . 109
T2, *It'll All Work Out In Boomland* 72
Taj Mahal 20, 22
   'Statesboro Blues' 22
Talking Heads 172
   Fear Of Music 206
   More Songs About Buildings And Food 172, 308–9
   'Take Me To The River' 308
   'The Big Country' 308
Taupin, Bernie 300
Tavener, John 63

Taylor, Derek 294
Taylor, James, *Mud Slide Slim And the Blue Horizon* 64
Taylor, John 241
TEAC 94
technician-musicians 233–4
Technics 94
Television 178
   Marquee Moon 158–64, 281, 305
   'Marquee Moon' 305
   'Torn Curtain' 305
   'Venus' 305
Teller, Al 239
Temperton, Rod 227, 228
Ten Years After 62
   Stonedhenge 39
   'Three Blind Mice' 39
ten-inch albums xiv
Tench, Benmont 318
Thank Your Lucky Stars 28
The Band *see* Band, The
The Man (concept) 54, 56–7, 58, 242
theme LPs xiv–xv
Thin Lizzy, *Live And Dangerous* 177
Thomas, Chris 98–9
Thompson, Paul 314
Thompson, Richard, *Henry The Human Fly* 291
Thompson, Richard and Linda
   I Want To See The Bright Lights Tonight 297
   Shoot Out The Lights 320
Thompson, Tony 312
Thorens 93
Thornton, Big Mama 29, 30–1
Three Degrees, *New Dimensions* 178
Thriller 267
Time 129
Time Out 52
Time Out's Book of London 48, 88
Time Warner 149
Times, The 10, 32
Tinsley Robor 77
Titelman, Russ 119
To Kill a Mockingbird 163
Tom Lehrer, An Evening Wasted With xiv
Tomelty, Frances 196
Tomorrow's World 235–6
Tony Bennett's Greatest Hits 273
Top Gear 20
Top of the Pops 90, 200
Topham, Chris 72, 95
Torry, Clare 98, 106
Toto 303
Tottenham Court Road sound equipment 93–6
Tower 249

Townshend, Pete 10, 11, 14, 35, 156, 174, 284, 286
    Empty Glass 314
    Quadrophenia 103
    Tommy 103
    Who's Next (Lifehouse project) 103
Traffic
    'Empty Pages' 284
    'Glad' 284
    John Barleycorn Must Die 50, 284–5
    Mr Fantasy 14
Travis, Geoff 201
Travolta, John 136
Tremeloes 18
Turner, Tina, *Private Dancer* 237
Tyler, Bonnie, 'Total Eclipse Of The Heart' 242
Tyrannosaurus Rex *see* T. Rex

U
U2 249
    Boy 315
Uncut 121
United States of America (group) 22
Unwin, Stanley 278
USC Trojan Marching Band 193
Utopia 114

V
Vallance's record shop 22
Van Halen, Eddie 229
Van Hamersveld, John 81–2
Van Peebles, Melvin 321
Van Ronk, Dave 246
Velvet Underground 39, 159
    The Velvet Underground And Nico 6
    'The Gift' 123
    Loaded 65
Verlaine, Tom 163
videos 217–21
Vietnam war 3, 32, 43–4, 56
Village Recorder 187
Village Voice 116
vinyl revival 261, 262–4
vinyl shortage 109–10
Virgin 249, 252, 255
Virgin mail order 51, 72
Virgin Records 51–5, 68, 100
Visconti, Tony 177

W
Wailers
    'Stir It up' 293
    Catch A Fire 293
Wainwright, Loudon III 65, 173
Waits, Tom
    Blue Valentine 309, 311

'Kentucky Avenue' 309
    'Somewhere' 309
Wakeman, Rick, *The Myths And Legends Of King Arthur . . .* 137
Walker, Johnnie 254–5
Walker, Scott 14
    Scott 274
War (group) 64
Ware, Martyn 212
Warhol, Andy 6
Warner Brothers 29, 57, 84, 110, 115, 149, 190, 272–3, 304
Warner Brothers Records 101, 143–4, 147
Warner, Jack 144
Waronker, Lenny 119
Washington Post 83
Waters, Roger 98, 104
Watts, Charlie 57, 291
Watts, Michael 121
Wavy Gravy 63
Weaver, Blue 301
Webb, Jimmy 11–12
Weir, Bob 51
West Side Story 238, 309
Wharfedale 93, 94
White, Barry 128, 134–5, 136
Who, The 10, 11, 239
    'Baba O'Riley' 285–6
    'Fiddle About' 281
    'Go To The Mirror!' 281
    Live At Leeds 58, 284
    'Pinball Wizard' 281
    The Who Sell Out 14
    Tommy 38–9, 281
    Who Are You? 174
    Who's Next 64, 285–6
    'Won't Get Fooled Again' 286
Will Davis Trio, *Have Mood Will Call* 130
Williams, Andy 9, 67, 111
Williamson, Robin 273
Wilson, Brian, 'Heroes And Villains' 11
Wilson, Dennis 191
Wilson, Tony 204–5
Winter, Johnny 276
    Second Winter 39
Winwood, Muff 37
Winwood, Steve 14, 285
Wishbone Ash 170
Withers, Bill 64
Wizard of Oz 105
Wonder, Stevie 227
    'I Wish' 301
    'Isn't She Lovely' 301
    'Pastime Paradise' 301

Index

'Sir Duke' 301
Songs In The Key Of Life 190, 301
'Superstition' 289
Talking Book 82, 289
Woodstock 32, 36, 40, 42, 44, 46
  official film 62–3
  triple album 62–3
Woodward, Bob, and Carl Bernstein, *All the President's Men* 121
Wright, Chris 178–9
Wright, Rick 96
'The Great Gig In The Sky' 98

X
XTC
  Black Sea 315
  'Living Through Another Cuba' 315
  'Respectable Street' 315
  'Towers of London' 315

Y
Yankovic, Frankie 28
Yes 84, 175
  Close To The Edge 167
  Fragile 72, 246
  The Yes Album 287
  Tormato 168
  Yessongs 102
Yetnikoff, Walter 228

Yom Kippur War 109
You Can All Join In 22
Young, Martin 247
Young, Neil 122, 133
  After The Gold Rush 283
  Everybody Knows This Is Nowhere 39
  Harvest Moon 254
  On The Beach 117, 296–7
  Rust Never Sleeps 188, 313
  Tonight's The Night 296
  Trans 320
Young, Paul, *No Parlez* 254

Z
Zappa, Frank 245
  Hot Rats 39, 279–80
  'Peaches En Regalia' 279–80
  We're Only In It For The Money 5
Zerostats 95
Zombies
  'Time Of The Season' 22, 276
  Odessey And Oracle 275
ZZ Top 64, 231–4, 232, 242
  Eliminator 233–4
  'Gimme All Your Lovin'' 242
  'La Grange' 210, 295
  'Legs' 242
  'Sharp Dressed Man' 242
  'Thug' 234
  Tres Hombres 210, 221, 295